STRAIGHT X EDGE

A CLEAR-HEADED HARDCORE PUNK HISTORY

TONY RETTMAN

Bazillion
Points

Praise for **STRAIGHT EDGE**:

"Tony Rettman's book is *the* choice for a first-hand account of the history, inner workings, and real truth of straight edge—one of the most important cultural influences of the last century. Straight edge kicked down the walls and opened the doors to music and choices that formed a new core of cool. This book ensures that legacy continues."—Al Barile, SS Decontrol

"I'm honored to be a part of this book that accurately recalls a counterculture which changed the course of many lives. *Straight Edge* serves as a crucial and authoritative glance into that world for fans around the globe, shining light on a time we will never forget."—Ray Cappo, Youth of Today

"Through a richly illustrated, fast-moving oral history, Rettman nails the X, and proves that each straight-minded generation is still having its say."—Mike Gitter, *xXx* fanzine

"A great book! Tony Rettman did it once again."—Mike Judge

Also by Tony Rettman, NYHC: New York Hardcore 1980–1990:

"A great oral-history book."—*New York Times*

"A fittingly bare-bones book, with fifty-two short chapters and no editorializing from the author. But the story it tells is not a simple one: this was, to quote the title of Cro-Mags' first album, an 'age of quarrel.'"—*The New Yorker*

"An essential document, the go-to reference for all fans of extreme styles of music. It started here."—*Huffington Post*

"A new oral history from crucial local imprint Bazillion Points, tells the tale of Agnostic Front, Cro-Mags, Reagan Youth, and the myriad other bands that helped put the scene on the map."—*Time Out New York*

"In a word: essential."—*Terrorizer*

"An excellent history"—*Austin American-Statesman*

"A journey into the heart of the chaos…a success"—*The Wire*

STRAIGHT×EDGE

IN MEMORY OF

DREW BERNSTEIN, DOUG BYRNES, SEAN MCCABE,
FRANK "SKIP" CANDELORI, SEAN MCGRATH,
PETER AMDAM, DAVE FRANKLIN,
AND JOHN "STABB" SCHROEDER

Crippled Youth brings K-Town mosh crew pride to a rabid Boston audience, the Rat, May 11, 1986. JJ GONSON

STRAIGHT EDGE
A CLEAR-HEADED HARDCORE PUNK HISTORY
BY TONY RETTMAN

Bazillion Points

Bazillion Points
New York | United States
www.bazillionpoints.com
www.straightedgebook.com

Produced for Bazillion Points by Ian Christe
Cover layout and design by Bazillion Points
Cover photo by Ken Salerno
Inside cover "Straight Time...A Short, Fast Visual History" by Brian Walsby

Photographs © Luke Abbey, Michael Andrade, Murray Bowles, Alison "Mouse" Braun, Bridget Collins, Chris Daily, Jamie Davis, JJ Gonson, Fred Hammer, Peter Hoeren, Casey Jones, Mikey Garceau, Pat Longrie, Dave Mandel, Vique Martin, Cari Marvelli, Kent McClard, Traci McMahon, Matt Miller, Justin Moulder, Jim Nargiso, Trent Nelson, Bessie Oakley, Angela Owens, Todd Pollock, John Porcelly, Dan Rawe, Robbie Redcheeks, Billy Rubin, Gail Rush, Ken Salerno, Chris Schneider, Bob Shedd, Dave Sine, Joe Snow, Anne Spina, Adam Tanner, Vicki Torch, Freddy Twice, Joe Whiskeyman, and Lenny Zimkus.

"I'm Not Perfect" © Anthony Civorelli 2017

Bazillion Points thanks Danielle Jelley-Rettman, Dianna Dilworth, Vivi, Roman, Civ, Daniel Ekeroth, 138, Ken Salerno, Julien, cubegrafik, Kong GmbH, and the letter X.

ISBN 978-1-935950-24-0

Printed in China

Cover: *Civ of Gorilla Biscuits dives into a Bold crowd, City Gardens, Trenton, NJ, July 9, 1989.* KEN SALERNO

TABLE OF CONTENTS

I'M NOT PERFECT

BY ANTHONY "CIV" CIVORELLI

I GREW UP IN QUEENS, NEW YORK, in the late 1970s and 1980s—old New York, as people call it now. The city then was a place where you stayed in your neighborhood and did what your siblings and friends did; which, in my case, was drinking and smoking pot by age 12. Being raised on rock 'n' roll and metal in a working class environment didn't leave much room for change or opportunity. So when I found graffiti in 1982, it lead me down a road of new art, music, and culture. Hip hop was punk in its own way, and incredibly inspiring in its early years, but it held the same trappings of drugs and alcohol use in the same peer pressure-based conformist system.

Seeking something new after a small bout with new wave, my childhood friends and I found punk and hardcore music. Like in the past, this world was also ripe with 40-ounce bottles, drugs, and junkies. By this time, such things were all becoming boring and redundant. But I quickly found bands like Minor Threat and Youth of Today. The idea of different scenes co-existing under the umbrella of hardcore made complete sense to me. The New York straight edge scene changed everything for me. It gave me a real sense of community based on common goals and nothing seemed unrealistic anymore like touring the world, playing shows and spreading the movement.

Straight edge isn't something I take lightly—that's why I'm thirty years into it. I still don't need a drink to get loose or wild. I don't need drugs to feel comfortable or to fit in. Straight edge gives me strength to deal with things head on, with no buffers, crutches, or masks. I have no clouded judgments or excuses to hide behind; just brutal clear-headed reality. I guess that might be why I come off like an asshole sometimes, with little patience for bullshit, but I'm not perfect. I'm just Civ.

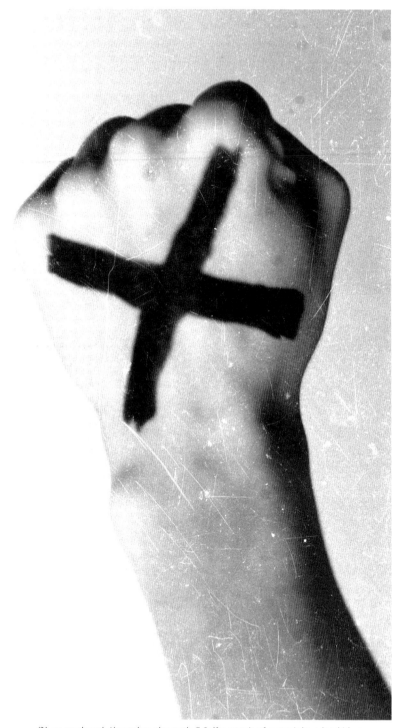

"X on my hand, I've taken the oath." Self-portrait of a straight edge kid. JOE SNOW

WASTED YOUTH

DAVE SMALLEY (DYS, DAG NASTY, ALL, DOWN BY LAW): First of all, you have to understand that the 1970s had a heavily drug-influenced culture. The drug culture started in the late '60s via the Beatles' *White Album* and all the San Francisco hippie stuff. It was a minority mind-set that eventually permeated the mainstream culture.

ANDY STRACHAN (DYS): In the 1970s everyone was stoned, even people's parents.

REVEREND HANK PEIRCE (ROAD MANAGER FOR C.O.C., SLAPSHOT, UNIFORM CHOICE): In the late '70s and early '80s, there was still this hangover of the '60s. Everyone was still into this idea of sex, drugs, and rock 'n' roll, but I honestly wasn't really impressed with it as a kid.

IAN MACKAYE (TEEN IDLES, MINOR THREAT, DISCHORD RECORDS): There was a social and musical revolution going on in the '60s that revolved around the exploration of substances. There was arguably a positive component to that in terms of mind and consciousness expansion, but I feel by the mid-'70s, people had a much darker relationship with substances. The counterculture evaporated and the only counterculture I was aware of was one of self-destruction.

KEVIN SECONDS (7 SECONDS, POSITIVE FORCE RECORDS): I grew up in relatively poor and working-class neighborhoods and lived in low-income housing until I moved away from home. Drugs, violence, crime, and sexualization surrounded me and became a normal thing to accept and consider in my own life. Despite that—and even though I tried and experimented with everything—there was another, wiser side of me. I knew that if I were to stay on that path with my friends, drinking, smoking, stealing, and doing drugs, I'd end up in prison or dead at way too early an age. I couldn't accept that.

ROB FISH (RELEASE, RESURRECTION, 108, THE JUDAS FACTOR): I grew up with my mother and father in Edison, New Jersey. During my younger years, we had foster kids living with us, but by the time I started elementary school it was just the three of us. My mother had specific mental and physical health issues. My father worked a tremendous amount of hours to keep everything together financially, and I didn't have a close personal connection with him. I also experienced sexual abuse, which led to some deep emotional struggles. Between all of this, I think it's safe to say that I was a troubled kid with a desperate need for a sense of control.

JOHN PORCELLY (VIOLENT CHILDREN, YOUTH OF TODAY, JUDGE): My older brother was the cool kid in high school. He played on the football team, and he was a huge partier. He would bring me to all these parties, and his friends thought it was funny to get me to drink because I was so young. They would give me Jack Daniel's, and two hours later I would be throwing up all over myself while they were all laughing. By the time I was thirteen, I was going to parties every weekend, and getting drunk on the regular. I honestly did not like or enjoy it.

STEVE REDDY (WOLFPACK, YOUTH OF TODAY ROADIE, EQUAL VISION RECORDS): I grew up in a small town west of Albany, New York, and I was the typical bad teenager. I would do whatever got me fucked up. I heard on the news that people were getting high from sniffing Pam cooking spray, so I tried it. Then I heard about sniffing glue. I thought you took the end of the glue bottle and stuck it up your nose, but someone told me you had to squirt it into a bag and strap the bag on your face. So I went home and did that. The only drug I didn't do at that time was heroin, and that's because I never found it.

JOHN PORCELLY: If you've ever seen the movie *Dazed and Confused*, that's what high school was exactly like at that time. Kids drove around in Trans Ams, smoking pot and going to keg parties held in the woods.

CHRIS BRATTON (CEASE FIRE, JUSTICE LEAGUE, CHAIN OF STRENGTH): In late-'70s and early-'80s suburban life, there really was no choice; you either got wasted with the crowd and partied fucking hard, or there was something seriously wrong with you. Your sexual orientation would be called into question in a public format by a bunch of fellows that were really heading for super things in their future lives.

MARK MCKAY (SLAPSHOT, STARS AND STRIPES, TERMINALLY ILL): High school existence at that time was all about Camaro sports cars and pot-smoking. The burn-outs at my high school wore untied work boots and flannel shirts. They all had lame attitudes, where they all were just looking forward to smoking in the quad between periods. I wrote off those people and all that stuff; it seemed like such a waste. It's not like I had some great life plan ahead of me, either—but if I was going to have any life ahead of me, it had nothing to do with that crap.

PAT DUBAR (UNITY, UNIFORM CHOICE): I was a skateboarder kid who was always in trouble. I became a disciplinary issue for my parents, so they sent me to a Catholic school in Santa Ana, California. We weren't Catholic, though, so the whole religion thing was a bit terrifying and made no sense to me. I had never seen anything like that. I remember the first mass I went to, wondering what was with all the gymnastics. All these guys were constant-ly getting up and down. It freaked me out. There was crazy shit happening around me with priests and kids, too.

The other kids at the school were driving Porsches. They were regularly breaking into their parents' liquor cabinets and getting fucking annihilat-ed. Everything there was all surface; no one at that school seemed to have any depth. They repelled me, and I didn't want to be anything like them. I was already pissed off I had to be there in the first place. I hated religion, I hated my school, and I hated the kids who went there.

DAVE SMALLEY: Maybe it was luck of the draw, but I never found any appeal in trying drugs. My dad worked for the government, so in seventh and eighth grade I lived in Paris. When I returned to the States in ninth grade, all the kids that I knew from sixth grade were now smoking pot all the time. That was shocking and depressing for me. People who were bright lights were becoming stoners, and their lights were going dim. I recognized that, and I grew wary of the whole thing; I never got involved.

IAN MACKAYE: When I was twelve, my father got a fellowship at Stanford Uni-versity, so he moved the whole family out to California for nine months. This was the year that I was in seventh grade. When we left D.C. I had one friend that smoked pot—he started when he was eleven—but by the time I returned a bunch of my friends in the neighborhood were getting high and drinking. Apparently they all went through some sort of transition during the time I was gone, but I missed it; I never got interested in the idea of partying. They were still my best friends and the people I rolled with, so I was around when they would do these things.

I remember kids going down to the park in the middle of the night and gathering on a bench in the field. Someone would produce a gallon of grain alcohol and the kids would proceed to drink themselves into puddles. I was usually the last man standing because I wasn't interested and I didn't partake. I never hated these people—I just didn't want to take part in the ritual.

KENT MCCLARD (*NO ANSWERS* ZINE, EBULLITION RECORDS): As a teenager, I was a loner with very few friends. I always felt like an outsider. Once I got into high school and started going to parties, I realized I didn't want to be like everybody else. I was uncomfortable with this idea that I could be suddenly accepted if I just did whatever everyone else wanted me to do. In theory, I guess that's what every kid wants—but if people were going to like me, I wanted them to like me on my own terms.

ANDY STRACHAN: I grew up in a little town called Marblehead, Massachusetts, about twenty miles north of Boston. My friends and I were all skateboarders who smoked weed and listened to the Rolling Stones. That was basically it. That describes pretty much the whole of the 1970s for me.

AL BARILE (SS DECONTROL, X-CLAIM! RECORDS): My high school life was pretty typical. From eighth grade through twelfth grade, every single weekend, we would drive around in cars, drink, fight, and go to parties. I didn't find it particularly interesting. I just didn't know what else to do.

JACK "CHOKE" KELLY (NEGATIVE FX, LAST RIGHTS, SLAPSHOT): I come from a tourist community, where there's not much to do but drink and smoke. In the summer there's a billion people and a lot to do, and in the winter there's nothing. Everyone just starts drinking. There wasn't much pot around, but it was a big thing for kids to take Quaaludes on the bus to school and field trips. I didn't want to be like everybody else.

SAB GREY (IRON CROSS): Looking at the background of what was going on at the time, Quaaludes were fucking huge. People were off their face on those things, bumping into walls, and this was the norm with kids.

IAN MACKAYE: It wasn't just kids getting high in the '70s, by the way. My parents were by no means hippies, but they were liberals who believed in civil rights and women's rights. They were opposed to the war in Vietnam. We spent a lot of time in the company of people that were challenging all sorts of conventional thinking. I think they were rebelling in part against what they perceived as "straitlaced America." So when I was growing up, I was pretty much surrounded by alcohol and drugs. My grandparents drank; my parents drank; my parents' friends drank; and my friends drank and got high. There was perpetual numbing going on.

JONATHAN ANASTAS (DYS, SLAPSHOT): I grew up in Cambridge, Massachusetts. My parents were very liberal college professors, so there was no real room for rebellion there. If I grew my hair, played hippie music, and smoked pot, that wasn't rebelling in my household. The great rebellion for me was to look at my parents and say, "You're fucking weak! You take drugs! You need a fucking crutch!"

IAN MACKAYE: My friend Henry Rollins and I were very into skateboarding in the '70s. This was the early days of skateboard culture. We took it very seriously. It wasn't a hobby or sport to us—it was a discipline that took us out of our houses, away from the teenage social scene, and put us into the streets and ditches. We were skateboarding before we had driver's licenses, so we often found ourselves on epic journeys in search of skate spots. It wasn't uncommon for us to take a bus for an hour, then skate another mile or two looking for some mythical drainage pipe. I reckon one of the main reasons that Henry and I got so into it was because skating was an alternative to high school parties and all of the substances that go along with that world. We were excused from the teenage rituals, because we were always out on a mission.

ANDY STRACHAN: Through skateboarding, we kept finding out more about punk rock. One of my friends' fathers was a Boston artist. He had known about new wave and punk rock from the start. He had a Ramones album. He told us, "You guys would love this stuff!" We were like, *Eh, whatever.* We just figured it was some artsy band. But we did love it.

We started to hear about the connection between skateboarding and punk going on in Southern California, where people were calling it "hardcore punk." We were interested—anything to just get away from that lame hippie shit!

IAN MACKAYE: I loved Ted Nugent, because he made a point to say he was sober. He claimed to never drink or do drugs, which was so radical at the time. I want to clarify we're talking about his *Gonzo* era, not the weird right-wing guy he is today. He was profoundly important to Henry Rollins and me. I also liked Led Zeppelin, Aerosmith, Parliament-Funkadelic, the Gap Band, Kool and the Gang, and ZZ Top. I loved heavy, rocking bands; but they were all Top 40 and all commercial, and so didn't represent me personally or my idea of a counterculture. I had given up on the idea of music representing a counterculture.

BRIAN BAKER (MINOR THREAT, DAG NASTY, BAD RELIGION): My only exposure to the whole hippie burnout thing came when about twenty percent of my class got into that shaggy Neil Young look and started smoking pot and cigarettes. But they were guys I grew up with and knew all my life. I didn't feel anything bad toward them. I just wasn't a part of that crew. The guys I hung out with, for lack of a better word, were nerds. We were more into Monty Python than Led Zeppelin.

IAN MACKAYE: I was pretty dismissive of punk rock when I first starting hearing about it, but this was largely based on the fact that most of what I knew about punk was coming from the commercial mass media. I hadn't actually done any studying on my own. In the fall of '78, I found myself arguing with high school friends about whether or not punk sucked— again, I hadn't ever really listened. So I borrowed records from some friends and from my older sister Katie. After sitting down with the music, I realized that this *was* the voice of the counterculture that I had been searching for.

The first punk show I ever saw was the Cramps, the Urban Verbs, and the Chumps at the Hall of Nations at Georgetown University in February of '79. That show, like most people's first shows, blew my mind. It was a room full of freaks and I thought, "Hey! I'm a freak too!" just for the fact that I didn't want to get high or drink. Now, some people there were getting absolutely destroyed, but I felt an immediate affinity with them because they were part of this counterculture.

JON ROA (JUSTICE LEAGUE, END TO END, EYELID): Before punk, everything seemed unreachable. I had nothing to relate to. Aerosmith had some relatable lyrics, but they were mostly about drugs and women. I liked it, but I couldn't relate to that. So punk came along and was totally relatable. But there were still elements that I couldn't relate to. Even something like the Ramones song "Carbona Not Glue" made me feel uncomfortable.

KEVIN SECONDS: Within punk rock, I knew I didn't look up to Sid Vicious of the Sex Pistols and Darby Crash of the Germs like so many of my friends did. I loved their music, but I detested the drugs and violence that they both glamorized.

DAVE SMALLEY: I always like to say that when American hardcore arrived during the early '80s, that was the total embrace and destruction of punk rock. That's what Americans are great at: fucking things up and making everything our own. We made punk harder and faster, so it would better fit what we were. The Buzzcocks and Generation X were great, because they were true to what they were. We took the punk rock ethos, made it our own, and said, "Well, this is who *we* are." And that's how punk became hardcore.

TOBY MORSE (H$_2$O, HAZEN STREET): The Sex Pistols were cool, but I didn't really know what "Anarchy in the U.K." meant. Kids like me weren't old enough to even comprehend anarchy or what the government was doing. What did *Never Mind the Bollocks* even mean? I love the Ramones, they're one of my favorite bands, but "Hey, ho—let's go!" wasn't saying much to me, either. Then you had the Dead Kennedys with "Too Drunk to Fuck." A lot of this music was all about "fuck this" and "fuck that" and "fuck the world." People can say punk came from England, but hardcore music is something that was made in America. Hardcore was about changing yourself and making the world a better place. It wasn't about "fuck your parents." My dad passed away when I was three, and my mom was working a couple jobs trying to raise three boys. I didn't hate my mom. I loved my mom!

REVEREND HANK PEIRCE: Hardcore punk in America was a reaction to the failure of the '60s as much as it was a reaction to the bureaucracy of Reagan. The mythos is that the revolution of the 1960s didn't work out, in part because it ended with everyone just wanting to get stoned. That's the reason I decided to stay sober; so I could stay focused on things that I felt needed to change, rather than getting wrapped up in all this other goofy stuff most kids did with sneaking beers and getting stoned.

TOBY MORSE: The thing that separates hardcore from punk is that punk was like, "Fuck this place." Hardcore was saying, "Let's make a difference. Let's make our minds stronger and focus."

DAVE SMALLEY: Punk rock started in nihilism and anarchy and shouting, "This place sucks!" but doing nothing about it. Sid Vicious dying of a heroin overdose set the tone as far as what people thought punk was all about. Drinking and drugs was such an established part of rock 'n' roll, and punk was really no different. The hardcore kids differed from the nihilists and the anarchists by trying to create a philosophy that said, "Yeah, this place sucks, but what can we do as kids to make it better?"

JOHN PORCELLY: Punk was all about being yourself, finding yourself, and bucking the norm. Punk gave me enough confidence to stand on my own two feet and say no to drinking every weekend. When you put all those punk ideals to the test like that in a preppy, suburban Westchester County, New York, high school environment, you realize a lot about yourself. I came to a turning point in my life and I didn't care if all the cool people in school were doing it. I just wasn't going to do it anymore. I felt like, if anyone wasn't going to like me because I didn't go out and get wasted with them, then fuck them!

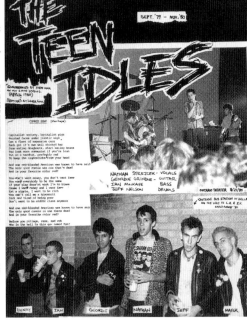

D.C.: SNEAKERS

IAN MACKAYE: Our mission was always getting into shows; that was paramount. The drinking age at the time in D.C. was eighteen, and that drove us crazy. The thing that made it most absurd was that most of us didn't drink, and we didn't want to drink. We just wanted to see the bands.

JEFF NELSON (MINOR THREAT, DISCHORD RECORDS): We had problems with bars in D.C. letting us inside to see shows. We were all under eighteen, which was the drinking age at the time. We were not the type of customers they wanted, anyway, because all we wanted to drink was Coke and water, and there's not much of a profit margin there.

IAN MACKAYE: A famous example of a near miss was in June of '79. I was seventeen years old and the Damned came to play in Washington, D.C. We loved the Damned and we absolutely had to be at that show. So I had to get a fake I.D. A friend of mine in my neighborhood was a naval sea cadet or something like that, and he got his hands on a bunch of blank sea cadet I.D. cards. He sold me one for ten bucks or something. I took a Polaroid photo of myself against a white sheet, then did a really shitty lamination job. When I got to the show, the doorman took one look at the I.D. and told me to get lost. Then one of my friends said, "Wait, you're not going to accept a U.S. military I.D.?" The doormen looked at each other, and then the guy that had denied me said, "Fine, you can go inside." I couldn't believe I had gotten away with it! The show was amazing. The Damned were incredible, of course, but even more importantly it was the first time I ever saw the Bad Brains.

I'm sure if I didn't get into that Damned and Bad Brains show, Henry Rollins or the other people who went would have reported back to me about how incredible it was, and I would have still gotten involved in the D.C.

punk scene—for sure. But thinking about the fact that I was born after a certain date almost prohibited me from being there for that cultural moment is wrong. It's clear to me now and it was clear to me back then.

NATHAN STREJCEK (TEEN IDLES, YOUTH BRIGADE): Ian MacKaye and Jeff Nelson started a punk band called the Slinkees. I knew Jeff from junior high school. Ian MacKaye went to Gordon Junior High School, but I think it closed down. He came over to our school for ninth grade.

Ian worked at the Georgetown Theatre, a place where the only movie they showed was *Caligula* by Bob Guccione. I worked up the street at the Häagen-Dazs. Way before he or Henry Rollins famously started working there, Ian would stop by the Häagen-Dazs to talk to me. The Slinkees' singer, Mark Sullivan, was leaving to go to college, and Ian asked if I wanted to sing for his new band. I was always dancing around at shows; I guess I looked like I would be a good front man. Our band became the Teen Idles. The first show was in my mom's basement, and we went on to play D.C. Space and other clubs around the area.

IAN MACKAYE: I always wanted to be in a band, but it seemed impossible. Punk made it possible.

NATHAN STREJCEK: Ian was one of the first people I met who didn't drink or do drugs and was proud of it. It was really cool because people would interview the Teen Idles and be puzzled. They didn't get it. They expected it to be all about sex, drugs, and rock 'n' roll. That stuff was so ingrained in people; they didn't understand why you wouldn't want to be part of that.

DAVE SMALLEY: When I started going to shows, these bands in D.C. like the Teen Idles were hitting chords with me both literally and figuratively. All of a sudden, I noticed a lot of the kids at these shows weren't drinking or doing drugs. That was probably one of the reasons I was latching onto it, even if only subconsciously at first.

IAN MACKAYE: From the very beginning, the Teen Idles fought to get our friends into the shows. We would arrive at these clubs with our crew, including people like my brother, Alec, who was fifteen years old. We would just tell the clubs, "They've got to come in—and if they don't come in, we're not fucking playing."

NATHAN STREJCEK: The Teen Idles song "Sneakers" really laid it out: Don't let people tell you what to do to be punk. It's okay to be different. You don't have to be the way everyone else is. You don't have to smoke or drink—just be yourself.

IAN MACKAYE: One of the first songs I wrote for the Teen Idles was called "Sneakers." On the surface it was about high school girls dating college guys, but in many ways I was writing about kids trying to act more mature and distance themselves from other kids by drinking and getting high. "Sneakers" was just saying: Take your time. Be a kid. You're going to get there no matter what.

NATHAN STREJCEK: Ian's sister had the *Whole Earth Catalog*, and that had the numbers and addresses of all these clubs, so we sent out tapes to punk clubs in California like the Mabuhay Gardens and Hong Kong Café. They replied back, giving us dates to play. We booked a show in L.A. and one in San Francisco, and we played them both!

IAN MACKAYE: We were supposed to play at the Mabuhay Gardens with the Dead Kennedys and the Circle Jerks, but we got dropped off the bill. But we ended up meeting all the punk kids from Huntington Beach who came up for that show, including Mugger, who became a roadie for Black Flag; Mike Brinson, who was a roadie for Social Distortion; Mike X Head from the *Decline of Western Civilization* movie; Tony Alva and his brother Mark; and this guy Gregg Gutierrez who ended up being in the bands the Salvation Army and the Three O'Clock.

We were all dancing at the Dead Kennedys show and they noticed our different style. We were clearly not from San Francisco. People there had a different look and were more partial to doing something like the pogo dance at that time. The Southern California kids were doing what they called "the crawl" or "skanking," which ended up being thought of as slam dancing. All of these differing dance and dress styles made obvious there were different factions in attendance.

We ended up hanging out with the H.B.s the next day and they came to see us when we played the Mabuhay Gardens the next night. Someone told me Tony Alva said we were the fastest band he ever saw. I was a huge fan of his skateboarding, so that made me feel incredible.

JEFF NELSON: All of us in the Teen Idles took a bus out to the West Coast to play those two shows, earning a total of twenty-six dollars. At the Mabuhay Gardens in San Francisco, they were putting a big X on the backs of the hands of kids who were underage, so they could get into the show and the bartender would know not to serve them alcohol. We were like, "Wow! What a great, simple system!"

IAN MACKAYE: When the Teen Idles went to California, there was a little bit of concern over whether we were going to be able to play the gigs because of our ages. We were blown away that Dirk Dirksen, who put on the shows at the Mabuhay Gardens, had developed this method of letting underage people into the shows by putting X's on the back of their hands. We went back to the clubs in Washington and really pushed doing this.

JEFF NELSON: When we came back, we got clubs to agree to let kids in with marked hands. Putting the X on your hand became almost a badge of honor. It showed everyone, "Yeah, I'm underage, and I don't even *want* to drink."

IAN MACKAYE: We even told them that we would put the X's on our hands ourselves to show how committed we were to our cause. Dodie Bowers, the manager of the 9:30 Club, gave it the okay and it worked out really well. The 9:30 was so supportive that we started doing all-ages matinee shows there on Sunday afternoons on a semi-regular basis.

By some point, a lot of us were already over eighteen, but I would still put the X on my hand. When bouncers asked for my I.D., I'd hand them a card from the Roy Rogers fast food chain's Buckaroo discount club for kids. I had written on the card in crayon, "I am eighteen," in childish writing. I would hand that to the bouncer. It might sound kind of prankish, but it was really a political statement about the absurdity of age policies at punk shows.

JOHN STABB (GOVERNMENT ISSUE): I still drank a mixed drink now and then, but I hated the taste of beer. Then came the whole thing with putting a Magic Marker X on your hand to show the 9:30 Club that you weren't drinking. I didn't stop drinking just because I was playing gigs with all the hardcore bands. I stopped because I got caught up in the physical energy of slam dancing and stage diving. I wore an X because I thought it was cool to have on my hands. Right away, a lot of people just did it as a symbol; even the punks who got drunk outside the club.

JEFF NELSON: When the Teen Idles got back to D.C. from California, we were very inspired by the *X*'s and also by the fashion sense of the Huntington Beach punks who had come up to San Francisco to see the Circle Jerks show at Mabuhay Gardens. That trip energized us to really do something of our own.

STEVE HANSGEN (MINOR THREAT, SECOND WIND): They came back from the West Coast with this thing they got from Huntington Beach. Ian MacKaye and Henry Rollins definitely filtered that through their own ideas, but wearing bandanas around your boots and the slam dancing came from the Teen Idles going out to L.A. There's no question.

IAN MACKAYE: The X on the hand was really about empowering youth. It was kind of a gang sign in a way. That's not to suggest that we were an organized violent gang, but it became a marker and an identifier for D.C. punks.

SAB GREY: The older punks in D.C. would look at us and say, "Look at these kids and what they're doing. It's so last year." That motivated us to do our own thing. We were like, "Fuck you! We're D.C. hardcore!"

STEVE HANSGEN: I got in just as everything was transitioning from being the D.C. punk scene to becoming the D.C. *hardcore* punk scene. There was a definite transition period between when the Teen Idles broke up and Ian and Jeff formed Minor Threat and Henry Rollins got S.O.A. together. The arrival of Minor Threat and S.O.A. was sort of the delineation.

JEFF NELSON: The Teen Idles broke up in November of 1980. We had recorded some songs, and we decided to release them with six hundred dollars we had saved up from shows. No one else was going to put our record out, so we decided to start our own label, Dischord. The first release on our label was the Teen Idles *Minor Disturbance* seven-inch EP. On the cover of the record was a picture of Ian's younger brother Alec, with his arms crossed showing his X'ed hands. On the cover of the first five or so records on Dischord, we always had a fist with an X on it next to the catalog number.

The District of Columbia flag is based on the crest of George Washington, which is three stars over two bars. All of a sudden, it occurred to us that if you substituted *X*'s for the stars it was triple X, like hardcore porn movies. *Hardcore* was the term for the upcoming offshoot of punk we were involved in, so it was very exciting how that imagery came together so easily.

Minor Threat spread straight edge to hardcore scenes around the country. From top: Minor Threat in Boston. BRIDGET COLLINS; *Minor Threat in Reno, NV. Note Kevin Seconds of 7 Seconds in sleeveless UK Subs T-shirt.* CARI MARVELLI

MINOR THREAT: STRAIGHT EDGE

BRIAN BAKER: I grew up in Washington, but I left after seventh grade because my dad got a job in Detroit. I came back to D.C. at the second part of ninth grade in February of 1980. While I was absent, a lot of my friends had discovered punk rock. So I got into punk to fit in, as strange as that sounds. My first punk show was seeing the Teen Idles opening for the Cramps in the summer of 1980. After that, it all happened so fast. I joined Minor Threat and we started to become a real band by the end of 1980. It was definitely a "right place at the right time" sort of thing for me.

JEFF NELSON: We formed Minor Threat after the Teen Idles broke up, and right away Ian wrote the song "Straight Edge." Ian's whole reason for writing the song was his disgust with the drinking, drugs, and sex focus of high school and American life at the time. He was turned off by what he saw, and the song struck a chord with people who were equally repelled by the focus on those things in music culture.

IAN MACKAYE: I wrote "Straight Edge" because I wanted to get it off my chest. I also wanted to sing it because maybe there were other people out there who didn't drink; I wanted to connect with them. I reckon the lyrics spoke to a lot of kids who didn't want to get high and didn't want to be a part of that world. When they saw there were kids saying, "Fuck that! We're not doing that!" that's all it took for them to say, "Yeah! I'm with you!"

BRIAN BAKER: I think the idea of straight edge in D.C. initially was just to build a community. We were all teenagers, and straight edge was a great tool to build this scene without having to deal with alcohol. Ian is such a fucking genius, because he was onto the idea at such a young age that alcohol sales should have nothing to do with art. I think that was the main drive behind it.

IAN MACKAYE: Why does this form of expression have to be dictated by the alcohol industry? Why do the laws pertaining to the consumption of alcohol have to be a part of it? Music is the only art form I can think of that has this sort of stricture. Do poetry readings have to be done in crack houses? Do art galleries have to be heroin dens? So why does rock 'n' roll have to be relegated to these places that serve alcohol?

BRIAN BAKER: I didn't drink or smoke because it just wasn't on the map for me at that point in life. The same was true for Minor Threat guitarist Lyle Preslar. But history has proven Jeff Nelson to be something of an iconoclast.

JEFF NELSON: I was the only one in Minor Threat who had tried pot before. I agreed with the sentiment of the song "Straight Edge" to a good extent, because I had already done lots of wrestling with my own little demons. To me, that's a different thing compared to Ian's approach. I've never met anyone who is like him. I've never met another person who just says, "No, I don't need it," and then wonders why others need it. Who else is like that? Who else is not susceptible to peer pressure or curiosity or boredom?

In terms of Minor Threat's intentions, "Straight Edge" was just a song. Then came another song, "Out of Step," which was sort of the sister song to "Straight Edge."

IAN MACKAYE: The song "Straight Edge" may have resonated with a lot of kids, but I think it was the song "Out of Step" that really freaked people out. Specifically, it was the line "Don't fuck" in "Out of Step" that seemed to cause people to lose their fucking minds trying to figure out what I was saying. The point of the song was pretty obvious to me: I don't do all these things, but at least I can think. I wasn't telling people what to do. I wanted the song to be succinct, hence the "At least I can fuckin' think" qualifier in the lyrics. This seemed to confuse a lot of people. Jeff and I had a long-running argument about whether or not the lyrics would be perceived as declarations or as rules.

JEFF NELSON: I was intent on not telling people what to do. I was uncomfortable being in a band that was being perceived as doing that. Ian and I really got into it, and he kicked a hole in the door of my room at Dischord House. I was laying out the lyric sheet, and I wanted to add parentheses around the *I*'s, to stress that Ian was saying, "*I* don't smoke, *I* don't drink, *I* don't fuck," with the band obviously backing him up, to a certain extent.

IAN MACKAYE: I was never against sex. I was against predatory sexual conquest behavior that I saw as destructive. It was a statement against the pressure put on teenagers to get laid and the terrible, unhealthy decisions people sometimes make in those situations. I used the word *fuck* to differentiate this kind of interaction from healthy sexual interactions, but some people took it literally and thought I was calling for abstinence. The reaction was interesting and entertaining to me. When I said, "Don't drink," in that song, people didn't think that I saying that people shouldn't consume any liquids. When I said, "Don't smoke," they didn't seem to worry that I was against curing meats or starting fires. When it came to sex, they had a harder time parsing the nuance.

BRIAN BAKER: Honestly, most of the time I didn't know what Ian was singing about. To this day, I'm not a lyric person. I'm more of a Van Halen type of guy. When you hear "Unchained," you really don't care what David Lee Roth is singing about, you know what I mean? It was always about the music for me. It wasn't like Minor Threat was united in some straight edge cause. We were just a band and "Straight Edge" was just a song. I wasn't about to hate a local band like Black Market Baby because they all drank heavily.

STEVE HANSGEN: Black Market Baby always got a pass because they were such a great band, and such an important band in the history of D.C. punk rock. They wrote great songs and they were what they were, so no one cared. They thought the straight edge thing was silly; then again, they were twenty-three-year-olds and we were sixteen. They thought we were silly—period! I've played in a band with Mike Dolfi and Boyd Farrell from Black Market Baby in the past few years. They've told me point-blank they thought us new kids were a joke, but eventually they realized we weren't.

SAB GREY: My band Iron Cross was a heavy-drinking band, too. There was always the line, If you got kicked out of Black Market Baby for having a drinking problem, just join Iron Cross. So yeah, I never considered myself straight edge, but I lived in the same house as the guy that wrote the song. People would say to me, "I heard Ian won't let anyone drink in his house!" I would reply, "Well, I live there. I can tell you that you're completely wrong, but I'm not going to bother because you're an idiot." We would watch football games, and those who were drinking were drinking, and those who weren't, weren't.

JEFF NELSON: I don't think there was anyone in D.C. who was actively waving a figurative straight edge banner. We were already sick of being asked about it by the time Minor Threat started touring.

TOM LYLE (GOVERNMENT ISSUE): When Ian MacKaye wrote the song "Straight Edge," the importance only came into play when other people took it out of context. It was never meant to be a movement. The song was never meant to be a rallying cry or anything. It was just about how Ian and some of our friends on the scene felt.

JEFF NELSON: When we went on our first big tour of the U.S., I remember Hüsker Dü made fun of us when we played with them in San Diego. Then we stayed at Jello Biafra's house in San Francisco, and someone who lived there put out a big dildo and fake joints. The whole thing was weird. We got teased by some fanzine editors when we were interviewed by them. Most often we were persistently fielding questions from kids who had a genuine interest in the straight edge idea.

JOHN STABB: "Straight Edge" is a great song, but it's a song about anti-obsession. It's not telling anyone not to drink, smoke, or fuck. The punks I grew up with in bands from the '80s get that—but the people in scenes from, say, Boston or New York took it to fascist levels, acting like bullies to others who had a beer or cigarette at a gig. They were just using the song's lyrics to be thugs. That was never what D.C. hardcore was about. You don't want to drink, smoke, or have sex? Fine, call yourself "monk rock." It's not a fucking religion—it's a song.

Straight edge is not a movement to me. There are peace movements, political movements, orchestral movements, animal rights movements; there are even bowel movements. Those I can take seriously. But a straight edge movement? That seems ridiculous.

JEFF NELSON: We were leaving on what would be our final U.S tour as a five-piece. We had a 1978 Dodge Tradesman van. Before we left, we noticed someone had written in crayon on the side of the van "Straight Edge Stinks." Right away after we left, we kept asking each other, "Who farted? That's disgusting!" The smell persisted for days and days and days. Eventually we learned our friend Roger Marbury, later bass player for Dag Nasty, had put a couple slices of Limburger cheese on the top of the engine manifold before we left D.C. The note didn't make sense to us until then.

Ian MacKaye seeing red at a backyard party in Reno, NV. CARI MARVELLI

D.C.'s
MINOR THREAT
all ages
N.J. **AUTISTIC BEHAVIOR**
CONN. **LOST GENERATION** 8:00
McRAD PHILLY at **LOVE** June 10 HALL
broad + Philadelphia., south st.s

WOULD WE FORCE THIS
MUTANT CHILD
TO WALK A MILE
TO SEE:
MINOR THREAT
NECROS
S.S. DECONTROL & THE F.U.'S?
DAMN RIGHT WE WOULD!!
AND WE'LL MAKE YOU DO IT, TOO.

ACHTUNG! Take the Red Line to Har-
vard Sq. Take the Watertown Sq. [71] or
Waverly Sq. [73] bus to Star Mkt., go up
Belmont, take 2nd right, Cushing, all the
way to the end, left on Huron, look for the missle
FRI. MARCH 4 8 pm V.F.W. Mt. Auburn
Post (Cam

HÜSKER DÜ
FRIDAY APRIL 8th Suburban Mutilation & NØ WIL-MAR CENTER
MINOR THREAT
SUNDAY APRIL 17th Die Kreuzen, Tar Babies SPECIAL 6:00 MAT INEE
Mecht Mensch, M.F.U.D. WIL-MAR CENTER
MILLIONS OF DEAD COPS
FRIDAY APRIL 22nd Die Kreuzen & Tar Babies NOTTINGHAM CO-OP 146 LANGDON

Clockwise from top: *Ian MacKaye of Minor Threat, the Gallery East, Boston, June 12, 1982.* BRIDGET COLLINS; *MacKaye takes a breather in Reno, NV.* CARI MARVELLI; *More action from Gallery East, with SSD bassist Jaime Sciarappa at right.* BRIDGET COLLINS

IAN MACKAYE: There was never really a straight edge scene in the early punk days in Washington. That was something that was perceived by people outside of town. Having said that, the D.C. scene put very little focus on getting high or drunk at shows, and I suspect people in other towns could see that from the outside and thought that was cool. They were interested in what they heard about what was happening in D.C. They saw the X's on the hands on the first Dischord releases, and they heard the song "Straight Edge," and wanted to be connected.

BRIAN BAKER: Minor Threat did not brand ourselves as a straight edge entity. The idea of having straight edge bands came after us, with the Boston people.

SSD's Al Barile gets lethal, Santa Monica Civic Center, August 6, 1983. ALISON "MOUSE" BRAUN

BOSTON: THE KIDS WILL HAVE THEIR SAY

JONATHAN ANASTAS: D.C. is responsible for the iconography of straight edge. They brought along the X's on the back of your hands so bartenders can't serve you alcohol because you're underage; and Minor Threat wrote the song "Straight Edge." Boston took it further by bringing that Boston-tough-guy thing into straight edge. Kids in D.C. were not slapping beers out of people's hands. They weren't preaching about lifting weights and eating red meat. We took it to a different place. The branding of straight edge was solidified in Boston.

MIKE GITTER (*XXX* ZINE): I think that Minor Threat wrote the script, and then SS Decontrol codified the message.

JAIME SCIARAPPA (SS DECONTROL, SLAPSHOT): In 1980, the Boston hardcore scene was in its infancy. There were maybe six or eight of us that kept bumping into each other. My first encounter with Al Barile was at a Dead Kennedys show. We connected briefly, then I saw him again the next time the Dead Kennedys came to town.

JACK "CHOKE" KELLY: When I discovered straight edge, it was like, wow, now there was a term for I was already feeling. In the summer of '81, it all started coming together. It was just sheer luck that I ran into people that were like-minded.

Black Flag played at the Mill Hill Club on Cape Cod, and I spoke to Jaime Sciarappa at that show. Black Flag also played again later in the afternoon at the Channel in Boston. Al Barile was driving down across the bridge heading toward the Channel and he saw me walking. I had a shaved head, so he pulled the car over. He was playing Disorder, and the first thing I said to him was, "Hey, Disorder, I like that band!" That was it. I hopped in his car and we were buds from then on. You couldn't miss Al at all those early shows. He was the biggest guy in the crowd.

JAIME SCIARAPPA: Choke was one of the first guys we latched onto. We met him at Newbury Comics. He was wearing a Black Flag button and we immediately connected. Choke, Al, and I became pretty inseparable in the early stages of the scene. That was the nucleus of what would be called the Boston Crew.

MIKE GITTER: The Boston Crew was a small handful of guys, probably about ten people. They were the guys at the first shows in the city at Media Workshop or Gallery East, and they created the foundation for Boston hardcore.

DAVE SMALLEY: The first Boston hardcore shows happened at Gallery East and the Media Workshop, which was this place up on the ten-millionth floor of this building that should have been condemned.

AL BARILE: The initial members of Boston Crew went to New York and saw Black Flag at Irving Plaza. Somehow I met Henry Rollins and he told me about the straight edge thing in D.C.

JAIME SCIARAPPA: Henry Rollins was the first one of the D.C. guys to talk to us. He said he heard from the Black Flag guys that the Boston Crew was cool. We hung out with him a little bit and Henry told us about the straight edge thing.

AL BARILE: Straight edge hit me at a point in my life where drinking wasn't really important. Personally, drinking was already over for me. So when Henry told me about straight edge, it just became a very natural influence. I didn't ever say anything to the people with me, like, "Hey, we have to stop drinking and be straight edge." That was *never* said. Ever.

To me, though, it was a light bulb moment, because I saw kids that looked cool to me and they were proud to be straight. I immediately saw the power of that, and for the first time ever I connected cool with being straight. I wanted to try to take that example of being straight edge and being cool, and bring that to Boston and basically spread it to the rest of the world. I wanted to run with it.

JAIME SCIARAPPA: I remember driving home to Boston that night with Al after the Black Flag show at Irving Plaza in New York. We had this talk that

Clockwise from top: *SS Decontrol annihilates home turf, the Gallery East, summer 1982; the short-lived Negative FX, debut vocal venture of Jack "Choke" Kelly; DYS bassist Jon Anastas (in sleeveless Venom shirt), Choke (Bruins jersey), and SSD bassist Jaime Sciarappa survey the damage during Negative FX's brief opening slot at Mission of Burma's final show, Bradford Ballroom, Boston, March 12, 1983.* PHOTOS BY BRIDGET COLLINS

we were going to make a conscious decision to take on this whole straight edge thing. We weren't big drinkers. We'd drink a beer here and there. But when we saw those D.C. kids and how cohesive they were, we wanted to model the Boston scene on the whole D.C. scene.

AL BARILE: I think Henry may have overstated the strong foundation of D.C. kids that were straight edge, numbers-wise, but I'm glad he did, because it left more of an impact.

IAN MACKAYE: Al wrote me a letter very early on saying how much he loved the Teen Idles and Minor Threat, and that he was down for straight edge. Then we spoke on the phone repeatedly. We were all isolated, so we were always looking for kids in other cities to share this with. I was psyched to be in touch with him.

AL BARILE: I respect Ian immensely, and I was always kind of surprised that he didn't embrace the subject. I know he believed in straight edge on a personal level, but whether he wanted it to be what it is today—I don't think that was ever his intention. But it was mine.

Straight edge was never a movement with DC, which people don't understand. It was just a song. I didn't live there, and I can't be sure, but my impression was that only a few people there didn't drink or take drugs. My feeling was that it was a *very* important thing. I felt that if they didn't want to deliver the message, I would.

JAIME SCIARAPPA: When Al and I bumped into each other again the second time the Dead Kennedys played in Boston, he said he was a guitar player trying to get a band together. I was a bass player trying to do the same thing. We exchanged phone numbers and pretty quickly got together and started fumbling around.

AL BARILE: SS Decontrol was already going by the time we went on that trip to New York. After that trip, I was resolute in making sure that I set an example in all facets of my life. It starts with one and you hope to get two, and hope to get three, and then just hope that the numbers grow.

JAIME SCIARAPPA: Almost every night Al, Choke, and I would hang out in Kenmore Square trying to make our presence known. I think we did, since three skinheads hanging around looked out of the ordinary at that time. We would hang out there, almost trying to recruit kids into hardcore.

AL BARILE: It wasn't about starting a gang or a club. It was about spreading the message of choice; hopefully people would think really hard about the choice of using drugs or alcohol, because that was the choice I was talking about.

CATHERINE GOLDMAN, AKA KATIE THE CLEANING LADY (*FORCED EXPOSURE* ZINE): The first SS Decontrol practices went on in my grandmother's house. Joe Mueller was the original singer for SS Decontrol, before they ended up getting Springa to sing.

JAIME SCIARAPPA: I'm pretty sure we got Joe Mueller as a vocalist through an ad we put in the *Boston Phoenix*. I think that's how we got our drummer Chris Foley as well. When it wasn't working out with Joe, we decided to ask David Spring, aka Springa, to be our singer. He was a scenester in Boston; we would see him at shows all the time. The first time I laid eyes on Springa was at an Elvis Costello show in 1979, when he was probably twelve years old. He always had a way of getting into every show.

DAVE SMALLEY: *SS Decontrol* stood for "Society System Decontrol," and they were already a band by the time I moved from D.C. to Boston to go to college in 1981. They should be recognized as the bedrock of the Boston hardcore scene. They were the first band that were really getting out there and doing it, especially in terms of being a straight edge band.

JONATHAN ANASTAS: Boston was just like every other city in America in 1981; Black Flag came to town and the entire world shifted. I missed the infamous first Black Flag show in Boston at the Paradise, since I was away at summer camp. I was working at Newbury Comics; everything was punk when I left for summer camp, and everything was hardcore when I came back. After summer camp, the first or second SSD show happened. The Rathskeller, or the Rat, had one or two shows before the bouncers beat up all the kids for slam dancing, and the club stopped having hardcore shows. There were also shows at Media Workshop and Gallery East.

ANDY STRACHAN: Black Flag played in Boston in July of 1981. My friends and I all went to that show after cutting all our hair off with clippers. There were fifty or sixty people there, and there was instant thrashing. We couldn't believe it. We all went to that show and met the rest of what would become the Boston Crew. They were blown that away we came from Marblehead, Massachusetts. There were maybe twelve of us, so they thought we were some big punk rock gang coming from there. We arrived

SSD at the Channel, Boston. GAIL RUSH

with shaved heads and high-top Nikes, wearing rolled-up jeans and sweat-shirts. Little did they know we were just these little kids who didn't know anything. Al Barile was there handing out flyers for a show with his band SS Decontrol. He was a big leader for our scene. He drove us around in his black van. He put so much work into building the Boston scene.

JONATHAN ANASTAS: Boston has always had this flinty, old-school work ethic. It's in our blood. We ran with that, because everything that the Boston Crew did, we did full-on. It was inspiring. If some new wave band put up a hundred flyers for their show, SSD would put up a thousand. If some touring band came in with a new Marshall amp, the next month we would have four full stacks. A lot of the guys played competitive sports before they found hardcore, or at least lifted weights. We were all trained in that mind-set. As they say in the gym, "Every day the weights are the same; the only thing different is you."

MIKE GITTER: The only reason I can give for why straight edge took off like it did in Boston is Al Barile. Al was and is a very strong, directed, and cre-ative person. Also, Al is a hockey guy. He has a competitive and aggressive personality, and I'm sure there was a degree of one-upmanship in him.

JACK "CHOKE" KELLY: Al had his own gravitational pull. He was one of the guys who organized and led the charge. He knew all the guys in all the other scenes, and he was the ringleader in Boston. He was the focus.

JONATHAN ANASTAS: Al had massive X's on the back of his hands, and he wore the jacket with "The Straight Edge" in big letters on the back. He wrote a manifesto, "The Choice," that was published in Glen E. Friedman's *My Rules* fanzine. He had a fucking manifesto! No other kid in America had a manifesto!

DAVE SMALLEY: Why was Boston so aggro and militant about straight edge? I don't know—maybe because Boston is a tough freakin' town! We had tough guys in our crew. We spray-painted our names everywhere, and got in fights, and got chased by jocks, and we ran from cops. That all hap-pened on a regular basis. Boston pits at shows were known to be really hard and aggressive. I can't count the number of elbows I caught in my eye and the number of times I started seeing stars. I'm not trying to glorify any of this, I'm just telling you this to describe things honestly. Our scene also had some great music that was centered around straight edge. Look no further than SSD and that first album in 1982, *The Kids Will Have Their Say*. Holy cow!

AL BARILE: I was trying to associate cool with being straight—that was the key concept. That's the big difference. I wanted that message to resonate with young people; that there was a different way to live your life. Hence the title *The Kids Will Have Their Say*. Back then, I think recorded music was more important than just merely playing live. You weren't a band in my opinion unless you made a record, so putting out the record was important to me. And doing it ourselves was *very* important.

I used a team of people that were around us; Phil N Flash did the photography and Bridget Burpee did the layout. I asked Ian MacKaye if it could be a partial release on Dischord. My feeling was that would make the label I was starting, X-Claim!, somewhat credible, and possibly help us get off the ground. I don't even think Ian reviewed anything; he just let me do it. He didn't have to do that—I know that Dischord is a DC label, and I'm eternally grateful that he felt SSD worthy to be on his label. I don't remember everything that went with it, but I think I sent him a bunch of records as part of the deal.

MARK MCKAY: I was in a record store out in the suburbs, and these thugs were in there selling their records to the store. That was Jaime and Al, and they were trying to sell this store the first SSD album. They played it on the speakers in the store, and I was just amazed. I gathered up the courage to ask if it was their record, and I bought a copy from them personally for three bucks. The straight edge content on that record was such a unified message. I didn't have an idea of what Minor Threat looked like. I just knew what they sounded like, and what their message was. But I could hold this record *The Kids Will Have Their Say*, with these rebellious shaved-head kids running up the Massachusetts State House stairs and this straight edge message and these militant themes, and it was really attractive.

NANCY PETRIELLO BARILE (PHILADELPHIA BYO): I bought SS Decontrol's *The Kids Will Have Their Say*, which I absolutely loved. While there was no doubt that their straight edge message was strong, I was more interested in the music. Their power was unmistakable; I wanted to see them live. I called the phone number and asked them to do a show in Philly. I ended up talking to Al for about two hours. He couldn't do the show, but he told me they would be playing in Staten Island with the Effigies and the Dead Kennedys. A couple of the guys from Autistic Behavior and I drove up to that show. I was blown away. To me, few bands had the sheer power of SSD. I remember talking to Al after the show. I didn't really smoke, but for some reason I had a cigarette. Al looked at me like I had a gun in my hand.

AL BARILE: I didn't say I was going to be militant, but I was certainly going to be intense and over the top, because that's how I live. Everything I do is one hundred percent—that's the only way I can do it with a hundred percent authenticity. Maybe that's where the militant intensity comes from.

Nothing was ever said to the other members of my band or the Boston Crew that we had to be straight, but certainly I wasn't going to participate in any activities that didn't involve being straight. So I guess while people were around me, they were going to be straight. What they did on their own time really wasn't my concern; it should have been their concern.

DAVE SMALLEY: Very quickly after SS Decontrol, our band DYS sprung up, as did Negative FX. One day I was walking around the Boston College dorm with a sleeveless white T-shirt with "Teen Idles" written on it in thick black marker. This kid came up and asked if I was in the Teen Idles. I said no, but we got to talking and we realized we both wanted to be in a band. I went down to Newbury Comics, which then was just one store that sold import LPs, a few punk records, and some buttons. I put up a little piece of paper on their cork bulletin board that said, "Punk singer and drummer with full equipment looking to form hardcore punk band." I had nothing, and the other guy sure didn't have a drum kit. We basically lied. But Jonathan Anastas called me up and said he was a bass player, and that he had an awesome guitar player who loved punk. That guy turned out to be a stoner who just wanted to play Van Halen riffs all day. So DYS was totally built on a lie. But Jonathan and I quickly jelled, and we eventually got Andy Strachan on guitar.

AL BARILE: The most important thing about DYS arriving was that we suddenly had a bunch of people with common influences. So we did encourage them. Having a bunch of bands was important to building our scene. We didn't want to have to play with a death metal band or something, but there was a period where we had to play with bands with whom we did not share a common fan base.

DAVE SMALLEY: SSD and DYS were definitely brother bands. L.A. had a scene with the Circle Jerks, the Adolescents, and Wasted Youth. That mirrored their culture and who they were. With Boston, we had SSD and DYS, and that reflected who we were. It was very modest and pure. I wanted to have a hardcore punk band that was centered on trying to make life better—trying to make the world a little better—and doing all that for straight edge. We had a certain evangelical ferocity. When DYS called our first record *Brotherhood*, it was about hardcore kids sticking together—straight edge or not. We walked the walk and we talked the talk.

ANDY STRACHAN: Seeing Al Barile play in SSD definitely inspired me to learn to play guitar. I was like, "Look at that guy. Look at the way he holds the guitar like a gorilla!" If he could do that, so could I. I joined DYS after only playing guitar for eight months. I think DYS was playing for a little while before I joined. Their guitarist was getting drunk, so they had to get rid of him. Our first show, we played a church in Cambridge opening for the Misfits.

MARK MCKAY: DYS was the band that always invited everyone to get up and sing along with them, and it was a real relationship. When you would see SSD, you'd feel it; but when you saw DYS, you were experiencing it. You were always afraid to get near SSD because they were so tough. DYS was more like, "Come up and join us!" You could go arm in arm with Smalley and sing. So DYS was more of a real influence on me than SSD, because I felt more camaraderie. Instead of being a witness, I could be a participant.

JONATHAN ANASTAS: All the older Boston punk rock bands seemed to have a problem when hardcore came to town. No one paid attention to the older bands except their friends in Boston. They might have been punk rock, but they still existed in the mind-set of wanting to gain attention from major labels. They wouldn't make a record until someone paid them to make a record. They weren't going to send demo tapes out, or get in a van and play for twenty-five dollars. They were still waiting to be "discovered" in the old model. We weren't thinking like that. If anything, we invented a new model. So I think there was incredible jealousy. These old bands were like, "Why are people in San Francisco talking about SS Decontrol? Why are people in New York talking about Gang Green?" No one talked about the older Boston punk bands outside of Boston.

DAVE SMALLEY: We were proud of being straight edge and making that a part

From top: *Early DYS wowing a crowd in Jersey City, NJ.* VICKI TORCH PHOTOS; *DYS vocalist Dave Smalley in top skanking form during Negative FX's notoriously bruising opening set for Mission of Burma, March 12, 1983.* BRIDGET COLLINS

Boston's straight edge crew seizes an ideal photo op, Tufts Medical Center, winter 1982. GAIL RUSH

of our mark, but there was no wider intent behind it. There was no pretense from anyone, because we were all figuring things out as we went. That's probably why each city was so distinct. Today, the Internet has blurred all the lines between distinctness in our country. It's hard to find an identity when every town has Starbucks and Target and Walmart and Staples. Back then every punk scene in America was pretty damned unique. Boston was very different from D.C., which was very different from Chicago, which was very different from Detroit, which was very different from L.A., which was very different from San Francisco. Each of those scenes was so distinct, musically, stylistically, and aesthetically. We were just showing who we were. We threw down the flag. You could pick it up if you wanted. You could step on it, too, if you wanted—but I don't think you would have gotten very far if you tried that.

ANDY STRACHAN: Not every band out of Boston was completely straight edge. That was just impossible! We could count the numbers of people who were straight edge in the Boston scene on our hands. There were drinkers and partiers that we knew all through growing up that were part of our crew. It's not like we were going to stop hanging out with them.

JONATHAN ANASTAS: Gang Green was in the Boston Crew, and they were a heavy party band. Jerry's Kids was somewhat of a party band. Even the F.U.'s were a bit of a drinking band. DYS and SSD were the straight edge bands, but there was no schism. You have to understand that no one was pure here. Media Workshop was a drug den, and no one talks about that. SSD would be putting on their straight edge shows while the owner sold beers out of a cooler and people probably sold God knows what else without anyone knowing. But SSD accepted it, because where else were they going to put on these shows?

DAVE SMALLEY: Some other bands weren't straight edge, like Jerry's Kids or Gang Green or the F.U.'s. They were part of the Boston Crew, but not the Boston Straight Edge Crew. They weren't straight edge and didn't pretend to be.

JONATHAN ANASTAS: The dirty secret about all these bands is that they were not even one hundred percent straight edge themselves. Not all of SSD was straight edge. Not all of DYS was straight edge. Not all of Negative FX was straight edge.

JACK "CHOKE" KELLY: I was the only person in Negative FX who was straight edge. But I wrote all the songs, so that made us a straight edge band.

REVEREND HANK PEIRCE: The songwriters were always the straight edge guys, and the rest of the guys in the bands usually weren't so much into it. Springa of SSD wasn't the most sober of people as I remember.

AL BARILE: I was going to spread this message, but I was going to do it by example. I never went to even my band and said, "Look, we have to be straight." Never said. Never done. I just felt that if my lyrics were going to be about something, it was going to be something important and meaningful, and I was going to help try and change how kids approached getting through those teenage years, a period of life that can be hard to navigate. I think everyone is influenced by what they see and what they think is cool, right? That was the message—the message was about choices. It was a message of choice.

I never took a straw poll and asked who was straight edge or not. I figured the best way was to continue to be steadfast. I never knew who else was and who wasn't. I just knew I was, and I was going to continue to set that example. Obviously I still had a lot of friends at home who went out on the weekends drinking. It's not like all of a sudden I despised my friends, or that I thought every bar in the world should be closed. It's not like I thought drinking or drugs were some tools of the devil that had to be eradicated from earth like during prohibition. I definitely do not have a puritanical view of life.

MIKE GITTER: Was straight edge the rule of thumb in Boston hardcore? Absolutely not! If you look at the scene, some of the best bands to come out of it weren't necessarily the ones who called themselves straight edge. It's similar to D.C., where bands like Scream or Void probably didn't adhere to the same ideological stances as some members of Minor Threat.

You had these musically phenomenal bands like Jerry's Kids or Siege, and history has been very kind to them. But they didn't stand for anything. I think the reason SSD, Negative FX, and DYS have held such weight in the punk rock pantheon is that they stood for something.

MARK MCKAY: With Boston, we have the same attitude with our scene as we do with our sports teams. We follow our sports teams to the gates of hell. I'm fifty years old, and I still watch the scores of the Bruins games just because

From left: *SSD singer David "Springa" Spring makes his point known at the Santa Monica Civic Center, summer 1983.* ALISON "MOUSE" BRAUN; *Negative FX singer Jack "Choke" Kelly.* BRIDGET COLLINS

it's something you hold onto. It's familiar and comforting, and straight edge is the same way. It's a source of pride; especially being in a town like this with a real active bar scene.

JACK "CHOKE" KELLY: When people would ask you where you were from, if you said Boston, you'd have to tell them, "We're north of New York." Sometimes it would just be easier to say you were from New York. So we were trying to get the name of Boston hardcore out there. In order to get people to listen, we had to go overboard sometimes. I guess I'll always be that twelve-year-old boy who wants to troll people. Sometimes I'll write a song and I won't mean it, but I'm not about to *tell* you that I don't mean it. If you're idiotic enough to believe it, then you're an idiot. It's not my job to spell everything out for you.

JONATHAN ANASTAS: With Al from SSD and Choke as his hatchet man, the brand of Boston straight edge solidified and the myth built on itself.

MIKE GITTER: If Al Barile was Grand Moff Tarkin, then Choke was Darth Vader.

JAIME SCIARAPPA: Boston started to get this reputation of being this super-militant straight edge city, and I think that was blown out of proportion a little bit. We would play a show in some town, and then hear afterward about things that went on, and everything was blown out of proportion.

JACK "CHOKE" KELLY: I remember a show in Ohio that SSD drove out to play. During the show, Al and I had flashlights. We were aiming them at people who were drinking, and shaking our heads in disapproval. We were just trolling people, to be honest. After the fact, people were saying the Boston Crew slapped beer bottles out of people's hands. No, we didn't. We never did anything like that! But we heard about that kind of stuff and saw the reaction, we would say, "Of course we did!" To me, it's not my job to correct the legend. It's my job to further it.

JONATHAN ANASTAS: Do you know about the T-shirt-sleeve hats the Boston Crew used to wear all the time? Well, it started out that you couldn't just make a sleeve hat; you had to tear a sleeve off someone's' shirt in the pit. It was like a trophy. You couldn't just go home and make one with a pair of scissors. It started as a joke, and then it wasn't. Then you really couldn't make a sleeve hat at home, and poor kids were going home shirtless.

JACK "CHOKE" KELLY: I think Al came up with the idea of the sleeve hat, or maybe Springa. We were always cutting the sleeves off our T-shirts, so it was the first recycling or repurposing, you know? What could we use those things for? It's kind of funny how they fit our heads so perfectly. It didn't provide any bit of fucking warmth, but it was another thing to put our stamp on. No one else thought of it, so we were going to do it.

Saying you had to earn your sleeve hat by ripping it off a punk's arm in the pit was one of those fun things we started to get a rise out of people. Like a sleeve is going to rip off that perfectly! We were always coming up with shit like that.

JONATHAN ANASTAS: Hüsker Dü came to Boston, and they sang backup vocals on the DYS *Brotherhood* record. They were grilling us. "We heard if we come with long hair, you guys will hold us down and shave our heads. We heard you guys slap beers out of people's hands." *That's* when we started saying all that stuff was true; when these guys came from out of town with all these rumors. "Yup, that's what we do!" And the stories just spread.

Slapping the beers out of people's hands—I liken that to Method acting, or being a professional wrestler. But at some point, we started taking the character home. It started as an ironic joke, and then the mythology took over. I think at some point, Ian MacKaye was like, "What the fuck are you guys doing? Are you guys fascists?"

IAN MACKAYE: SS Decontrol first came to D.C. in January of '82 to play a show at Woodlawn High School. They drove down in a snowstorm, and, at the time, I was driving a newspaper truck for the *Washington Post* delivering bundles. I had come home from work and probably gone to bed at four in the morning or something like that. At the Dischord House, my room was directly above the front door, and I was woken up at ten in the morning by all this stomping. I came downstairs to see all these bald guys wearing shirtsleeves on their heads, stomping the snow off their boots. They all seemed huge and super muscular to me. That was the first time I met them and it left a real impression.

JEFF NELSON: We were friends with SSD, and I liked them, but there was a jock aspect to them. They called themselves the "Boston Crew"; the minute you start using the word *crew*, it constitutes a lot to me.

IAN MACKAYE: SSD's show ended up being controversial, because the Boston Crew was so violent on the dance floor. I reckon that their idea of the D.C. punk scene was that it was going to be really tough. While we might have been tough, we weren't bruisers. Most of us didn't go to shows looking for a fight. On the other hand, we wouldn't really back down from one. But the Boston guys definitely showed up to stomp some ass, and a lot of the D.C. kids just weren't into it.

JAIME SCIARAPPA: SSD would do this thing called a "pig pile," where we would just jump on each other and it would get to the point where the bodies would be eight high. I think in D.C. a kid got a broken rib or something. Then it went around that we were bullies, and we beat the kid up. Don't get me wrong, we liked to go to shows and make our presence known. We had a few guys in our crew that were pretty insane, but we would never injure a kid on purpose, especially not in D.C.

IAN MACKAYE: It was fucked up and some people were mad at me for bringing them down here to play. People were saying, "Fuck those Boston guys!" and I kept saying, "No, they're nice guys! They're my friends!"

My recollection is that, after the show, Al Barile said something to me like, "I'm really disappointed in D.C." I asked him what he meant, and he said that he had figured that our scene was going to be this huge army of bald guys throwing their X'd fists in the air or something. I think he was surprised to find so many weirdos, wimps, and women.

JONATHAN ANASTAS: Compared to what happens today, or what went down in Los Angeles, it was really nothing. Everything was also more about factions than an overall scene war. Boston, for sure, did its best to create it. SSD would stuff their vehicles with as many kids as they could hold, then roll up to Irving Plaza or the Rock Hotel in New York. Someone would grab a Sharpie and say, "Everyone draw an X on your forehead so you'll know who *not* to punch in the face." Choke would lead a straight edge chant on stage between songs; things like that.

BRIAN BAKER: There was a feeling at the time in D.C. about the Boston bands that had us thinking, "Wow, this is being a little bit misconstrued." But it's a long-running D.C. punk tradition to think we're doing it the right way and the way you're doing things is just the *wrong* way. D.C. likes to take ownership of things once we see other people want it.

The Boston crew first travelled to D.C. to support SS Decontrol playing with locals Government Issue and Iron Cross at the Chancery, February 20, 1982. Clockwise from top: *Straight edge traffic stop. Note Al Barile's stellar jacket; SS Decontrol vocalist Springa leans against a pole while the Boston Crew takes it easy; Jack "Choke" Kelly of Negative FX and his crucial wardrobe element, the sleeve hat.* PHOTOS BY BRIDGET COLLINS

Members of SSD and DYS in Boston's seedy "combat zone" district, circa 1982. GAIL RUSH

DAVE SMALLEY: There was a respectful relationship between D.C. and Boston. We were the two cities that were marked by this thing called straight edge. Both places were either hated or loved for it.

JACK "CHOKE" KELLY: Dave Smalley and I were living in the same house, and he was pen pals with Ian MacKaye. Ian wrote a letter to Dave that read something like, "You guys in Boston are too militant about straight edge." I was like, "Oh really?" So I decided to write this drill sergeant–style chant about straight edge, and recite it before SSD played with Minor Threat at Irving Plaza. Again, I was just trolling, but people fell for it hook, line, and sinker. It had lines in it like "Kill anyone with a beer in their hand." I mean, c'mon, really? We were having fun with it all. I don't understand why a lot of people don't like me. To me, punk rock was always about pushing the envelope and stepping on toes. Did anyone think Sid Vicious was a Nazi because he wore a Nazi armband?

SAB GREY: I don't want this to turn into a bunch of middle-aged guys stomping their feet and complaining, but most of those Boston guys were a bunch of fucking hockey jocks who got turned on to punk. They were jocks before punk, do you know what that means? They were always assholes! I was the weird kid who played sports, but I was a weird kid first. Why would you punch someone for drinking a beer? They're not bothering you. I don't like it when right-wing fascists do it. I don't like when the Christian right does it, so why should we allow hockey jock punks to do it? It's called bullying and I don't like it.

BRIAN BAKER: As the Boston guys took straight edge into this militant factionalized thing, all I could do was be a smart-ass and say, "Yeah, way to misread it." But I didn't realize maybe straight edge was very attractive to these people because they might have had problems with drugs or alcohol, or had a shitty upbringing where they got beat up by drunk parents. I never thought about it like that. I didn't really think further that maybe this could be an awesome, empowering thing for them. And if so, who was I to interrupt the way they felt?

From top: *Early three-piece line-up of 7 Seconds rocking the Reno scene; Just a couple of "young rads"—Kevin Marvelli (left) and brother Steve (right) in the early '80s.* PHOTOS BY CARI MARVELLI

7 SECONDS: COMMITTED FOR LIFE

DAVE SMALLEY: 7 Seconds was the first band we heard about from outside of Boston and D.C. that was into this straight edge thing. I've often used the analogy that straight edge was my gang—not in the sense of drugs and money laundering, but in the sense of brotherhood. Once we started to hear about bands like 7 Seconds across the country, we felt like the "gang" was spiraling into something. If we found out a band was straight edge, or had a straight edge guy in the band, we gave our extra support.

KEVIN SECONDS: At the time that we formed 7 Seconds in 1980, we were blown away by what we were hearing about the D.C. scene. Here we were, young pups; we didn't party or want to be like all of our other younger friends getting wasted and doing stupid shit with absolutely no purpose. Now we met kids across the country with similar feelings. It was terribly gratifying and revelatory.

MIKE GITTER: Discovering 7 Seconds was interesting. Here were some guys from Reno, Nevada, that espoused a familiar ideology to what we knew in Boston, but they did so with a certain sensitivity and a humanity that was rare at the time. They embodied the personal outlook of Minor Threat, but took that to a more humane place. Hearing that kind of voice echo back with a different enunciation from the other side of the country; especially in the pre–social media era, we felt a creative and ethical kinship.

KEVIN SECONDS: The seeds for 7 Seconds were planted in the early part of 1979, when my brother Steve and I got turned on to bands like the Dils and D.O.A. that had a harder, faster, more intense edge than the British and New York punk bands. We started a group called X-Banned, but we couldn't find a drummer in Reno who could play as fast as we wanted. Then a kid I worked with at Montgomery Ward named Bob Seeds told me he was a drummer and wanted to join a band. We would sit up all night, playing records for him. We started practicing at a friend's basement. We never really played gigs, but we started to sound pretty good.

Everything was moving along until Bob joined the navy near the end of 1979. Not long after, Steve and I were in a record store in Sparks, Nevada, and we noticed a long-haired guy in a big parka covered in punk rock band buttons. We were so excited to find yet another punk fan around. His name was Tommy Borghino, and we hit it off instantly. He invited us to come listen to records at his friend's house, and we were blown away. Between Tom and his friend, they had the biggest punk rock and new wave record collection we had ever seen.

Tom bought a drum kit, and by January 1980 he was our new drummer. At the time, I didn't want to sing. I wanted to be the guitar player. Tom's younger brother Jimmy tried out with us and we liked his style and spirit. We played our first show at a redneck biker Top 40 bar on March 2, 1980. We started playing parties around town as 7 Seconds, and by the summer of 1980, a really fun little underground scene grew from those parties. Within a year, I was singing and playing guitar for the band. Other bands sprouted up during that time, like the Thrusting Squirters and the Wrecks—an all-girl band who were sort of our sister band.

BESSIE OAKLEY (THE WRECKS, *PARANOIA* ZINE): At the local library there was a book about British punk, and my friend Jone Stebbins and I would pore over it. We really studied that book; the edgy style piqued something in me. We tried to find records by those bands, or records that looked cool, and we came upon stuff like Generation X, the Buzzcocks, the great British compilation *Live at the Roxy*, the B-52s, and so on. We saw Devo on *Saturday Night Live*, and I loved the theatricality, the clever beats, and the curious phrasing. That music made me want to move around—not like a rocker or cheerleader, but more like a robot, and just do weird stuff. I just had to be myself; being different was easier and less intimidating than trying to follow someone else's formula and failing.

When I was fifteen and Jone was fourteen, in February 1980, our parents drove us to see our first live show. The band was called the Beat, from California. They were fast and fun, and Jone and I got up and danced around by the stage while the rest of the audience sat at little café tables. These two guys were jumping around, too, and—importantly—they wore leather

Photos from top: *Kevin Seconds.* CARI MARVELLI;
7 Seconds live in Nevada circa 1984. CASEY JONES

jackets. They talked to us after the show, and were really friendly. We learned that they were in a band, and the next week was going to be their first gig, an afternoon matinee. The taller guy had this giant button on his jacket with the name of their band in that punk style of cutout letters: 7 Seconds. We saw them the following week, and exactly one week after that they played again with the Zeros from San Francisco, the first out-of-town punk band to play Reno.

After the first time I saw 7 Seconds, I had an experience that really sealed the deal. Jone and I were hanging out in a moving truck with Kevin and Steve, and Tom and Jimmy "Dim Menace" Borghino; the two sets of brothers that made up the original 7 Seconds. There were a few other people in there. A joint started being passed around. I had never smoked pot or done any drugs and I didn't really want to. I thought something like, "Ugh, the moment has come where I *have* to smoke pot." When it got to Kevin and Steve they said, "No thanks." They were inspired by the anti-drug stance of Chip and Tony Kinman of the Dils. I was sort of incredulous. Both Jone and I passed on the pot as well. And I felt like, *Wow, I didn't lose any cool credibility; there's room in this scene for me just the way I am.*

TONY KINMAN (THE DILS): People should realize that a drug dealer is no cooler than a liquor store owner or a pharmacist. But for some strange reason, these people have attained the status of folk heroes and they don't deserve that at all. They're businessmen.

KEVIN SECONDS: I think being a message-oriented band just resonated with fellow frustrated young people. We played fast and spoke up for and against things. I suppose the common thread, which we shared with those East Coast bands, appealed to kids thinking and feeling the same way.

BESSIE OAKLEY: The Reno scene was always sort of different. We were a bit rough-and-tumble, and rugged in a Western sort of way. No one was really pretentious, and we laughed a lot. And the bands were really energetic. Out-of-town bands could feel it. Kevin Seconds, I think, coined the term *rad rock* very early on to describe the Reno scene and differentiate it from punk. We used that and the word *rads* instead of *punks* for a while.

KEVIN SECONDS: I was fascinated by the idea of all these cities having punk rock scenes with their own flavor and identity, and I wanted like hell for

Reno to be represented, so I came up with silly shit that I hoped other kids would pick up. The black eye makeup thing was just my own naive way of communicating how I felt that society and the mainstream and authority figures were doing everything possible to keep down people with a more rebellious spirit and attitude. We might be getting pummeled and we might have bruises, scars, and black eyes, but inside, nothing would ever change us. If anything, we were becoming more anti-societal and rebellious. Eventually, other Reno kids adopted the black-eyes look, and it just went from there.

JOHN PORCELLY: Hardcore always had this nihilistic vibe that I didn't like. Don't get me wrong, I was angry—but I wasn't into this "kill your mother, kill your father" thing. If you were a kid back in the days of the punk scene, you could be heading to a dark place. There was heroin and sniffing glue. Any kid could have easily fallen into that trap, and a lot of kids did. Many people from that early scene died in the gutter. So a band like 7 Seconds changed my life. I could have gone two ways when I was a young, impressionable kid in punk. I'm so glad bands like 7 Seconds came along to give me a positive direction in life.

BESSIE OAKLEY: I distinctly remember Kevin using the word *hardcore* in an interview we did with 7 Seconds for the first *Paranoia* zine. When asked what kind of music they played, he said, "Call us hardcore rock 'n' roll. If we're still playing in a year, I want to be twice as hardcore as we are now. I want to keep going till we sort of self-destruct, so there's no more. I want people to know us as one of the hardest hardcore bands. I think it's important, there are very few hardcore bands around, and I think those bands should be noticed. I want people to think we contributed to hardcore." That was summer or fall of 1980.

KEVIN SECONDS: Henry Rollins was the first D.C. hardcore kid to make contact. He wrote to us around 1981, saying he had gotten a copy of one of our early demo tapes from Jello Biafra, and he wanted to trade a copy for his band S.O.A.'s new seven inch. Soon after, we heard from Ian MacKaye in a similar way. We started writing letters back and forth, trading tapes and records, and filling each other in on what was going on in our respective cities. I still have and adore those letters.

I never imagined we would last five years, let alone almost forty. I suppose back when I was twenty-one or twenty-two, I didn't think that bands were suppose to stick around for long periods. That was something the Rolling Stones and the Grateful Dead did. Not hardcore bands.

CHRIS BRATTON: Although 7 Seconds were from Reno, Nevada, they might as well have been from Southern California—they played here constantly and became a massive influence on all of us. They were the very first band in the Western United States to be influenced by East Coast hardcore. That was very important, because they were the band we could see, touch, and be at their shows talking to them in person, in real time, on the regular. Later, Justice League actually got to play shows with them. They made the fairy tale of East Coast hardcore seem real and attainable for us little West Coast kids. 7 Seconds put the dream within our grasp, encouraging us with their infectious positive mental attitude to go out and make it all happen for ourselves.

KEVIN SECONDS: Personally, I've never been comfortable with the tag of straight edge. I don't do drugs. I don't smoke. I don't smoke pot. I don't drink. I'm not into it. But for me, I was never into it as an action or a movement. I was never trying to prove a point. We've never been comfortable with the straight edge thing. I think that happened because some of the early stuff had some lyrics. People affiliated us with Minor Threat because we were friends and we played together a lot.

STEVE LARSON (INSTED): Even though they never really considered themselves a straight edge band, 7 Seconds from Reno had a lot to do with straight edge taking off in Southern California. They felt like a California band, even though they weren't. They had a completely different vibe. Kevin Seconds was positive, and obviously played a huge influence on Insted. He was fun and inclusive. That mattered a lot to hardcore in Southern California.

PAT LONGRIE (UNITY, UNIFORM CHOICE): I was initiated into straight edge through Minor Threat, and obviously I gravitated toward that band. But 7 Seconds *really* got me into straight edge. I had been corresponding with Kevin Seconds and his brother Steve Youth from day one. When they came to play Southern California for the first time in 1982, we hit it off really well. They came back a year later and stayed at my house.

JON ROA: There were older people in Los Angeles, like Al Kowalewski from *Flipside* magazine, who took us with a grain of salt. Maybe he figured, "Let's wait and see what these kids can do." We weren't hurting anyone, so why not? But 7 Seconds seemed more inclusive. They were older, but they didn't seem like a big machine. They toured in this small VW van, and they would help other people whenever they could. You could approach Kevin Seconds and say, "Hey, can you take my band on tour?" He'd say, "Here are the phone numbers, if you can book it, you can go"; which is exactly what happened with Justice League. His behavior was a big influence on me.

KEVIN SECONDS: Looking back, it's shocking how dangerous and stupid going out in a van and touring the entire country for two months straight in 1984 really was. We had no money, no car insurance, nothing to fall back on. Bands rarely got gig guarantees back then, so you never really knew what you were walking into and who was trustworthy or not. Cops hated you. Rednecks hated you. Kids in the ghetto neighborhoods where you were playing hated you. Even fellow punk rockers hated you. To make things even more ridiculous, we traveled the country in a friend's 1958 VW bus with just about the shittiest gear imaginable. We were hungry every day, and lucky if we got showers. Every gig was different. We broke down several times. But I'll tell you this: It was one of the most incredible and thrilling times of my life. We met some of the greatest people on the planet, saw the best bands, stayed at the coolest houses, and even managed to get laid every once in a while. I'd do it all over again in a heartbeat.

DAN O'MAHONY (CARRY NATION, NO FOR AN ANSWER, 411): Only three names are not subject to debate with me. I marched willingly for years to the beat of Kevin Seconds, Pat Longrie, and Pat Dubar.

RYAN HOFFMAN (JUSTICE LEAGUE, CHAIN OF STRENGTH, CIRCLE STORM): 7 Seconds was melodic, the lyrics were heartfelt and uplifting, and Kevin was amazing. Now 7 Seconds was a big band; each night they played, Kevin would learn about the newer local bands in the area. Right before he would hit the stage, he would either put on a shirt of the local band or mention the local band during their set. That was influential and sent a very powerful message that encouraged people like myself to start a band.

KEVIN SECONDS: I'm glad we did stick it out. I think we make great fast punk rock music, and we have some interesting opinions worth sharing. I don't think the majority of kids buying into rebellious subculture know or care about who we are, but there will always be people into what we do.

Ron Baird of Stalag 13, West Los Angeles Federal Building, February 4, 1984. ALISON "MOUSE" BRAUN

SOCAL: IN CONTROL

JOE NELSON (TRIGGERMAN, IGNITE, THE KILLING FLAME): In the early '80s, Southern California had a huge punk rock scene; possibly the biggest in the world at the time. But when Minor Threat came through, at least twenty dudes were so moved that they wanted to form bands, including Pat Dubar and Pat Longrie from Uniform Choice; Brad "X" Xavier from Doggy Style; Gavin Oglesby and Casey Jones from No for an Answer; and Ryan Hoffman from Justice League.

CHRIS BRATTON: By 1981, Riverside County and the Inland Empire in Southern California were the United States' leading production and distribution capital of the crystal methamphetamine, often referred to as the world's most dangerous drug. As suburban kids growing up wearing a kind of enforced blinders, we all felt that there was just no other choice than to do what was heavily expected of us. That's just the way it was.

RON BAIRD (STALAG 13): I was an East Coast hardcore snob. I didn't like many of my peers' bands much, like Decry or things like that. I respect those guys now, but at that time I thought L.A. punk was total shit! The Midwestern hardcore band the Necros stayed at my house. I said to their singer, Barry Henssler, "I live in a cultural backwater." He thought I was crazy. Here I was in Southern California, seeing Black Flag numerous times, and all I could think was, "I wish I was in D.C.," or, "I wish I was in Boston."

I went to see the Ramones at the Hollywood Palladium in August of 1981. Henry Rollins had just moved out from D.C. to sing for Black Flag, and he was hanging out. I was hanging out with the guys from Circle One, and they were hanging out with Rollins. I started chatting with him. He was cagey and intense. In hindsight, it was probably nerves. He was a young guy in L.A.—a big, crazy city—and he had joined a band that was already legendary. I think he was just nervous. Rollins was talking about straight edge and all these bands from back in D.C.

CHRIS BRATTON: By 1982, at the age of thirteen, I had graduated from listening to Devo, Adam and the Ants, the Clash, and the Sex Pistols into Black Flag, Circle Jerks, TSOL, and the Germs. But even those technically hardcore bands still had for me the somewhat nagging feeling of "older brother" punk. Before long, I was exposed to an absolute gift to my future life—from my crystal meth dealer, ironically. While I was scoring and doing meth at his house, he played me the yellow-sleeve press of the debut Minor Threat seven-inch, the D.C. hardcore compilation *Flex Your Head* on Ian MacKaye's Dischord Records, and also the similar Boston hardcore comp, *This Is Boston, Not L.A.*

This was the real underground, even more so than Black Flag or the Circle Jerks, because the very few punks at my junior high school were already sporting that shit. This was way deeper. Forget all that older-brother punk, this was the fucking soundtrack to my life; a shotgun blast by dudes almost three thousand miles away that somehow could miraculously fucking read my innermost thoughts.

RON BAIRD: A few days after I met him at the Ramones show, Henry Rollins's first L.A. show with Black Flag happened—a matinee at the Cuckoo's Nest in Costa Mesa. Seeing him up there was the point where I said, "I want to do this," and I started Stalag 13. I always look at my hardcore journey as first converting to punk rock, and then converting to straight edge. I talk about the changes in religious parlance because they were deeply quasi-religious experiences that changed me into the man I am today. Talking to Rollins for the first time about straight edge was conversion number two in my punk rock journey.

KEVIN HERNANDEZ (INSTED): Stalag 13 was one of our favorite bands. We'd drive up to Santa Barbara to see them quite often. I think they are a very underrated band that doesn't get the accolades they deserve.

RYAN HOFFMAN: Stalag 13 and America's Hardcore started the Southern California positive hardcore scene.

PAT DUBAR: I loved Stalag 13. I didn't know them personally, but I wore out their record *In Control*. They were the only straight edge band in Southern California in 1984.

Stalag 13's Ron Baird, Cathay de Grande, Hollywood. ALISON "MOUSE" BRAUN

CIRCLE ONE 7 SECONDS
STALAG 13
SHATTERED FAITH
KENT STATE

FRI FEB 18
$6 7:30 PM

MANDIOLA'S BALLROOM 6130 PACIFIC BLVD. HUNTINGTON PARK

12XU PRODUCTIONS

HEART ATTACK
(FROM NYC)
MIA
(FROM LAS VEGAS)
STALAG 13

JERRY'S KIDS
JUSTICE LEAGUE
CHILD HOODZ

SUNDAY, MARCH 11

MATINEE SHOW—STARTS 4 P.M.

$5. NO INS
AND OUTS!

SUN VALLEY
SPORTSMANS HALL

FROM SAN FRANCISCO DIRTY ROTTEN IMBECILES

STALAG-13
DR.KNOW
BASIC MATH
NIP DRIVERS

The original lineup of Pomona's Justice League shouted, "Don't Forget the Kids!" PHOTOS BY CASEY JONES

CHRIS BRATTON: Stalag 13 was huge. They were the first established Southern California band to take Justice League seriously and see us as more than just a bunch of fourteen-year-olds with X's on our hands. Their singer, Ron Baird, took us under Stalag's wing, putting Justice League on their shows and wearing Justice League shirts constantly onstage, which thankfully was documented in a lot of photos and videos.

RON BAIRD: Obviously, we didn't think we were progenitors of anything. Looking back, I guess we were the forerunners for West Coast straight edge. Doing my Ph.D. on youth subcultures, I looked at a lot of this hardcore stuff, and I can see we're in the time line of influential bands from that first wave. That's really cool.

JON ROA: Justice League started around 1983, about six months after Stalag 13. That's when you started to see people getting into straight edge and putting X's on their hands, and straight edge started to take hold in Southern California.

RON BAIRD: Stalag 13 played the Federal Building in West L.A. in February 1984. You could get a permit for twenty-five dollars to put on shows there—so I guess the government wasn't completely fucked. The building had this big, beautiful lawn, and was so much fun to play. In the footage from that day, you can see all the Justice League guys onstage singing along. They were the main guys to look at us and take something from it.

RYAN HOFFMAN: Justice League was highly influenced by Stalag 13, Minor Threat, and SSD, and also by America's Hardcore.

JON ROA: America's Hardcore needs to be mentioned when it comes to more youth-oriented bands coming out of Southern California. America's Hardcore wasn't a straight edge band per se, but they were the first Southern California band that was more inspired by what was going on in hardcore in other parts of the country. They took the aesthetic and work ethic of other scenes and did things with it; that was really important.

CHRIS BRATTON: America's Hardcore are absolutely godfathers of Southern California straight edge hardcore. They practically invented the concept of merchandising in hardcore, as their T-shirt graphics were killer and revolutionary, looking like nothing that had come before. Plus they were super DIY, making and distributing their own shirts, which we all completely took note of and learned from. That America's Hardcore shirt was everywhere in 1983 and '84. Look at photos of Texas hardcore band D.R.I. from around that time. Then Minor Threat drummer and Dischord Records co-owner Jeff Nelson had one on the back cover of Minor Threat's swan song seven-inch, *Salad Days*.

DANNY SLAM (AMERICA'S HARDCORE): We formed under the name Section 8 in the spring of 1982. After a while, we thought our name was too generic. My little brother, Jason, suggested we use America's Hardcore. The name comes from the labels I would put on these cassette tape recordings I made for friends of all the great music I was buying. I was hugely influenced by S.O.A. from D.C. We covered their song "Public Defender," and that shaped our style in their mold of aggressive hardcore.

We played our first show as America's Hardcore in January of 1983. We had already written a song called "America's Hardcore," about the incredible hardcore bands from all across America. The name was perfect for us. After our guitarist Drew Bernstein joined, we became a lot more serious. Drew always talked about how we had to be "dedicated." He was very hardcore about what he was into, and he became the driving force behind making America's Hardcore stickers and T-shirts.

JON ROA: Even though they didn't wear *X*'s on their hands, America's Hardcore promoted this youth-oriented scene.

DANNY SLAM: Drew was serious about being straight edge for a while, but it was never my thing. I liked to drink then, and I still do. But we definitely picked up on the positive attitude vibe that Minor Threat sang about. That was always a big theme with us. We were fixated on positivity and not being rock stars—meaning we got up there and raged through our sets without fucking around between songs like rock stars do.

Our lyrics were a mix of the L.A. "fuck you" punk attitude and an idealistic positive outlook. So our immediate environment had an influence. Part of that was going to shows and getting drunk, and then going crazy when the music hit our guts. But as we listened to more and more bands from all over, and read the lyrics, we started caring more about putting out a positive message, going to the shows, and supporting our favorite bands.

JON ROA: They were so young, just teenagers, but they went on tour when no other L.A. bands were going on tour, not even Bad Religion. America's Hardcore played shows as far away as Arizona. When they came back, we

Via a handful of compilation appearances and a few bad-ass T-shirt designs, America's Hardcore made a huge impact on Southern California hardcore. Guitarist Drew Bernstein left AHC to play second guitar in a short-lived five-piece lineup of East Bay peace punkers Crucifix. He also acted in Penelope Spheeris's 1983 film Suburbia, *and founded the clothing company Lip Service, famed outfitter of Sunset Strip hair metal bands.* Clockwise from top: *vocalist Danny Slam and Bernstein urge the kids to use their heads and open their eyes; AHC vocalist Danny Slam; AHC bass player Scott Kosar.* PHOTOS BY ALISON "MOUSE" BRAUN

just kept asking them how they did it. At that point, Black Flag seemed like the only band that could go as far as Arizona—but Black Flag seemed like men, and America's Hardcore were kids! America's Hardcore made everything seem more accessible. When they made shirts, they were very direct and rudimentary. I said, "Oh! Now I know how to do it!" I realized you just try to do the best you can to get your message out.

DANNY SLAM: We played with Minor Threat and 7 Seconds; our experience was incredible. Also memorable was our little tour in September 1983 with the Circle Jerks to Las Vegas, Tucson, and Phoenix—where I sang from the top of a wrestling cage. We felt like we had really made it, playing shows away from home. All the gigs were a huge rush, with tons of butterflies in our stomachs as we got on stage. Then came the amazing feeling of letting go and raging through our set with unabashed enthusiasm, screaming the lyrics as loudly and energetically as possible.

We were practicing a lot at Sin 34's Spinhead Studio, getting ready to do some sort of album, when I quit. I blame myself for the band's demise. I was in a weird space and I thought, foolishly, at nineteen years old, that I needed to be a responsible dude and not go running off on this big U.S. and Canada tour we were planning. I didn't want to leave my live-in girlfriend and our four dogs to fend for themselves. Funny thing is, that girl was out of the picture not long afterward. Not going on that tour or doing the album are big regrets in my life.

RYAN HOFFMAN: America's Hardcore was short-lived, but they really influenced the next generation of bands, especially in the way they marketed themselves with T-shirts and stickers.

PAT DUBAR: I only ever saw America's Hardcore once, but I remember thinking the graphics on their shirt were cool—obviously!

RYAN HOFFMAN: The scene was pretty violent, and there was a lot of intimidation from skinheads and punk gangs. Being straight edge was not cool. Mostly the scene was influenced by European punk bands like G.B.H., Discharge, Toy Dolls, and the Exploited. At that time, the straight edge scene wasn't very big.

IAN MACKAYE: The early L.A. hardcore scene was so fucked up. Those guys in bands like Stalag 13 and America's Hardcore were playing on the front lines of some serious debauchery.

RON BAIRD: The violence in the early L.A punk scene was very real, even before the gangs. The Dead Kennedys played at the Whisky on Sunset and there were fights front, right, and center. Anybody with long hair was laid out. The Hollywood punks might have been more open-minded than us. I was fighting a lot. I saw so many riots. There was a big one when Black Flag played a rehearsal studio in Hollywood. Punk rock was crazy, man! I'm not proud of a lot of that shit.

Hanging out at Oki-Dog once, I was involved in beating the living shit out of this long-haired homeless guy. The guy pulled a knife and Mugger from SST Records just clocked the guy with no fear. They chased the guy across the street and everyone was laying into him. Somebody picked the guy up, dragged him across the street, and tossed him through the order window of a Der Wienerschnitzel. In hindsight, it was fucked up.

JOE NELSON: I loved the danger of those early L.A. punk shows. A perfect example is when the Exploited played Fender's Ballroom around 1985. The rumor around our high school was that the local white-power skinhead gang was going to stab their singer, Wattie, to death onstage. We all went to that show just to see that happen. Recently, I heard that show broke the attendance record for Fender's at the time. Fender's probably held 2,500 people; but they had 2,800 in there who just wanted to see Wattie get killed onstage. I told my mom I was going to the movies, but actually I was going to a show in hopes of seeing some guy get killed by a bunch of white-power skinheads. That is fucked up!

PAT DUBAR: California was a really violent scene. I didn't realize how bad it was until Uniform Choice did our first U.S. tour. We would be in a town like Madison, Wisconsin, or Salt Lake City, Utah. Some little fight would break out and everyone would be making a big deal out of it. I would just laugh. I never felt too threatened on that tour. For us it was the equivalent of training to be a Navy SEAL and then being sent out to play paintball.

DANNY SLAM: Yes, the L.A. hardcore punk scene of the early '80s was very violent. At most shows there were fights, usually ten dudes kicking the crap out of one poor guy. There were a handful of dudes that you did not want to piss off who were known to love to fight, including John Macias from Circle One, Mike Muir from Suicidal, Oliver from the LADS, Sean Emdy from FFF, Mugger, and others. A lot of fights just spontaneously erupted from clashes in the pit.

PAT DUBAR: I can't even put a number to the amount of fights I was in at punk shows in Southern California. I never gave them a second thought, because you had to survive. As I get old, I think most of what I did was crazy, but it was all done in the spirit of doing the right thing.

DANNY SLAM: Many kids grew up familiar with gang life in L.A. and started creating copycat punk gangs. Partly, the gangs were justified, as being a punk was a bit treacherous. I went to a huge high school of two thousand kids, and about ten or fifteen of us were punks. Not a day went by when somebody wasn't fucking with me. But the punk gangs were also just another way of being antisocial, and having safety in numbers to do stupid shit like spray-paint walls, break shit, steal shit, fight with other punks at shows, et cetera. I was most familiar with the FFF gang, which was made up of all the punks where I lived in North Hollywood. FFF copied the style of Mexican gangbangers with khaki pants and buttoned-up Pendleton shirts, and the kids adopted nicknames like Oso, Flaco, and Shorty.

RICH LABBATE (INSTED): If you went to shows at places like the Olympic Auditorium or Perkins Palace, there were a couple thousand people there made up of all these cliques from different neighborhoods. It reminded me of that movie *The Warriors*. You would affiliate yourself with a gang just to stay safe. Even I was affiliated with a gang in my little town, just so I would have a decent amount of people around me.

STEVE LARSON: When I first started going to shows in Southern California, it was frightening. If my parents knew what I was involved in, I don't think they would have let me go. East Coast guys would always come out and talk about how crazy New York was. Then they'd go to a show at Fender's and shit their pants. The huge amount of people, and the huge amount of gangs out here was a totally different vibe.

JON ROA: I remember when Justice League first started playing out, people would offer us Coke cans with beer in them. I started thinking, "Why do you find this to be such an affront?"

CHRIS BRATTON: I clearly remember an older punk dude coming up to me at a huge, packed, August 1984 show at the Olympic Auditorium with Suicidal Tendencies, SSD, the Minutemen, and the Red Hot Chili Peppers. That punk dude saw my Minor Threat shirt, and he just had to come over and tell me, "You know what? That stupid fucking Minor Threat band is just a cheap, watered-down, shitty black-and-white photocopy of the Damned. Every single song they play sounds like a fast, shitty version of 'Love Song.'"

PAT DUBAR: D.C. punk was always the shit for me. I liked some California bands, but the D.C. shit seemed harder to me. It seemed more real. I just gravitated to that. The message and the music locked into me. I already felt the same way about religion and drinking, so Minor Threat was a perfect fit. I felt like I was moving *toward* something instead of moving away from something. If I could have moved my family to D.C. in the early '80s, I would have. I've never made any apologies for saying Ian MacKaye's music changed my life.

When my friends and I actually saw Minor Threat, the energy was insane. We couldn't control ourselves. All the atoms in our bodies were smashing against each other at the same time. As kids, we were fearless. That's why they draft kids at nineteen to go to war; you don't feel your mortality. You might be scared, but fearlessness will overcome.

A shaggy Dave Smalley of DYS GAIL RUSH

EAST COAST: HOW WE ROCK

MIKE GITTER: By 1985, all the original straight edge bands on the East Coast were done. The Boston straight edge temple bands SS Decontrol and DYS had moved on musically, and Minor Threat had broken up altogether.

JEFF NELSON: When Minor Threat broke up, there might have been some continued frustration on my part about being perceived as a monk, due to songs like "Straight Edge" and "Out of Step." But the bigger issue was the types of songs that Brian and Lyle were writing. I thought it was some of the best stuff we had ever written, but it was very different music than what we'd been doing before. Ian was an excellent shouting singer in Minor Threat, and these songs would have required him to break out of that mold.

IAN MACKAYE: As Minor Threat got more popular, our aspirations and ambitions became different. Lyle and Brian had specific ideas of what they wanted; Jeff had specific ideas of what he wanted to do; and so did I. My ambition was to grow big and refuse the model; not to do the typical rock thing. Lyle and Brian wanted to become more official. They wanted to use contracts and get a manager and a record deal. That wasn't what I wanted to do. All this wasn't an issue at the start of the band, because there was no fucking way we thought were going to be big. Basically, Minor Threat broke up because we were kids who couldn't agree on which way the band should go.

JEFF NELSON: To spread your wings and mature musically in hardcore was really hard to do gracefully, without sucking or alienating your fans. I was burned out on the slam dancing and macho aspects of hardcore by '82, and I would say I was burned out on super-aggressive hardcore music by '83. That's around the time Minor Threat broke up.

IAN MACKAYE: In many ways Minor Threat's most brilliant moment is when we broke up, because it made us unimpeachable. I don't think there's a bad song in the batch, and we never compromised at all. We don't have that embarrassing third album that a lot of other bands had.

JEFF NELSON: It seemed at the time like there were only a couple different directions to break out of hardcore punk. One was heavy metal and another was new wave; both had been the enemies of hardcore punk early on.

IAN MACKAYE: A toxic element came into the Washington punk scene. A new group of people arrived who were more aggressive and violent and into partying and fucking shit up. It didn't represent what we were about, and we couldn't relate to it. It was a drag, because we were really invested. Then came these people who appeared to be a part of it, but I didn't agree with them on any kind of philosophical or spiritual level. Some people said, "Fuck it," and were done with the scene. But we were not done. We started another scene. We wanted things more wide open. Bands like Embrace, Rites of Spring, Beefeater, and Kingface were a response to the context of the situation.

MARK MCKAY: D.C. moved on. The bands evolved, and people started taking social action toward things they saw as wrong. They took part in political protests or started working for homeless shelters. Their music evolved very quickly and became something a little bit different. The messages became more aware of the world and personal politics.

JEFF NELSON: The stuff that started coming out of D.C. would be labeled as "emo core." The bands went in a more sensitive direction, where the Boston guys went more heavy metal.

RICH LABBATE: At some point, it all got weird. I was into Dischord Records, buying S.O.A. and Minor Threat. All of a sudden they starting putting out this stuff like Beefeater and Rites of Spring, where I was like, "What the fuck is this shit?" Then in Boston, DYS and SSD became full-blown cock rock. Even New York's Agnostic Front was onto a metal phase by 1986 with their second album, *Cause for Alarm*. Everything was changing and it seemed like people were giving up on hardcore.

AL BARILE: At the time, music genres were very clear and distinct, and hard rock and heavy metal people did not like hardcore punk.

REVEREND HANK PEIRCE: When I moved to Boston in 1984, the straight edge thing was already dying out.

MIKE GITTER: The last great first-wave Boston hardcore show was in January of 1984 at the Fraternal Order of Eagles hall in Malden, Massachusetts. That was literally the last night of DYS playing the songs from *Brotherhood*, and was also probably the last time the F.U.'s played as a straight-up hardcore band.

MARK MCKAY: We put on this show at an Eagles hall in the town where I grew up. DYS played, and they tore it up. That was the last great hardcore show in Boston ever. Then in the spring of 1984, DYS came out with their metal sound. SSD were going down that same road. By the next time we heard them, it felt like the door had slammed on hardcore.

MIKE GITTER: The invasion of the second guitar players started it all. SS Decontrol got François Levesque. Ross Luongo joined DYS. Then Steve Martin joined the F.U.'s on lead guitar as they were transitioning from the F.U.'s to Straw Dogs.

JAIME SCIARAPPA: Hardcore had run its course with us. We were looking for something else. We were attracted to really heavy stuff. As far back as 1981 when we heard the song "Damaged I" by Black Flag, we thought slower was definitely heavier. When we were writing that later SSD stuff, we always said the songs had to be slow and powerful.

JONATHAN ANASTAS: We all loved our rock and metal from day one. We never stopped loving it. We used to go to Van Halen and Def Leppard shows. The only person I ever wanted to be was Joe Perry. When I was in DYS I thought, "I can't be in Aerosmith, but I can play this!" But when Metallica played the Rat in July 1983, the world changed again. It was just like when Black Flag came to town in '81. Hearing Metallica's *Kill 'Em All* was as transgressive to me as Black Flag's *Damaged*.

ANDY STRACHAN: We saw Metallica and were like, "Oh my gosh!" We wanted to go in that direction. It all seems so lame now.

DAVE SMALLEY: I think there has always been a very close relationship between hardcore and hard rock. They're both hard-edged forms of music with lyrics that raise eyebrows among most people. What's the difference between the first two Metallica records in attitude compared to SSD or DYS? It's all

Kevin Seconds of 7 Seconds senses the new wind in the air on the night the air conditioning broke at City Gardens in Trenton, NJ, summer 1987. PHOTOS BY KEN SALERNO

the same fucking attitude, which was: *Fuck your world. We're taking over.*

AL BARILE: We weren't trying to be metal per se. I don't even really like metal. If metal is bands like Iron Maiden, then we were definitely *not* trying to be metal. We were just trying to be hard and good at what we did, including trying to write songs that were memorable and had a longer shelf life.

JONATHAN ANASTAS: We were genuinely excited about what Metallica was doing. We were excited about what Venom was doing. To this day, I still don't understand how Venom got on our radar, but, all of a sudden, we were listening to more Motörhead, Metallica, and Venom. And we could actually play it now!

DAVE SMALLEY: We were listening to Judas Priest, Venom, and Metallica. Then Jonathan Anastas and I and a lot of the other Boston Crew guys got into working out. We were hardcore into weight lifting and we'd listen to all that stuff while lifting.

JONATHAN ANASTAS: We were a tight group of people egging each other on. We'd hear a song SSD wrote, and then we'd push it a little further. Then they'd push it a little further. Then Al bought a Marshall stack. Aerosmith was broke, so I bought a Marshall bass stack off Tom Hamilton because he had no money. The backline started growing, and the guitars started getting nicer.

REVEREND HANK PEIRCE: People were getting better at their instruments, so they said, "I don't need punk rock any more! Now I can do what I really want to do."

MARK MCKAY: A lot of the kids in Boston were all of a sudden interested in Judas Priest. Once playing abilities became more than trying to play as fast as you could for a minute and a half, the attraction was there to slow it down a little bit and try to emulate this other form of music. All of it was still aggressive, but to me it had nothing to do with punk rock. I was looking to get away from Kiss, Rush, and these indulgent bands. I was looking to jettison Lynyrd Skynyrd from my life, in favor of this scene that was fresh and exciting.

DAVE SMALLEY: In the same way people were getting better at their instruments, I said to myself, "Wait a minute, I know how to sing." I sang in church choir, and in musicals in high school, so I knew I could do a little bit more. We all wanted to stretch as musicians. The growth was organic.

AL BARILE: We were just getting better at our instruments; we were trying to write better songs. I never considered SSD particularly good at playing off-the-charts-fast music, so it was a matter of finding our power groove. The next phase of SSD was our third record, *How We Rock*. I know what the goal was. In many ways, I'm not sure if we accomplished that goal. The goal was to bring music and vocals into a powerful blend, and I don't think we achieved that vision for the band.

MIKE GITTER: SSD's *How We Rock* was an aggressively polarizing record. Not only did the cover look like Judas Priest's *Point of Entry*, the back cover looked exactly like AC/DC's *For Those About to Rock We Salute You*. Musically, they were on their way to being a hard rock band.

JONATHAN ANASTAS: No one was pushing against this direction, because we were feeding off each other. We would be at rehearsal, and everyone there was loving it. So the people closest to us really liked it. Then we took it out to three hundred people and they didn't like it. It went from positive reinforcement to negative reinforcement as we moved outside of the core of our friends.

AL BARILE: Reluctantly, some SSD fans went along for the ride. I'm not sure if they understood what we were trying to do, but we did.

MIKE GITTER: The people who were already fans and acolytes of SSD and DYS went along with the changes.

JACK "CHOKE" KELLY: I was friends with all those guys, and I can truly say I hated that shit! I hated what was happening. They were my friends and everything, but that doesn't mean I had to like where their bands were going. AC/DC and Metallica weren't my thing.

JONATHAN ANASTAS: When SSD and DYS played the Rock Hotel in New York together, the crowd was booing our gear! We weren't even onstage yet! How was our gear wrong? We ended up getting beaten up by half the audience; at least *I* got beaten up by half the audience.

ANDY STRACHAN: When we decided to play heavy metal stuff, we took such a beating. Looking back, we all jumped too far too quickly. Bands get really into growing, without realizing that the people in the scene move slower. *Brotherhood* came out in 1983 and the second DYS album came out in

1985. To us, it was a long time, but not to others. People weren't ready.

We started doing "Last in Line" by Dio and "Everybody Wants Some" by Van Halen. We were growing out our hair. I remember looking into the crowd when we played "Closer Still," that ballad off the second record, and seeing my friends with their jaws on the ground. That song started out as a joke at practice. We were really into solo Ozzy, and we thought "Closer Still" sounded like something off one of his recent records.

AL BARILE: The last time I listened to the later SSD records was a long time ago. They seemed slow and sluggish, and lacked the energy, innocence, and spirit of our *Get It Away* EP. That's important, because we really didn't know what we were doing with *Get It Away*. We weren't trying to do anything. After *Get It Away*, we saw the possibilities of where the SSD sound could go. That's when we tried to do something and things got fucked up. To me, *Get It Away* was a very innocent record, and that's what made it what it was.

MIKE GITTER: Individually, I think SSD became something of a boogie-less boogie-rock band. They tried to be something that they weren't really good at. I think DYS made for a better metal band. If you go back and listen to their second record, there is more of a direct lineage to their original sound on songs like "Held Back," "Late Night," or "No Pain No Gain." Those are the songs they played live before the record came out.

DAVE SMALLEY: The punk purists and the San Francisco anarchist crowd hated the second DYS record. The review in *Maximum Rocknroll* was scathing. But what did we really expect from a narrow-minded fuckwad who wanted to hear the same three chords over and over again? There was a lot of dismissal, but the biggest thing in punk rock is to be honest about who you are, and say, "Fuck it." That's what we did, but we were dismissed because of that.

ANDY STRACHAN: The back of the second DYS record was so lame. Jon had on makeup and Dave had a salamander on his shoulder. Ross the other guitar player and I didn't know what was wrong with them.

JONATHAN ANASTAS: We played a showcase for the talent scout Michael Alago, but we never talked deal points or anything. Michael signed Metallica, and we were getting comparisons to them. We were going to Canada to shoot this multi-camera video. Things were starting to happen a little.

DAVE SMALLEY: We were hated, but we were just being who we were. At the same time, bands like C.O.C. and D.R.I. were bringing metal into hardcore as well, but they were loved by all the same people who were giving us hell.

ANDY STRACHAN: I recently listened to that last SSD record, *Break It Up*. All I could say was, "Wow!" They really took it as far as any band at that time, going for the heavy metal thing.

JONATHAN ANASTAS: Our more metal sound changed little about how I, or DYS, behaved at home or on the road. The big black *X*'s may have been gone from the backs of our hands; our shaved heads may have been grown out into long hair or mullets, but the gym workouts remained—and the commitment to our lifestyles remained. There are no drug references on our second album beyond the song "Graffiti" and the metaphor it uses for our love of tattoo needles.

AL BARILE: We were trying to find a vocal style that fit in powerfully with the music. Later, we found out that wasn't going to be achievable, and that's why we broke up. It wasn't going to happen, but there was no way to turn the clock back to *Get It Away*. Probably the best that could ever come out of our early sound was *Get it Away*. In hindsight, if we just kept on putting out a second, third, and fourth version of *Get it Away*, and we didn't try to improve, the band would have continued and the fans would have been happy. We would have never tried to fix our problems or find the missing pieces. It was as obvious to me then as it is right now what those missing pieces were, and the issues were unsolvable.

ANDY STRACHAN: SSD flew to L.A. in August of 1984 and played one of their last shows with this music to a group of kids expecting hardcore punk. Instead, they got Springa with all these bandanas on and everything. You've got to hand it to them: That took guts.

JONATHAN ANASTAS: At SSD's last show at the Olympic Auditorium in L.A., they were playing Alice Cooper's "I'm Eighteen," and Springa was under three pin spotlights on the top of the P.A., looking like David Lee Roth.

JAIME SCIARAPPA: Al and Springa were fighting like cats and dogs. They were constantly at each other's throats. Springa got into theatrics, and Al and I did not. The bullshit he would do would drive us crazy, so he hid it from us. Then in the middle of the set, he would come out in some wacky outfit or waving some stupid prop. Once, he came out with a pig's head he had picked up from a butcher. He threw it out into the audience, and someone threw it back. It hit me in the leg, and one of the pig's teeth ripped open my leg and I was bleeding. It stopped being fun, and fun was the whole reason we were a band. It certainly wasn't for the money or the fame.

ANDY STRACHAN: The last SSD show in Boston was so weird. They played at this college, and we had to sit in seats.

JACK "CHOKE" KELLY: SS Decontrol's last show in Boston was so hard to watch. Good Lord, I was embarrassed for them. But they didn't see it. They were like, "Fuck you! We're gonna do what we want to do, whether you like it or not!" All I could say was, "No! No! No!"

AL BARILE: The last SSD show was at Suffolk University in Boston. There was no sadness; it felt like a relief to get it over with. In a way, I was disappointed that we couldn't do what we wanted to do. The fact was, we couldn't write the songs we wanted to write.

MIKE GITTER: Meanwhile, even on the West Coast, bands like 7 Seconds were musically evolving.

KEVIN SECONDS: We weren't attempting to bail on hardcore or punk rock. We just got caught up on our many influences and were pretty shell-shocked by the amount of violence we were seeing at punk rock and hardcore shows, especially in Southern California. I had written a lot of the material for *New Wind*. I pondered starting a whole new side project that would be a more melodic, midtempo type of thing, but when I played the songs for the guys they seemed to love them. We decided to record them as 7 Seconds. That probably wasn't the smartest thing to do after the success and popularity of *The Crew* and *Walk Together, Rock Together*, but we weren't thinking about being smart at the time.

No one took the amount of shit from the hardcore scene that we did. People were pissed, sending us death threats. I remember several shows where kids would stand up front, just visibly bawling their eyes out, they were so disappointed and disenchanted by us. It was really frustrating and depressing, and it did get under our skin. Ultimately, though, it helped us grow a thicker skin.

We were young, sincere, idealistic, and we still felt very much a part of the team. We did everything we could to strengthen hardcore. We took young bands on the road with us, put out their records, promoted them in interviews, and always did what we could to make the community fun and strong. Being dissed by the hardcore scene at the time really bummed us out, but it never came close to killing the spirit for hardcore, for punk rock, and for our band and fans. We just had to accept that we might be on our own for a little while we waited for kids to catch up.

MIKE GITTER: After all these bands changing and breaking up, there was still a hunger for the straight edge stuff. And when something echoes back, it usually echoes back louder than when it was first spoken.

Despite being weighted down by an excessive amount of hair, DYS bassist Jonathan Anastas grabs mighty air during the band's later days. GAIL RUSH

Pat Dubar and Uniform Choice, straight and alert in Hart Park, Orange County, as Ryan Hoffman of Justice League and Chain of Strength and Jon Bunch of Reason to Believe and Sense Field appear to believe. CASEY JONES

UNIFORM CHOICE: SCREAMING FOR CHANGE

PAT LONGRIE: Growing up in D.C., Boston, New York, or Chicago I'm sure was unique. Orange County, California, was shockingly different from all of those places. Orange County straight edge was informed by Minor Threat and 7 Seconds, but was germinated by our own thought patterns and how it affected our lives. From there, we started forming our own bands.

CHRIS BRATTON: When America's Hardcore and Stalag 13 broke up, it left the newly emerging audience wide open for Uniform Choice to be crowned the heavyweights, mostly through Pat Dubar's leadership qualities and undeniable onstage electricity and magnetism. Orange County kids would have jumped off a cliff if he told them to.

RICH LABBATE: I didn't consider Stalag 13 a straight edge band. Their singer was straight edge, but they didn't have super in-your-face straight edge songs. But when Uniform Choice entered, they were considered a straight edge band. There were *X*'s everywhere. They were promoting that lifestyle. And they were in your face.

PAT LONGRIE: I went to Catholic high school, where I met Pat Dubar and Dan O'Mahony. Freshman football brought us together. We all shared a love for this aggressive music, and we liked the idea of a positive, gang-like thought pattern. We were young people rebelling against parents and trying to figure out who we were. You're not really a kid anymore, but you're not an adult yet. Punk rock was this wonderful outlet for what we were experiencing at the time.

Punk rock wasn't shunned in my high school. It was embraced like you wouldn't imagine. Pat Dubar and I played football, baseball, and basketball. When we started forming bands and playing shows in people's backyards and garages, the whole football team would show up. That was a very unique thing for punk rock. We had none of these negative experiences where we got beaten up for being into punk, or anything like that. It was a positive vibe.

PAT DUBAR: I moved to Orange County from Missouri when I was nine, the summer before fourth grade. I was the king of the dorks. I moved to a place where everything had to be Ocean Pacific, and I was wearing Toughskins, Wallabees, and number shirts from Kmart. The only person in our neighborhood who wanted to be friends with me was a big kid named Pat Dyson. Then I went to my first day of fourth grade and Pat wasn't there. The only friend I had made had already moved away.

Fast-forward to my freshman year of high school; I was riding on the bus with Mike Pritzl, a guy that I had played Little League baseball with. He was sitting behind me, listening to Black Flag's "Jealous Again" on his headphones. That weekend I rode my bike to a record store and found the little punk rock section with forty or fifty records. I bought the *Jealous Again* EP, *Group Sex* by the Circle Jerks, and *Never Mind the Bollocks* by the Sex Pistols. I also bought an Exploited record, just for the cover. I fucking wore those records out.

I got some older dudes to drive me to Zed Records in Long Beach. The first time I went in there, I was so overwhelmed by a store that was pretty much all punk rock. I asked the guy behind the counter, Big Frank Harrison, if there was something he would recommend. He handed me the first Minor Threat seven-inch. I took that home, and the first song I heard was "Filler." Since it was all about religion, and I was stuck in this Catholic school that I didn't understand, that song became my battle cry.

Very soon afterward, I was at the T-Bird Rollerdrome seeing Suicidal Tendencies and Descendents. I got up on stage, did my thing and flipped off the stage, and wiped out all these people. I took out one motherfucker that was huge. All of a sudden, someone was picking me up by my shirt. I looked down at the guy who had me off the ground. "Pat Dyson? It's me, Pat Dubar!" We became friends again. I told him I was singing in this band. He had a band too, and he asked me to try out to be the singer.

PAT LONGRIE: Pat and I were not musically inclined at all. We flipped a coin to see who was going to buy a P.A. and who was going to buy a drum set. Pat ended up buying the P.A., and that was it. I bought the drum set and started hammering. We found a couple of other guys and played some shows under the name Labelled Dead. Then Pat was asked to join the original lineup of Uniform Choice.

PAT DUBAR: I went to Pat Dyson's house to try out to be in Uniform Choice, and the band was playing really bad pop punk. I tried to sing a song called "Don't Take the Car." After the practice, I told Pat I couldn't do it. He suggested that we do a band ourselves. So we put an ad in the *Recycler* and Victor Maynez showed up. We kicked the original guitarist out and continued as Uniform Choice.

PAT LONGRIE: The lineup of Uniform Choice that Pat tried out for had been around for a few years, but they were nothing like what Uniform Choice would become.

PAT DUBAR: I didn't like the name, to be honest, but we worked with it. The guitar player was writing the pop punk shit, so we kicked him out. I was surprised to learn later how far back that original Uniform Choice went.

JON ROA: When people started talking about the Pat Dubar lineup of Uniform Choice, I was like, "You mean that band that played the Cuckoo's Nest all the time?" But after Pat they had a whole new group of members.

PAT LONGRIE: When Pat joined Uniform Choice around 1983, I started a band with Joe Foster, a kid named Rob Lynch, and a bass player; we were Unity. Uniform Choice and Unity started the Orange County straight edge scene. We would always go to each other's shows and open up for one another; it was a real family thing.

KEVIN HERNANDEZ: I played basketball with Chris Smith and Brad Xavier, who ended up forming Doggy Style. They were really good friends with Pat Dubar, a really well-known local high school baseball pitcher in our area. His photo would be in the newspaper regularly. So Uniform Choice sparked my interest. It was interesting to me to see guys who played high school sports, yet were into hardcore.

GAVIN OGLESBY (CARRY NATION, NO FOR AN ANSWER, BLOOD DAYS): "Uniform Choice" was the only thing written on the wall in the weight room of our high school. Their name was there the entire time I was at the school. I had no idea what it meant, or what it was, until some time later.

RYAN HOFFMAN: Uniform Choice and Unity were great! The scene was very small in the early '80s, so most of us knew each other really well. Almost every weekend we would meet up to see the touring bands like Agnostic Front, SNFU, Necros, Cause for Alarm, M.I.A., Marginal Man, BGK, 7 Seconds, Scream, or D.R.I. It was really a nonstop assault. It's amazing how influential those bands were. They created the next wave of bands from those of us who were in the crowd. After meeting at those shows, kids formed all kinds of bands, including Infest, Unity, Uniform Choice, Scared Straight, NOFX, Excel, Justice League, Pillsbury Hardcore, and Final Conflict.

JON ROA: Unity was the first band to hand out printed lyrics sheets before their shows. We thought that was such an awesome idea. How else could you get the message out? How else would they understand your lyrics and where you were coming from? Unity would give out demo tapes for free, too. They didn't sell them for a dollar; they gave them away to spread the message. They became a big force.

PAT LONGRIE: Rob and Peter Lynch were two brothers who were stalwarts in the Orange County straight edge scene. They were at every fucking show, and they were the coolest guys you'd ever want to meet in your life. But Rob came home one day and opened the garage door to find his older brother hanging there. That was shocking, and the band kind of ended there.

CHRIS BRATTON: America's Hardcore's sudden absence from the embryonic straight edge scene left a total void that was quickly jumped into by Uniform Choice.

JON ROA: When Uniform Choice came out with their "Use Your Head" T-shirts I was like, "Those shirts look exactly like America's Hardcore's shirts!"

CHRIS BRATTON: They latched on to America's Hardcore's T-shirt designs and graphics and used them for their own.

PAT DUBAR: Orange County always had a faction of punks who loved D.C. hardcore. Since those bands either never really came out here or broke up by the time we started playing, the kids who liked that sound would come see us instead. A little movement started out of that, even though that wasn't our intention.

KEVIN HERNANDEZ: Uniform Choice took it to the next level. Not only were they playing shows regularly, more importantly they were at every show supporting other bands. Pat Dubar could always be found in front of shows passing out flyers. He'd do this thing where he would look someone up and down and then hand them a flyer; almost as if he was surveying who he would allow to go see his show. We'd mimic that gesture a lot afterward, and laugh about it.

JON ROA: Even though there were a few bands before them, Uniform Choice was the catalyst for any straight edge scene starting in Southern California. My band Justice League did not have the same work ethic as Uniform Choice. I was in high school, and I took my schooling very seriously. But Pat Dubar just did it. He's the one who made straight edge viable and accessible to the kids. He was a very productive, sincere guy.

PAT LONGRIE: I was sitting in my dorm room on a Friday night after Unity broke up, and I got a call from Pat Dubar saying they kicked their drummer Pat Dyson out of Uniform Choice. He said, "We need to play a show in Riverside tonight and you need to play drums for us." I said, "I'm in L.A., and I don't know your songs." Pat said, "Whatever. We're going to stop by your house and pick up your drums for you, so call your dad and tell him we're coming over. We'll play you the demo tape on the way to the show and you'll learn the songs." That was how I joined Uniform Choice.

KEVIN HERNANDEZ: Go back and look at Uniform Choice. You had Pat Dubar with a shaved head and wearing Vans. Then you had Vic Maynez, the guitarist, who was this average Joe. Then you had Dave Mello, the bass player, a surfer. The drummer at the time, Pat Dyson, was an ex–football player. The mix intrigued me. You could get a surfer guy coming to the show, saying, "Hey, that bass player looks just like me." Then some jock could see Dyson and be lured in and get into the message.

BILLY RUBIN (HALF OFF, HAYWIRE, *THINK* ZINE): Young kids were enamored with Pat Dubar because he was in shape, he was an athlete, and he was charismatic. He was a pretty big, tough guy. Kids wanted to go to punk shows and not get beat up. It was nice to know that if you went to see this band play, someone from this band would stop the show and handle any trouble that happened.

PAT DUBAR: You name any L.A. punk gang; they were at all the early Uniform Choice shows. Back then, there were skinhead gangs like the Family and the O.C. Skins. You had the Sons of Samoa and Suicidal and the L.A. Death Squad, or LADS.

The kids who wanted to come see us were normal kids from Orange County into skateboarding. These kids would ask me, "If I come to your show dressed normal, am I going to get my ass kicked?" I would be like, "Of course not, punk rock is all accepting! Come and do your thing!" I was naive about that in the beginning. Sure enough, one of these kids would be the first to be attacked by one of these gangs. Afterward, I said, "No one who is coming to see us is getting their ass kicked." I mean, they might get their ass kicked, but at least I would get my ass kicked too, defending them, you know?

STEVE LARSON: Pat Dubar would be standing in the middle of a tense scene, basically putting up his middle finger and saying, "Fuck you! I like sports and I'm straight edge!" That was comforting. When I saw Pat Dubar come out with his head shaved, pegged plaid pants, no shirt, sweating his ass off—he scared me but I also felt comforted. Pat Dubar feared no one, and Uniform Choice was like a protective big brother.

JOE NELSON: Pat would protect all the kids that were straight edge. Shows in California were infamously violent, so having someone like Pat protecting you made you feel okay to be up front. If some skinhead or member of L.A.D.S. fucked with you, you knew he would stand up for you. Pat was a tough dude with a hero complex. He was cool to throw down with some dudes while a bunch of little straight edge kids stood behind him going, "Get 'em, Pat!"

PAT DUBAR: We weren't into violence. I'm not going to say we were pacifists, but we weren't going out looking for violence. In the middle of all this chaos I wanted to come out and say, "Hey, this scene is mine, too." That's the kind of scene we wanted to build. We didn't want to play to a group of people who were exactly like us. We just wanted everyone to be included. I didn't care if you drank. But if you drank and acted like a fucking idiot, then there was no "Get Out of Jail Free" card. Drinking isn't an open invitation to be an asshole. We weren't out to hurt anybody, but we weren't skipping through the daisies either. Uniform Choice wasn't positive youth. That's not what we were about.

High on life: Pat Dubar of Uniform Choice PHOTOS BY CASEY JONES

JOE NELSON: There's actually a great video of Pat Dubar's brother Courtney doing a stage dive during a Uniform Choice set. He goes off camera and ends up getting pummeled by the L.A.D.S. in the crowd. In the video you see all the kids run to Courtney's aid, only to have all of them come scattering back onstage into the video. Pat, however, stayed right smack in the middle of it. You can actually hear him punching dudes with the mic. He must have hit and dropped ten dudes.

We're not talking some dumb jocks from the suburbs either. We're talking about dropping guys who if they didn't get killed two or three years later, are now all lifers for murder, armed robbery, or some other major crime. I mean these people were hard-core criminals.

PAT DUBAR: One of the dudes from Sons of Samoa pulled a knife on our drummer before a show. Then while we were playing, they were grabbing the mic and screaming their area codes into the mic and shit. We got in a big fight with those guys afterward. My main problem was that they didn't give a flying fuck about the music. They just came to fight.

PAT LONGRIE: There were fights all the time. In the middle of the set, there'd be fights onstage where we would have to jump in and grab people. If no one got stabbed, then everything was fine and we moved on with our set. It was just a way of life.

PAT DUBAR: When these guys would put up their arms to *Sieg Heil*, I'd say, "You need to put your arms down, or else I'm coming off the stage." They would keep it up, and I would drop the mic, get off stage, and start swinging. By doing that, we slowly eradicated those elements from coming to our shows.

BILLY RUBIN: I always thought Uniform Choice had more of an appreciation for diversity within punk rock. Those guys grew up going to shows in Hollywood and seeing bands that were in no ways straight edge. Someone like Dave Mello, the bass player for Uniform Choice, was a complete outsider. He could not have cared less about that straight edge crap. He just wanted to be in a band and have fun. He and his bandmates were just stoked that Pat Dubar was motivated to get them shows, rather than playing in an average punk band of the time where nothing happened because everybody was on drugs.

JOHN PORCELLY: When we went out to the West Coast the first time, touring with 7 Seconds in 1986, there seemed to be a parallel straight edge scene forming out there around Uniform Choice. Seeing them for the first time at Fender's Ballroom was incredible. Pat Dubar got onstage and began this whole intro rant, while running from one side to the other like a demented motivational speaker.

KEVIN HERNANDEZ: Uniform Choice had a show at Flashdance on a Sunday. For the whole night before they played, Pat Dubar wore his hoodie over his head. When band started playing its intro, Dubar was still in the back of the venue. Then he ran up, jumped over the crowd, landed onstage, ripped his hoodie off, and revealed his head was completely bald. The place went fucking *nuts*.

PAT DUBAR: We recorded *Screaming for Change* with Chaz Ramirez, a semi-cult hero in the Southern California punk rock world. He had done stuff for Social Distortion. We knocked the record out pretty quick. I did all my vocals in two days. We were supposed to mix, and he kept blowing us off for months and months. Finally, we nailed him down and he admitted that he had erased all the vocals by mistake. So I had to rerecord all the vocals. We were so pissed off. We really should have known better than to trust him. While we were in his studio, this band Detox had also been recording. They wanted a gunshot sound on their record, so they were in the studio shooting a real gun with real bullets into cinder blocks.

For some reason, I just assumed we would be on Dischord Records. That led to another delay for the record. I thought, "I'll just send this off to the guy from Minor Threat, and he'll put it out." I called Ian MacKaye, and he was super cool. But when he told me Dischord only put out bands from D.C., my whole world came crashing down. I asked him, "Now what do we do?" He simply said, "Just do it yourself, man. You can do it." I didn't know how to put out a record, but he said, "You'll figure it out. We did. That's what you have to do. Build your scene and put out your own fuckin' record." And we started our label, Wishingwell Records.

PAT LONGRIE: There weren't many labels around. There was Touch and Go in the Midwest and Dischord in D.C., but nothing out here except for BYO, the Better Youth Organization. We weren't gravitating to them at the time. So we said, "Let's do this," and we started Wishingwell.

My previous band Unity had opened for Uniform Choice at plenty of shows, so Pat and I decided the first thing we would do was the Unity *You Are One* seven-inch. The guitarist Joe Foster was cool with it. We got John Lowe to play bass and Pat Dubar took over vocals. We got our friend Gavin to do the artwork. My mother did her calligraphy for the song titles. That was the first Wishingwell release.

ROB HAWORTH (NO FOR AN ANSWER, HARD STANCE, FARSIDE): The start of Wishingwell Records felt like the start of a Dischord Records for the West Coast. The model went beyond just trying to start your own label, and included setting up your own shows and tapping into other people to network. What we saw going on with Wishingwell inspired us and resonated with us as younger kids who looked up to Uniform Choice.

PAT LONGRIE: We needed distribution, and before that we needed someone to give us credit to print lyric sheets and album covers. We went up to Hollywood and made a deal with a character named Tabb Rexx. He was going to extend us credit to some places he knew, and he promised to pay us a certain amount of money. He was fascinated with the hardcore stuff. He ripped us off, of course, but we knew that going into it. We just wanted to be able to have a record in our hands that was ours.

PAT DUBAR: After all the missteps, the first Uniform Choice album, *Screaming for Change*, finally came out two years after it was recorded.

PAT LONGRIE: After we made the deal with Tabb Rexx, he called us to say, "I have a proposition for you. I have a rap band that I want you to collaborate with. They're called N.W.A." He described them as really aggressive rap music, and saw a connection between us both. I said, "Sure, we're in." N.W.A. also said yes. They were intrigued by us, too. But that never worked out.

BILLY RUBIN: At the time, Uniform Choice were the only ones. Initially, there was no flag, and they weren't leading anything, because there wasn't anything else yet. Pat Dubar had a vision and wanted to do things. It wasn't about straight edge being a movement at that point.

RICH LABBATE: Pat Dubar had his brother Courtney out in their garage, screen-printing Uniform Choice T-shirts. They had the means of experimenting, so they'd say, "Hey, let's print this on a hooded sweatshirt" or on a long-sleeve shirt, or on a short-sleeve, or on a pair of sweatpants. A lot of bands didn't have access to that kind of equipment, but they did. They made

Clockwise from top: *Pat Dubar summons an intense pit for the delight of Southern California punk legend "Big" Frank Harrison.* BILLY RUBIN; *An early photo of Unity guitarist Joe D. Foster.* COURTESY OF FRED HAMMER; *Victor Maynez, David Mello, and Pat Dubar live and direct from the O.C.* CASEY JONES

more of what worked; they realized merchandising is a key element of this whole thing.

PAT LONGRIE: Our take was that if we were going to charge someone $7.50 a shirt, we might as well print stuff on the front, back, and the fucking sleeve. We made nothing off of them, since we were printing them on Hanes Beefy-T brand shirts that cost us six dollars. I loved coming up with the sayings that we printed on the sleeves of the shirts, like: "Drugs & Booze a Sure Way to Lose"; "No! I Don't Want Your Drugs!" and "For Those Are None as Blind as Those Who Will Not See."

CHRIS BRATTON: Uniform Choice was the first hardcore band to fully realize and utilize the importance of band merch. By 1987, they were touring with fifteen fucking shirt designs available at their shows! Pat Dubar's brother Courtney, who printed and handled their merch, went on to cocreate and then own the massively successful company Affliction Clothing.

PAT LONGRIE: Courtney Dubar was fourteen, working behind his parents' house in Fountain Valley in a shed he made *himself* out of plywood, printing our shirts with an eight-color silk-screen press he bought himself. We paid him fifty cents a shirt to print them, and that little psychopath is a now billionaire entrepreneur.

When we went on tour, all those shirts saved our ass. We would be somewhere like Green Bay, Wisconsin, making $125 for playing the show, but we could sell T-shirts for sure at the venue. We were in Saskatoon, Canada, and Pat's mom and dad's camper blew up. Well, thank God we had money from selling shirts, or we would have had to cancel the tour.

On our first tour, we played at the 9:30 Club in Washington, D.C., with Die Kreuzen. Ian MacKaye was not happy that we had all these T-shirt designs, because he didn't believe in merchandising and all that. I remember thinking, "Motherfucker! I've been eating peanut-butter-and-jelly sandwiches every day on this tour, and surviving on that and the cases of Shasta soda we brought from home with us. Are you serious?"

RICH LABBATE: Uniform Choice's *Screaming for Change* in 1986 planted the seeds in the ground in Southern California. From that, bands like Insted and Half Off sprouted up. The combination of Uniform Choice and Youth of Today coming out here that first time built up the straight edge scene in Southern California. That brought the next wave locally.

ROB HAWORTH: I was attracted to this stuff, because it was more positive than the compilations *Maximum Rocknroll* would put out, filled with songs about how the world's fucked and we're all screwed. That was bumming me out. I wanted to know there were positive aspects to hardcore, that we could come together and make things work.

GAVIN OGLESBY: Unfortunately, Uniform Choice was either unwilling or unable to tour as heavily as they might have. I think their legacy would be totally different now. I don't think there was a band in the country that could touch them around the time that record came out. Uniform Choice was a great band, and they had fanatical fans.

Youth of Today at the Rat, Boston, spring 1986. Crippled Youth/Bold vocalist Matt Warnke and xXx Editor Mike Gitter are front and center. JJ GONSON

NEW YORK HARDCORE 1987

YOUTH OF TODAY

WAR ZONE

SIDE BY SIDE

FRI SEPT 28 AT THE ANTHRAX

FREE... FREE AT LAST
YOUTH OF TODAY + WARZONE
AND SPECIAL GUESTS
SUNDAY APRIL 5th

CBGB and OMFUG
315 Bowery (at Bleecker) (212) 982-4052

BRING 16 yr old ID!

DOUBLE RECORD RELEASE PARTY

Pied Piper Presents:

YOUTH OF TODAY

ALL AGES!

PLUS RxIx's NERVE

at: Lupo's
377 Westminster St.
PROV. R.I.
(401)-351-7927

on: FRIDAY, MARCH 11th

(Yo, Cindy, Happy B.D.)

YOUTH OF TODAY: TAKE A STAND!

DJ ROSE (EARTH CRISIS, PATH OF RESISTANCE): Minor Threat made it clear you didn't just have to read the newspaper and complain; you could do something and express your frustration in an artistic way. When Youth of Today came along in 1985, they sensed that no one was carrying this banner.

JOHN SCHARBACH (BREAKTHROUGH, GIVE, MOB MENTALITY): Straight edge was born in the early '80s and began to make its way around in various forms. D.C. started it, Boston took it a little farther, and then New York branded it.

ARTHUR SMILIOS (TOKEN ENTRY, GORILLA BISCUITS, WARZONE): I maintain that two people—Ray Cappo and John Porcelly—are largely responsible for what started happening in the hardcore scene around 1985 and lasted roughly three years. They had played in a few bands, including Violent Children and the Young Republicans, in Connecticut. Nineteen eighty-five is when they formed Youth of Today.

JOHN PORCELLY: I met Ray Cappo at the Anthrax club when it was still in the basement of an art gallery in Stamford, Connecticut. I walked in and saw him holding a skateboard with an X on his hand, and I was like, "Oh my God! A kindred spirit!" Even skateboarding wasn't a big thing back then. I ran up to him and asked, "Are you straight edge? Do you skateboard?" and he said yeah to both. We went outside to skate, and became instant best friends. A month later, by the end of 1984, I was playing guitar in his band Violent Children.

RAY CAPPO (VIOLENT CHILDREN, YOUTH OF TODAY, SHELTER): In February 1985, the whole hardcore scene and everything that I loved was over. For all practical purposes, there was no such thing as straight edge. I was completely made fun of for being straight edge.

JOHN PORCELLY: Straight edge was dead in 1985. Minor Threat broke up, and SSD and DYS had gone metal and broken the hearts of kids all the way from New York to California. So straight edge wasn't respected. People would say to me, "You're straight edge? Really? Why are you still holding on to that? The guys in Minor Threat don't even care about straight edge anymore."

RAY CAPPO: The other guys in my band Violent Children were straight edge, but they were really into heavy metal. The whole scene was going metal.

JOHN PORCELLY: The vibe at the time was that old-style hardcore was dead, metal was in, and Corrosion of Conformity was the most cutting-edge band on the scene. I didn't like C.O.C., and I didn't want to play that kind of music. I would rather listen to SSD or 7 Seconds than any of those bands. Everybody was like, "Why don't you guys move with the times?" Our answer was firmly "No!"

ARTHUR SMILIOS: Porcell confirmed for me that their impetus was to play pure hardcore, not the metal that had really made inroads into the scene at the time. Personally, I was never a fan of metal. To me, it was mindless "dude" music. I had no interest in Satan or wizards, or whatever nonsense the lyrics were promulgating. I wanted nothing to do with it—and I certainly bristled and chafed at the thought of metal infiltrating the scene that had given me a home.

JOHN PORCELLY: Ray Cappo played drums for Violent Children, and he also wrote most of the lyrics. He wrote songs like "Skate Straight," that were really positive straight edge songs. But the singer didn't want to be in a positive straight edge band. He wanted to have a joke band like the Meatmen. I remember one show where he threw dog biscuits into the crowd, and Cappo and I were cringing.

RAY CAPPO: My whole dream in a hardcore band was to preach straight edge for the benefit of the world. That was the most righteous thing I could think of. I just wanted to do something good with my life. I thought life was stupid, basically. I thought the world was a lousy place with so many illusions and problems. Straight edge seemed right. It seemed like a good cause.

JORDAN COOPER (REVELATION RECORDS): Ray and Porcell loved punk and hardcore. They had their own little culture that formed in Connecticut, where Ray

From top: *The classic Youth of Today lineup of Ray Cappo, Porcell, Craig Setari, and Tommy Carroll bring it to the Boston crowd on May 11, 1986. They opened for California's Youth Brigade, then touring in support of their "departure"record,* The Dividing Line. JJ GONSON; *A suspender-clad Ray Cappo and a stoked Porcell bring the East Coast mosh to Southern California.* CASEY JONES

and Violent Children seemed to be in the center of things. They liked straightforward hardcore more than the post-hardcore or progressed hardcore stuff. There was a kind of tongue-in-cheek mocking of the less "hard" stuff that extended to clothes styles, dance styles, and really everything within the hardcore culture. Violent Children broke up because some members of the band were either losing interest or not interested in making the band about straight edge and positive hardcore proselytizing. Ray and Porcell wanted to put *more* energy into the band and focus harder on that message. They left Violent Children and started their new band with those goals in mind.

RAY CAPPO: I told Warren Kennedy, the bass player from Violent Children, that I wanted to go on tour. He said, "No, I don't wanna go on tour." So I quit the band. I was really fired up. I knew Porcell would want to be in a new band. He wasn't into this metal stuff, he really wanted to be in a straight edge band. He couldn't stand living in this same stupid town his whole life. I told Porcell I had some good news and some bad news. The bad news was that Violent Children broke up, so we didn't have a band anymore. The good news was that we were going to start a new straight edge hardcore band; our dream band! I would sing, Porcell would play guitar, and we were going to be called Youth of Today. The band would be completely generic. The sound would be a slap in the face to all those metal bands. He was like, "Yeah, forget those guys!"

SEAN MARCUS (AWARE): In the middle of the woods of Connecticut, there was a skate ramp called "the Bitch" that had "Violent Children" spray-painted on it. One day, the Violent Children tag was gone. Ray Cappo had painted just the words "Youth of" on the ramp at that point. I don't know why he stopped there; maybe he ran out of paint or something. He said, "Youth of Today is me and Porcell's new band. Fuck that Violent Children shit, this is going to be better."

JOHN PORCELLY: We had very clear ideas; we wanted to meld together the lyrics of 7 Seconds and the music of Negative Approach. We named the band Youth of Today because it was the most generic name we could come up with. That was our way of saying powerful straight-up hardcore was still near and dear to our hearts. We put big X's on our hands so would be no question of what we were into.

Pretty quickly, a buzz formed around us. At our second show, at the An-

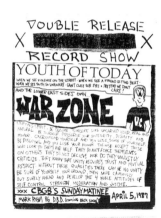

DOUBLE RELEASE
X ~~STRAIGHT EDGE~~ X
RECORD SHOW
YOUTH OF TODAY
WHEN WE SEE VIOLENCE ON THE STREET · WHEN WE SEE A FRIEND GETTING BEAT ·
WHEN WE SEE YOUTH SO UNAWARE · CAN'T CLOSE OUR EYES · PRETEND WE DON'T
AND THE LOWER EAST SIDE'S OWN   CARE

WAR ZONE

xxx CBGB'S SUNDAY MATINEE   APRIL 5, 1987
MARK RYAN '86 D.B.D. (coming back soon)

POSITIVE FORCE
records
no.3 7 SECONDS
       'Blasts from the Past'
       (blue vinyl)   7" E.P.
no.4 YOUTH OF TODAY 7" E.P.
       'Can't close my eyes'
       connecticut h.c.
coming: YOBS 12" E.P.
OUTCRY 12" E.P. (FROM MINN.)
VERBAL ASSAULT
            12" E.P. (FROM RHODE IS.)
'ANOTHER SHOT FOR
    BRAQUEN' north amer.
        comp. lp featuring
YOUTH OF TODAY   7 SECONDS OUTCRY
T-SHIRTS   DISSONANCE, YOUTH
$6 P.P.   OF TODAY AND MORE

ALL 7" 3.00   IF YA ORDERED
12" $4.50 P.P.   BUT HAVEN'T GOT
EUROPEAN ORDERS   ANYTHING LET US
ADD   KNOW!
1.00
                        RAY OF
                        TODAY ROM
P.O. BOX 9184 RENO NV 89507

From top: *John Porcelly jumps for joy as Youth of Today tours the West Coast with heroes 7 Seconds in the winter of 1986; Ray Cappo wins over the crowd on Youth of Today's first tour of California at Ronnie's in Monrovia. Ryan Hoffman of Justice League and Chain of Strength is visible front and center singing along.* PHOTOS BY CASEY JONES

thrax, Mike Gitter drove all the way down from Boston to interview us for his fanzine, *xXx*, one of the biggest zines at the time. I think things happened because there were a lot of kids that felt the same way we did. The older generation was declaring hardcore dead and looking down on all of us. We said, "Fuck you!" to the older generation. Hardcore was awesome! If it was dead, we were going to bring it back to life. That was our mission statement.

MIKE GITTER: I found out about Youth of Today through their original bass player Graham Phillips, who went to Boston University with me. When I heard the first recordings, I thought they had the intensity of old Boston hardcore with some New York style thrown in there, and a message that was easily identifiable and appealing.

RICHIE BIRKENHEAD (UNDERDOG, INTO ANOTHER, YOUTH OF TODAY): In 1985 one faction of hardcore was going in the metal direction, and another faction wanted to keep hardcore the way it had been in 1982. That latter faction went neo–straight edge, and the one band they rallied around was Youth of Today.

WALTER SCHREIFELS (GORILLA BISCUITS, WARZONE, YOUTH OF TODAY, PROJECT X, QUICKSAND): I felt all the good shit had already happened. I appreciated the heaviness of the metal stuff, but it wasn't what I wanted. Then Youth of Today came out, and they sounded like the New York hardcore band Antidote. They had this image and expression of old-school hardcore. That was a relief from the whole crossover metal thing, so that really attracted me.

DAVE ZUKAUSKAS (*RUN IT!* ZINE): Hardcore was becoming a "party" thing; arrive at the show, hang around the parking lot, drink some beers, ignore the new bands that were playing, and don't go back inside until the older bands started playing. Basically, punks started to look like every stereotype that parents had of punk rockers. They wore leather, they were drunk, and they weren't motivated to do anything. Ray and Porcell were like, "To hell with that, let's get kids into it. Let's lead by example and show that hardcore kids can do something positive."

STEVE REDDY: I went away to college in Albany and started going to hardcore shows there. I got a flyer for an Ill Repute and Scared Straight show right down the street from where I lived. When I got to the show, I heard Ill Repute and Scared Straight weren't showing up, but a show was still happening with two other out-of-town bands I had never heard of: F.C.C. from

New Jersey, and Youth of Today. Probably about thirty people came to the show, and maybe half of them left when they found out that the headliners had canceled. I stayed.

Youth of Today was pretty intense. Their roadie Rat Boy was moshing around in a circle, super low to the ground, grabbing everyone's legs as he went by. After the show, everyone hung out on the steps outside the hall. When I met Ray and Porcell, I was psyched. I could tell they were jocks, and I was definitely on the jock side. The hardcore scene was not a place for jocks, so I felt a connection with these guys.

JOHN PORCELLY: While most punks were lifting beers to their mouths, we were straight edge as fuck and lifting weights. I played football, and Ray was on the wrestling team. We were young and trying to find our own identity amidst a scene filled with Mohawks and combat boots.

JEFF TERRANOVA (UP FRONT): Youth of Today supported this idea of a positive, unified scene with songs like "One Family" and "Break Down the Walls." But they looked like the kids who beat you up in high school. It was kind of a mind fuck, because the visual didn't match what you were experiencing.

DAVE ZUKAUSKAS: I got to know Ray Cappo and Porcelly just as Youth of Today was getting started, early in the summer of '85. I had just put out the first two issues of my zine, *Run It*, and Ray contacted me. In the second issue of the zine, I interviewed the Dead Kennedys. Part of the interview was about two skateboarders who were causing trouble at their show in New Haven; jumping onstage, messing with the band, and so forth. It turned out the two kids were Ray and Porcell; so Ray wanted to introduce himself and say, "Hey, you didn't know it, but that was us!"

JOHN PORCELLY: We were straight, loud, proud, and outspoken. Ray had a jacket that said "Straight Edge in Your Face" on the back. Once when the Dead Kennedys played, I jumped onstage and grabbed the cigarette out of the bass player's mouth and stomped it into the ground.

RAY CAPPO: We were really bold, and we would challenge the crowd all the time. We would make fun of the crowd and put down the crowd. A lot of people hated us right from the beginning, which made for a good start.

STEVE REDDY: Youth of Today opened for G.B.H. in Albany. Tommy Carroll was playing drums for them. Someone heckled one of Ray's speeches between songs. Tommy was only fourteen or fifteen, but he got up from the kit and said, "I'm going to come out there and stick your Mohawk right up your ass!"

JORDAN COOPER: Youth of Today got a lot of criticism for calling themselves straight edge. Most of the older punk or hardcore guys weren't straight edge; or even if they were straight, they didn't make a major point of it. Drug abuse didn't seem to be epidemic in the Connecticut scene—though they existed, for sure. But even before Youth of Today drugs might have been even less prevalent within the scene there than in the population generally!

JOHN PORCELLY: We polarized the scene from our first show. There was this old, bitter, jaded crowd who thought what we were doing was really juvenile. When we threw being straight edge on top of it, we were considered very uncool. That would make us go out and say, "Fuck you! You guys suck! You're old! You're out of shape! Go ahead and drink your Guinness and get fat. We're going to do push-ups and sing about straight edge."

MATT WARNKE (CRIPPLED YOUTH, BOLD): When you see pictures from that time, certain people with highly visible X's on their hands did give an evangelical bent to the whole thing; like passing out loaves and fishes or whatever metaphor you might want to use. That led to resistance, and other strong personalities who pushed against it.

DAVE ZUKAUSKAS: I remember the initial reaction to Youth of Today being hatred. I loved Youth of Today from the very beginning; that message was what I wanted to support at the time. Maybe someone will step in now, decades later, and say that I had the wrong impression. At that time, pretty much every band and scenester you could name had negative shit to say about Youth of Today.

CRAIG SETARI (STRAIGHT AHEAD, YOUTH OF TODAY, AGNOSTIC FRONT, SICK OF IT ALL): Youth of Today is the only band I ever quit just because I felt like it was trendy and corny. I felt like I was being pushed into something with that band. Not doing drugs is great. I used to be a burnout kid, so it helped me in a big way. But hardcore is grimy. I got into it because I was a grimy kid, and that straight edge thing started to come off way too clean for me.

DAVE SMALLEY: When Youth of Today came around, I was like, "What the fuck is this? This wasn't the point. We weren't trying to be a religion." We were just trying to give kids an alternative to feeling the pressure to be a part of a certain lifestyle.

BRIAN BAKER: By the time bands like Youth of Today and Bold came around in 1986 or 1987, I knew I had nothing to do with that. It was obvious they were taking the straight edge thing to a whole other level, and making it a totally separate entity of their own.

IAN MACKAYE: By the mid-'80s, I was just in a different place. It was legitimate and real for them, but for me it was weird. It didn't seem like a progression. It seemed regressive to me and I didn't agree with some of the fundamental aspects—they were what I had been accused of being for years, and it was exactly what I never intended.

I didn't look down on it, but I didn't appreciate the judgment from some of those people that what we were doing in Washington was wimpy with bands like Rites of Spring and Embrace. To me, those bands were the progression.

DAVE SMALLEY: Now, I realize Youth of Today had great songs. They were carrying forward a tradition we set. I don't know if we passed a torch, but we certainly helped light that torch and that's great. That's what I wanted. I didn't want straight edge to be something that lasted from 1981 to 1985 and then never existed again. Then all those problems that made straight edge necessary in the first place would come right back. I'm glad there were bands that picked it up and did it their own way.

BRIAN BAKER: At the time, I was a smart-ass and smug because Minor Threat was still so fresh in my mind. So I wasn't too charitable to those bands. I didn't see them as a tribute. I was more in the mind-set of: "Can't you get your own fucking idea?" I didn't realize back then that part of being influential is allowing people to be influenced by you and not being so shitty about it.

DAVE ZUKAUSKAS: The more that the veteran punks pushed back against Youth of Today's message, the more motivated they were to speak up and be more vocal. If everyone had been more open to what Youth of Today was saying, they probably wouldn't have found it as necessary to be so brash and forceful.

JORDAN COOPER: The pushback Youth of Today got in Connecticut in the early days was pretty minor; snide comments, heckling, and stuff like that. The Connecticut scene was a kind of family and the family seemed to support Youth of Today generally, even if people didn't universally align with the entire message.

ARI KATZ (ENUF, UP FRONT, LIFETIME): The straight edge thing that blew up on the East Coast in the '80s came from suburbs. If you had a rebellious nature, straight edge was the easiest way to separate yourself from the suburban high school party scene. I think that's why it blew up the way it did on the East Coast.

RAY CAPPO: Youth of Today brought a suburban element to the hardcore scene and made it easier not to be a badass to hang out. You didn't have to be a criminal or a drug addict. There were kids who thought, "I can relate to hardcore, but I can't relate to the negative elements." Straight edge let you become a part of the hardcore scene and still have ethics, morals, and integrity.

STEVE LARSON: The first time Youth of Today came out to California in 1986, they automatically got points with all of us out here, simply for coming through with 7 Seconds.

JOHN PORCELLY: Violent Children played with 7 Seconds early on. That first time they played at the Anthrax club, Cappo and I moshed like no one had ever moshed before. We'd be doing seven stage dives per song! There's no way Kevin Seconds could have overlooked us.

KEVIN SECONDS: I met Ray and Porcell when 7 Seconds toured the East Coast in 1984. I might be wrong, but my earliest memory of us all hanging out was at a show at the old Anthrax club, back when it was a tiny basement. Ray asked if he could sing our song "Trust" to his then-girlfriend, Becky Tupper. From then on, we just became buddies. He and John were omnipresent. They showed up everywhere we were, yet they weren't pesky or lame. We loved seeing and hanging out with them.

JOHN PORCELLY: Kevin was one of the few guys from the older generation who recognized what Youth of Today were doing and sort of championed it. He asked to put out our first EP, and then asked if we would tour the West Coast with them. Being asked by Kevin to go on tour with 7 Seconds in California was literally a dream come true. But our drummer came out and said, "I'm not going to fucking to do that!" He thought it was insane that we were just going to jump on a plane and play these shows. He quit the band and went back to college. Luckily, Kevin said, "Just come out here. I'll play drums," which worked in our favor. 7 Seconds was one of the biggest bands in hardcore. Everyone saw Kevin Seconds playing drums for us and people got interested.

RICH LABBATE: One day I was at a local record store in Pomona, California, called Toxic Shock. Bill Tuck, the singer of a band called Pillsbury Hardcore, worked there, and he was on the phone with Ray Cappo. Ray was talking about his band Youth of Today and how it was very reminiscent of Antidote. I was a huge fan of Antidote so I was immediately interested. I went to go see them when they showed up on the West Coast on tour with 7 Seconds. They brought a style of hardcore to Southern California that we never really heard before. They had the East Coast mosh, and that was very welcomed.

JORDAN COOPER: The first tour Youth of Today and 7 Seconds did together was fairly early—before the first Youth of Today seven-inch was even out—but the hardcore purist network was aware of Youth of Today and welcomed them warmly. Having 7 Seconds hosting and being on Positive Force Records obviously helped a lot, too. A very small percentage of people at each show were hardcore purists, and even fewer called themselves straight edge, but enough that Youth of Today made friends in most places they played. The response to Youth of Today at every show wasn't always huge, but the people who were there to see them were enthusiastic, even in the beginning.

BILLY RUBIN: When Youth of Today came out west the first time, I had heard records by Agnostic Front, Cause for Alarm, and Antidote, but never seen that kind of hardcore played live before. So when these little bald-headed guys with funny accents came out and started playing songs with breaks for moshing, it was really thrilling.

JOEY VELA (BREAKAWAY, SECOND COMING): Man, I will never forget the first Youth of Today show in Northern California. We had never heard of them before. The show was at New Method in Emeryville, and all we knew was that they were some band from back east and that Kevin Seconds was playing drums for them. They took the stage and their presence was just so strong and powerful, it just blew us all away. Ray had everyone singing along to all of the songs, even though no one had even heard them before.

RAY CAPPO: We played in New York with Agnostic Front and Damage at the end of 1985, right before our single came out. I'm a bigmouth. Back then, no one was straight edge in New York. We had a little bit of an attitude. We left and went to California and toured with 7 Seconds. They put out our single on their label, Positive Force. We got back and everybody was straight edge. It was unbelievable.

DAVE SCOTT SCHWARTZMAN (ADRENALIN O.D., PLEASED YOUTH): It's funny, because every city had a straight edge scene and New York's came last. I was a straight edger without a straight edge scene; but by the time straight edge happened in New York, I was already smoking pot. I was like, "Thanks! Where were you when I needed you?"

JOHN PORCELLY: At one point, you had CBGB booking agent Johnny Stiff saying, "If you put an X on your hand, you're going to get your ass kicked." Then, out of nowhere, straight edge was the biggest thing to ever hit CBGB.

PAUL BEARER (SHEER TERROR): The Youth Crew thing didn't appeal to me. I'll admit it: I was a fucking lunkhead. I liked to get drunk and do stupid shit like smash windows. A lot of people didn't like what I did, and that's understandable, but a lot of my friends were troublemakers, too. It was what it was.

ARTHUR SMILIOS: I wore X's on my hands and took it very seriously. My high school was filled with drugs and alcohol and I didn't partake. At that age, where you aren't secure with who you are, having something with which to identify is important. It gave me a sense of belonging, as well as pride that I was living in a way that was not the norm of my socioeconomic group.

STEVE REDDY: When straight edge got a foothold in New York, I was astonished. My first exposure to New York was shows that didn't start until eleven o'clock at night at the Rock Hotel and that was some scary shit. A younger group of kids bubbling under didn't want to be a part of that, but wanted to be part of the hardcore scene. The straight edge thing was inviting to them.

JOE SNOW (PHOTOGRAPHER): By 1985, I had already gone to some shows at the Ritz. Everyone there was a hardcore urban punk, and I didn't feel like I fit in. I remember standing around in front of those shows trying to put on a tough-guy face around punk rockers that were living in squats and eating out of garbage cans. I was a suburban kid from Connecticut who felt intimidated. I felt like I was crashing their party, and that eventually they were going to figure out I wasn't really one of them.

STEVE REDDY: Youth of Today carried themselves well, and made you want to be a part of what they were doing. Before that, it was like, "I'm straight edge," and that was it. But now it was, "I'm straight edge and we've got a movement going on here."

Choke of Slapshot, putting Boston back on the map DAVID SINE

SLAPSHOT: BACK ON THE MAP

MIKE GITTER: Slapshot formed in 1985 as a celebration of the Boston hardcore tradition, which had been absent on the scene for a couple of years.

JACK "CHOKE" KELLY: After Negative FX broke up, I formed Last Rights in 1983. We never went anywhere, I honestly think because we came in just at that era in Boston where everyone was going metal. SSD were on their way out and DYS was doing the same thing.

MARK MCKAY: I had seen Negative FX only once; they opened for Mission of Burma's final show in March of 1983 and it broke into a total riot. After that, my friends and I just thought Choke and his crew were thugs and a menace to society. We hated Choke. I remember him giving me shit in the parking lot of some show once. So when I saw him up onstage with his Last Rights band, I was like, "Oh God! This guy again? He's a fucking menace!" No one could get near the stage, because Choke was swinging the mic stand into the crowd, looking to hit someone. But the music was unstoppable! To this day, Last Rights are my all-time favorite hardcore band. For the mere six songs they made, it's perfection.

MIKE GITTER: After Choke disbanded Last Rights—who only ended up playing one legendary show—he ducked out of the limelight for a while. People were wondering what Choke was going to do next.

REVEREND HANK PEIRCE: Choke was like, "Everybody sold out! They've all gone metal!" He asked me if I played drums, and I told him no, but my friend Mark McKay could. Choke was like, "That guy?"

MARK MCKAY: I didn't become friendly with Choke until late 1984. He was dating a friend of mine. She told me, "I'm dating this guy and you have to meet him." When she told me who it was, I was like, "Seriously? You've got to be kidding me! He's a fucking menace!" He hated me right off the bat. He thought I was this positive, goofy suburban kid without a brain—and I knew he was a menace. But we started getting used to each other and we formed Slapshot.

JONATHAN ANASTAS: After six months of being out of DYS, I realized I wanted to be in a band again. I missed the camaraderie and the teamwork. I missed playing onstage. So when I was asked to be in Slapshot, I jumped at the chance.

REVEREND HANK PEIRCE: I was on tour roadying with the Straw Dogs, and a lot of people were asking about Slapshot. Mike Gitter was writing about them in *Thrasher*, *Maximum Rocknroll*, and magazines like that before they even started practicing, I think. Gitter was and still is a great publicity machine.

MIKE GITTER: Slapshot gained popularity in the Boston scene quickly, because it was an all-star band. First off, you had Choke, who was an irascible button-pusher and was definitely down to say all the right—or wrong—things to garner interest in the band. You had Jonathan Anastas, who was the charismatic bass player of DYS. You had Steve Risteen on guitar and Mark McKay on drums, who were two second-generation Boston hardcore guys hungry to carry the torch. Then you had Jaime Sciarappa from the undisputed kings of Boston hardcore, SS Decontrol. So there was instant attention and interest in Slapshot.

MARK MCKAY: Honestly, the genesis of Slapshot came from hearing all the great Boston bands playing metal music and singing introspective lyrics about whatever the hell they were singing about! These guys were just shutting it all down. They were already bored with hardcore after a year or two. The first song Slapshot wrote was "Back on the Map," which was all about getting our Boston hardcore scene going again. All the bands had gone metal and the kids didn't care. Gang Green was the biggest band in town, and that wasn't the greatest message to be getting out to people. We wanted things to be back to where they were.

REVEREND HANK PEIRCE: The song "Back on the Map" was a statement. We were going to go out, see the world, and show everyone what Boston hardcore was really about.

Slapshot riles up the crowd with a singalong at CBGB, New York, 1988. BOILING POINT ZINE

JACK "CHOKE" KELLY: Slapshot filled a void, because there were no other hard-core bands to support in Boston. We formed in the fall of 1985, and we were already playing shows by Christmas. We got huge shows. I look back now and think, "Damn! How did we get as big as we were?" We were mediocre at best.

JONATHAN ANASTAS: Sonically, my head was somewhere else. If I lived in L.A. at the time, I probably would have been in a band like Guns N' Roses. But I liked Choke's concept for Slapshot a lot. I liked doubling down on the straight edge thing and the hockey imagery. Jack is the ultimate provocateur. Slapshot was very much like professional wrestling thematically.

MARK MCKAY: With Slapshot's interpretation, straight edge became a pro wrestling thing. We said the most obnoxious things that could possibly be said, and they went into legend. Being shocking and pushing buttons was a Boston punk rock tradition. The F.U.'s did a great interview in *Maximum Rocknroll* where they took Tim Yohannan and that crew for a ride, thinking they were these pro-American assholes. You can talk to any of those guys to this day—they're all wonderful people with great families and all that stuff. It was part of that Boston hardcore punk rock shock tactics thing. That's why Choke had the name Choke! It made everyone say, "What the hell's Boston all about?"

MIKE GITTER: At his core, Choke is a punk rocker. His response to everything is, "Oh yeah? Well, fuck you!" He always wanted to take it one step further. In the early days of Slapshot, there was a very humorous undercurrent. It wasn't self-parody, but there was a dark sense of humor at play. With a song like "Straight Edge in Your Face," Choke was very serious about what the song was about, but there was a sense of humor to it.

JACK "CHOKE" KELLY: We played the whole wrestling heel role right up. But that was my thing. Why be the positive guy? We were the dark side of straight edge! I've never been into that whole positive thing.

MARK MCKAY: When Youth of Today first came out, I loved them. They reminded me of me of all the Boston stuff from five years before. They were intense, they were into it, and they had learned from their elders.

STEVE REDDY: When Slapshot played one of their first shows in Albany, Porcell and I did between five and seven hundred pushups that day. We wanted to be all yoked up when we met Jon Anastas. Then we saw him, and he was like four-foot-eleven or something! He probably weighed one hundred and twenty pounds! He was still super cool, but it was a funny situation.

MARK MCKAY: Youth of Today took things to the next level. They loved the music and they wanted it to be pure and mean something. They played from the heart and I took to them right away.

JACK "CHOKE" KELLY: I would write back and forth to Porcell when he was going to school in Albany. At the time, I thought we were all buds and all on the same page.

REVEREND HANK PEIRCE: Initially, we all thought it was great that a bunch of other straight edge bands were coming up. Then this big schism happened between Slapshot and Youth of Today.

JONATHAN ANASTAS: At some moment Youth of Today got bigger than Slapshot. The purity of their brand helped them.

MARK MCKAY: Choke was not into Youth of Today. He had been doing this straight edge thing in Boston since 1980. He had done Negative FX and been done with it. He had done Last Rights and been done with that. So Slapshot was his third band, and he was looking at Youth of Today like, "Oh, these new kids!" He still had that old Boston scene mentality of keeping it tight, and not letting in anyone new. He didn't like the whole positive attitude they had, because he's a real negative guy.

JOHN PORCELLY: A couple of things happened with Slapshot. First, we played in Boston at the Rat. The guitarist for Slapshot, Steve Risteen, was bouncing while we played, and he was punching and kicking kids—just being a dick! I grabbed him and told him to lay off the kids, and he totally backed down.

Second, we played at T.T. the Bear's Place in Boston a year or so later, and had an incredible show. After the show, Steve Risteen got all up in my face. I couldn't believe this guy was doing this. Back then, I was lifting weights and I was in good shape. We were going back and forth. All of a sudden, a Slapshot roadie we called "the Experiment" came out along with Choke. That guy we called "the Experiment" was huge! There was no fight, but from then on, we were like, "Okay, Slapshot are our fucking enemies!"

JACK "CHOKE" KELLY: At our first show at CBGB, it all went down the tubes. We were friends with Youth of Today and Crippled Youth, until suddenly we weren't. It all came out of left field. Youth of Today or Crippled Youth didn't show up on time, because they wanted to force us to play before them. They thought we should be opening the show. I can't speak for them and what actually happened, but from what I gather, they purposely showed up late so we would have to play first.

MARK MCKAY: Slapshot played at CBGB with Crippled Youth and Youth of Today. At the end of the show, both bands tried to short us on the money. So Steve or someone else said, "We came down all this way, and you're not going to pay us this paltry sum we asked for? Why not?" Ray said, "Well, the other bands need to get paid, and they drew more people to the show than you guys." Ray was trying to insinuate the New York bands drew all the people, and we didn't deserve the money. He said something like, "If there was a show across the street with the New York bands playing and Slapshot playing CBGB by themselves, no one would come see you." I was ticked off by that. I had been friends with Ray and all these guys. They would take me aside and be like, "Tell us stories about the old Boston scene!" To go from that to, "You don't mean anything in New York, so we're not going to pay you," I felt hurt. But unfortunately, they crossed the kind of guy that would take something like that to the grave, and that's Choke. We harbored a grudge. We all thought these guys really let us down, but Choke was like, "Fuck those guys!" and really went with it.

REVEREND HANK PEIRCE: We had assumed we were going to headline. But we got there and it was like, "Why don't you guys play first since Crippled Youth are using our equipment?" We were like, "What?" We had this assumption we were going to headline, since that's the way it was billed. It was a matter of pride, which always gets in the way.

JOHN PORCELLY: In all honesty, Bold were way bigger than Slapshot in New York, but Choke was like, "What the fuck? We have to play before a bunch of fifteen-year-old kids?" That's what ignited the whole rivalry.

RAY CAPPO: We invited Slapshot to play a show at CBGB. They were friends of ours. No one had heard of Slapshot at the time. At Some Records on East Sixth Street, they had sold maybe three Slapshot records, while they had sold seventy-five copies of our record *Can't Close My Eyes* and tons of Crippled Youth seven-inches. Crippled Youth were really popular in New York. Slapshot was billed over Crippled Youth, but I said, "I know you guys are from out of town, but Crippled Youth is a local band and bigger than you guys around here." They got really bummed out that I said that. I was like, "I know they're only thirteen, but they're really popular here." Slapshot put up a big stink, so we were like, "Okay, whatever." At the end of the night, I found out Slapshot had more money than Crippled Youth, and I said, "Wait a second! No one even knew who those guys were!" So I went to Slapshot and demanded they give Crippled Youth more money. After that show, they hated our guts. That's when they put stuff on their records like "Thanks to Youth of Today for ripping us off." We didn't rip them off—they gave us the money!

JACK "CHOKE" KELLY: I was like, "Okay, you started this!" and it was war from then on. We didn't fire the first shot. In classic Jack Kelly fashion, I went overboard and really, really made enemies. Now, everything is just water under the bridge. We just had a goofy town rivalry. But doing stuff like that haunts me to this day.

REVEREND HANK PEIRCE: The beef between Youth of Today and us played well with the whole vibe of us being angry old men and them being the happy, positive young guys.

CURTIS CANALES (CHAIN OF STRENGTH, CIRCLE STORM): We played in Boston with Youth of Today, and Slapshot showed up with their goon squad and threw raw meat all over the sidewalk. I guess they were indignant with Ray's vegetarianism? Or maybe they were upset because Slapshot was becoming irrelevant?

STEVE LOVETT (RAID): We heard a story that Slapshot threw meat at Youth of Today while they were playing. I don't know if it was true or not, but we knew that they were not vegetarian. Slapshot played our town and our crew planned on throwing tofu at them. They waited until the show was over, and did a drive-by on Slapshot while they were loading out their equipment. Several pounds of tofu hit them, and they yelled, "They're throwing tofu at us!" The surreal part was that I was talking to Choke across the street while the rest of the band got hit. I pretended that I didn't know anything about it. Despite that, I remember Choke being super cool about it all.

JOHN PORCELLY: A couple years ago, Judge played the This Is Hardcore festival in Philadelphia with Slapshot. I hadn't seen Choke in years. I was outside and I saw him. For a second, I thought he was going to give me some shit.

But he came up, gave me a big hug, and said, "Don't take anything I ever said personally. I had nothing against you or Youth of Today, you guys were just the easiest targets. I am just an asshole and I like being an asshole!"

JACK "CHOKE" KELLY: People don't really understand; I'm not my band and my band isn't me. A lot of people think, "Choke doesn't like my band, so he must not like me." It has nothing to do with that! Just because I don't like your band doesn't mean I don't like you. But just because I like you doesn't mean I think your band is awesome. These days, there are plenty of times when I'm like, "I like that band, but they're fucking assholes." But people still believe all these stories.

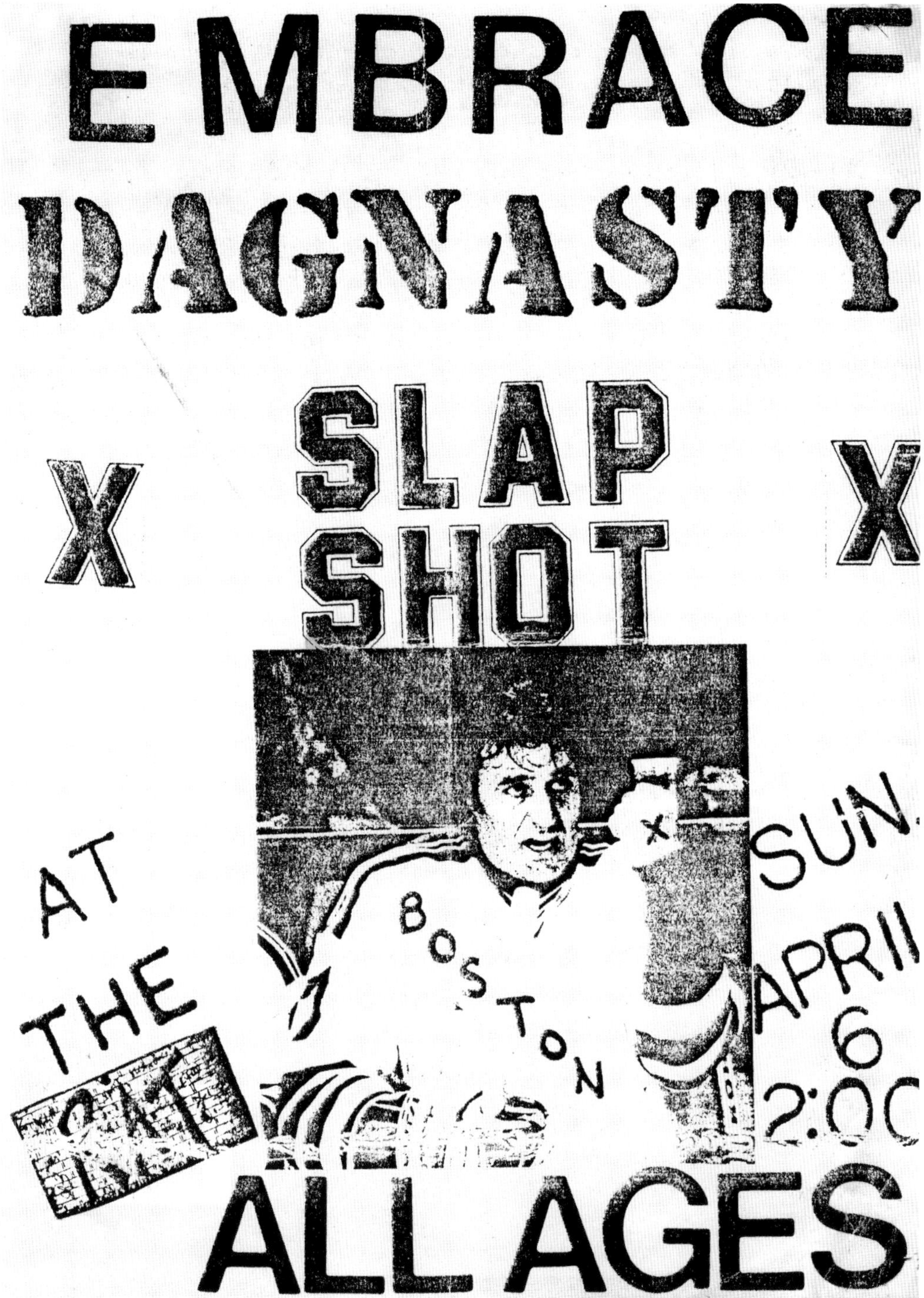

EMBRACE DAGNASTY

X SLAP SHOT X

AT THE OK

BOSTON

SUN. APRIl 6 2:00

ALL AGES

Matt Warnke of Bold keeping it LIVE at the Anthrax. JOE SNOW

BOLD: JOIN THE FIGHT

RAY CAPPO: Crippled Youth, who later became Bold, was basically a local punk rock band made up of thirteen-year-olds. We were really excited to hear them. They played at the Anthrax, opening for the Descendents, and everybody loved them.

MIKE GITTER: Crippled Youth were twelve-year-olds playing straight edge hardcore. That was such a great, uncalculated marketing idea. Who wouldn't want to see a band of prepubescent kids playing their interpretation of old school hardcore?

DAVE ZUKAUSKAS: When Crippled Youth started out they were more punk. They had a song called "Desperate for Beer," and they did Black Flag covers. But I guess even by the time of their first show they had positive youth type songs like "Stand Together," and that's what really impressed Ray and Porcell. At the time, there were no other straight edge–type bands from the area. I'm guessing that Youth of Today saw Crippled Youth, who were all thirteen and fourteen at the time, as the one band playing the Anthrax with whom they had something in common.

RAY CAPPO: Even when Violent Children was active prior to Youth of Today, we had always wanted a brother band to play out with.

STEVE REDDY: The scene was so small at that point that discovering these four-teen-year-old kids from Katonah, New York, playing hardcore was crazy. And the first time I met Crippled Youth, they were real punks. They had their hair gelled up into spikes and stuff like that.

JOHN PORCELLY: They were these seventh graders that had Mohawks and played in a punk band.

MATT WARNKE: Ray, John, Darren, and Graham from the early Youth of Today were all at Crippled Youth's first Anthrax show. The fact that we were all from nearby and were into 7 Seconds, Agnostic Front, and Dischord Records made them interested in us. Also, we all skated at that point. We started hanging out, and those guys lent us so many great records by SSD, DYS, Jerry's Kids, Negative Approach, Reagan Youth, the Abused, and Antidote. We knew of the bands, but having access to the records was critical and fortunate, and definitely helped to influence our sound and sensibilities.

RAY CAPPO: Crippled Youth lived right near Porcell and we became friends. I had a ramp in my yard and we would skate it. They were young kids and wanted music. We'd give them all the good records and say, "It took us years of buying the stupidest records. I wish someone did this for me. Here's a stack of nothing but the greatest records!" They became our younger brothers.

DREW THOMAS (BOLD, YOUTH OF TODAY, INTO ANOTHER): I believe at the time Youth of Today tried to align themselves with what SSD had done as far as taking a leadership role in the scene. With that said, I think in Bold, we saw our-selves a bit more as a "younger brother band" like DYS, if there had to be analogies drawn.

DAVE ZUKAUSKAS: Plus Crippled Youth needed someone to drive them around! They weren't old enough to have their licenses yet, so it made it convenient for Youth of Today and Crippled Youth to play shows together.

JORDAN COOPER: Ray and Porcell probably consciously wanted Crippled Youth to be a little-brother band, and they ended up becoming longtime friends. As for their "role," Bold was probably the closest band to Youth of Today as far as mutual support and camaraderie.

JOHN PORCELLY: In the beginning, the Youth Crew was Youth of Today and our small circle of friends: the kids from Crippled Youth; Dave Stein and Steve Reddy from Albany; Rat Boy; Dave Run It; Herbie Straight Edge; this kid Travis from my high school; and a few Connecticut skater kids. There were only a handful of us, because we were literally the only straight edge kids in the tristate area at the time. So, it was us against the world. I think straight edge kids will forever be the minority, and still feel like that even today.

Youth of Today's Tommy Carroll and John Porcelly show support for their little brother band Crippled Youth at the Rat, Boston, spring 1986. Soon after this show, Crippled Youth became known as Bold. JJ GONSON

Matt Warnke of Bold, Scott Hall, New Brunswick, NJ, November 1988. Note your fifteen-year-old author peeking through to take a picture with a crappy Instamatic camera. Amateur! KEN SALERNO

MATT WARNKE: Crippled Youth came upon resistance and resentment in the same way Ray and Porcell had. Crippled Youth had a one-page feature in *Maximum Rocknroll* right around the release of our seven-inch EP *Join the Fight* in 1986. Our label New Beginning Records arranged that. I was just completely psyched, looking forward to being in this zine in which I had read about so many bands. The piece was fairly innocuous. One of the questions was something along the lines of, "How do you feel about yourselves and other straight edge bands getting flack for stating your beliefs?" Drew responded by drawing the analogy between us and other straight edge bands championing our beliefs and day-to-day habits, and a band like Murphy's Law, who sang proudly of their party-loving ways. No one questioned them for that, he pointed out. I remember reading that and having a bad feeling in the back of my mind that this would not go unnoticed.

Fast-forward to say six weeks later, I was at a show at the Ritz. I'm not sure who headlined, but Murphy's Law was playing. About midway through the set, Jimmy Gestapo introduced a song, possibly "Care Bear," and he basically called out Crippled Youth for having the audacity to say something about his band. I felt like a spotlight was shining right on me. Everyone who was near me stepped back about six feet. I was thinking, "Thanks, Drew."

Mark Ryan from Death Before Dishonor and Supertouch came up to me, and he was like, "Don't worry, I'll talk to those guys and straighten this out." Murphy's Law's set ended, and Mark insisted we head backstage to iron things out. I remember the intense looks I got from Petey Hines and Joe Bruno. I was trying to be tough, but I was like fourteen years old facing these cats. Anyway, nothing was really resolved that night.

I stayed over in New Jersey, and the next day we headed into Manhattan to the CB's matinee as per usual. I remember being in the back of Mike Ferraro from Judge's Camaro. I don't think we really talked about it too much, but there was a sort of underlying concern of what could happen. We had no real way to know. I remember walking down Third Avenue toward CB's. Then I think Mark again had a word with Jimmy G, and Jimmy just came over and shook my hand. He made some joke, and that was that.

JOHN PORCELLY: The whole Youth Crew thing is still relevant. Being the new generation back then, we were young and considered naive and dumb for

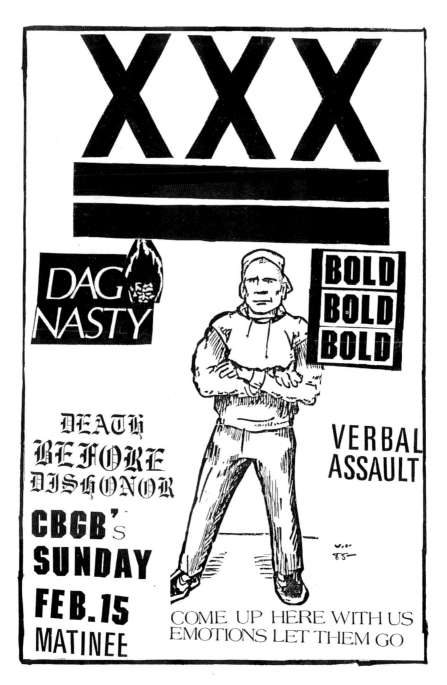

XXX

DAG NASTY

BOLD BOLD BOLD

DEATH BEFORE DISHONOR

CBGB's SUNDAY FEB.15 MATINEE

VERBAL ASSAULT

COME UP HERE WITH US EMOTIONS LET THEM GO

Bold closed out its set at this matinee with a cover of Minor Threat's "Filler." Upon hearing a song he helped write, Brian Baker worked his way out to the side of the stage, watched for a few seconds, and then proceeded to make the ultimate stinkface before retiring to what could only loosely be called the "backstage" area of the club.

taking such a hard stance against drinking and still clinging to fast hardcore with breakdowns, instead of more "mature" music with complex songwriting and musicianship. Most of the older generation had moved on. But we loved that early mosh-tastic, super-hard hardcore. To this day I think young, energetic alternative kids find it the most powerful, moving music ever.

The final touring line-up of Bold, containing John Porcelly and Tom Capone, delivers the goods at City Gardens in Trenton, NJ, during the summer of 1989. KEN SALERNO

GORILLA BISCUITS

From NEW YORK!!!!The Amazing!-

PLUS LOCALS-

PAINFUL
X-TREMETIES

STRAIGHT
FROM THE
HEART

WHERE:
EAT AT MARV's SKATEPARK
(off of Deadwood Ave. and
Pool Dr.. across the street
from the Windmill truckstop)
call for details-(605) 341-0721

WHEN:
July 26t

TIME:
6:30 pm
COST:
$2.00

Who could help but lose their minds when *Gorilla Biscuits* and *Bold* toured together in the summer of 1989? Clockwise from top: *Proof of the mayhem at City Gardens, Trenton, NJ.* KEN SALERNO; *Gorilla Biscuits flyer from Eat at Marv's Skatepark, South Dakota; Walter Schreifels (complete with faux neck tattoo) living it up on the West Coast in the summer of 1989.* DAVID SINE

YOUTH CREW ACROSS AMERICA

JOE NELSON: In the same way Black Flag toured the country in 1981 and spread hardcore around America, Youth of Today spread straight edge. They toured everywhere, planting seeds, and full-on straight edge bands started popping up all over the country.

JOHN PORCELLY: I booked our first tour myself when I was eighteen. Promoters were ringing my dad's phone off the hook to get us to play. The shows were all small clubs and basements, but there were a handful of straight edge kids in each city, totally psyched to see us.

JORDAN COOPER: Even before Youth of Today started, it felt like there was a sub-scene within the overall punk scene with usually younger kids who were new to hardcore or more into straightforward hardcore; let's call them hardcore purists. In that sub-scene, straight edge was generally a little more popular than in the overall scene. Ray was pretty active trying to connect with hardcore purist kids when he was in Violent Children, and he continued to do that with Youth of Today trying to promote both that sub-scene and straight edge.

RAY CAPPO: We thought straight edge was an important message. We wanted to take it seriously and travel around the world. It was a lofty idea. We wanted to put out a record and travel around America. That was our dream.

JOHN PORCELLY: Cappo and I really wanted to start this hardcore recruitment tour! We wanted to know what hardcore was like in Virginia and all over, you know? We wanted to spread straight edge everywhere.

TIM MONROE (UNIT PRIDE, BREAKAWAY): Youth of Today really weren't like anything I had seen. I started going to shows when I was fourteen, and the scene was much different. There was a lot of violence and drugs at shows. I was pretty apprehensive going to shows in San Francisco. But these guys were speaking out and standing up to all the bullshit in the scene—I was hooked. Just the message and how they presented it really hit home. They opened with "Expectations"; from the first chord of that song, people just went nuts. It was amazing. They were the perfect alternative for a lot of kids like myself to some of the other punk bands' messages at the time. I mean, I loved bands like MDC and Christ on Parade, but what Youth of Today was singing about meant more to me than dead cops and anarchy.

JASON PETERSON (YOUTH UNDER CONTROL, WIND OF CHANGE): We met Ray and Porcell when Youth of Today first toured the West Coast in a station wagon. They played the Electric Rhino in Phoenix. They needed a place to crash, so we snuck Youth of Today into Jason Palmer's walk-in closet without his parents knowing. The next day we all skated in Tempe. They had great stories about the New York scene. We got so amped when Ray told us about starting his record label, Revelation. Meeting them gave us the energy to kick our scene in the ass.

JOEY VELA: I don't think Youth of Today's impact on the scene really took shape until their debut LP *Break Down the Walls* came out in 1986 and they went on that nationwide tour. *Break Down the Walls* was widely anticipated, and the band delivered better songs, better production, and really just a perfect formula all the way around. That record had so much heart—it moved you. Straight edge or not, you heard that record and it made you want to go off.

JOHN PORCELLY: The period right after *Break Down the Walls* came out in 1986 was super weird for us. We'd roll into some town, and there would be dozens of kids dressed like us. But they were straight edge, and wanting to set themselves apart from the rest of the punk kids with whom they were at odds. Every movement needs a uniform, and, somehow or other, people chose the way that we dressed as the uniform.

JOHN COYLE (BACK TO BACK, STRAIGHT ARM, OUTSPOKEN): The first time I saw Youth of Today at Fender's Ballroom in 1986 it was ninety percent punks; by the time they came back the second time, a year or so later, Fender's was 120 percent full of straight edge kids in cutoff sweatpants and basketball shoes. Youth of Today changed everything. I can clearly see their show as the moment the scene changed. I may be wrong, but that's how I remember it.

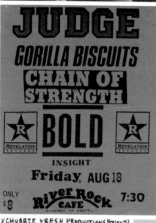

New Jersey Straight Edge titans Turning Point hit the road in 1989. The entire spring of that year seemed to revolve around them and fellow locals Release playing VFW halls or Philly clubs like Pizazz. Kids were hungry for the edge, and Turning Point delivered. COURTESY OF DARREN WALTERS; *Connecticut's Pressure Release in the family station wagon.* CHRIS DAILY; *Various flyers show the national reach of straight edge at the time.*

BILLY RUBIN: When Richie Birkenhead was in the band, and *Break Down the Walls* had already come out, Youth of Today more or less moved to Southern California for a while, living in the home of Dan O'Mahony. This whole crew of people spent a lot of time at the beach, totally fascinated by the fact there were actually girls walking around in bikinis. After that, people who came later into the Orange County scene, like Joe Nelson and the guys who formed the Sloth Crew, really latched onto that East Coast character that Youth of Today brought with them.

JOHN PORCELLY: Things had changed by the time we toured again for *Break Down the Walls*, with the mighty lineup of Ray Cappo, Richie Birkenhead, Mike Judge, Walter Schreifels, and me. There were a ton of edge kids at every show, singing every word like their lives depended on it. I mean, what are you going to do with a lineup like that? You're either going to fight us or you're going to join us.

STEVE REDDY: My band Wolfpack played Buffalo with Agnostic Front in 1986. We played there two weeks after Youth of Today had been there, and there were twenty kids with the Ray Cappo haircut and their sweatpants rolled up and everything. There was a band playing called New Balance, which changed its name to Zero Tolerance. I just thought, *Holy shit!* That was the first sign Youth of Today had disciples!

WALTER SCHREIFELS: Going on tour in Youth of Today was amazing. We came from New York with a message. It was such a cool counter-argument to what was going on at the time, which was either crossover or waiting for G.B.H. to come around again. You could either see these punk dinosaurs or cross over to metal. We would play, and every night would be the fucking best show, you could just hear people in the audience thinking, "I'm going to write a fanzine!" or "Fuck, I'm going to start a band!" Every night was like that. It was awesome.

TIM MONROE: The guy who would end up being the singer of Unit Pride ran away from home in Northern California and ended up staying in Queens, New York, with Walter Schreifels. This was probably late 1986. When he came back, I think he magnified the New York influence on us. Youth of Today and the New York stuff definitely inspired Unit Pride as far as the sound and attitude and lyrical content. It was a lot easier to sing about your friends and making good choices in life instead of political stuff.

MARK STARR (INSIGHT): Jeremy Chatelain and I were already playing in a band called Past Tense by the time Youth of Today came to Salt Lake City, but that show changed our whole direction. Although we were already going that direction with Past Tense, seeing Youth of Today was very inspiring. I had seen a lot of bands that blew me away, but I think the energy they all had and probably just how positive they were blew me away. I remember the place going crazy, and Youth of Today not stopping with energy. To be honest, I don't remember too many bands that came up right after that. I feel like Insight were the only band in Salt Lake City doing that for a bit; soon there would be more straight edge bands popping up like Right Side Up, Headstrong, and our close friends Better Way. We had a great music scene, and a lot of talented musicians. Guys from the Salt Lake City straight edge scene went on to be in lots of bands, including Jets to Brazil, the Gimmicks, Rival Schools, CIV, Himsa, Helmet, Iceburn, Eagle Twin, and J. Majesty.

CAINE ROSE (TOUCHXDOWN): In early summer of 1987, I called Ray Cappo to see if they would play a show in Richmond, Virginia. On July 5, they were at my home, ready to play their first local show—the most memorable of all the shows I've ever been involved in. Their roadies were R. J. Vail from New Jersey and Civ from Gorilla Biscuits—an unknown band to us at the time. My band What If! and D.C.'s On Edge, who would later turned into a band I would front called TouchXDown, opened up for the most explosive and spirited show I had ever seen. The following day, we all went to a local amusement park, and most of Y.O.T. gorged themselves on junk food and sodas—much to Ray's chagrin. That was a time to remember.

JASON PETERSON: Youth Under Control played with Youth of Today in '87 at a dance club called Prisms in Chandler, Arizona. At the time, Arizona had a major skinhead problem. Most of the shows at Prisms ended in fights with the skins. Many times the bouncers tried to protect us from the waiting skins by escorting us to our cars. It got so bad that the promoters, the Victor brothers, who ran Placebo Records, didn't let skins into shows anymore.

During the Youth of Today set, one of the skins kicked my thirteen-year-old neighbor in the head. Ray stopped playing and called the skin out; then Richie Birkenhead jumped offstage and got into the skinhead leader's face. They went back and forth, then decided to throw down behind the local McDonald's at 11 p.m. I remember being in the van with all those guys; Richie and Porcell were going nuts. Everyone was screaming, we were so amped up. We got to the McDonald's and waited at least an hour, but the skins never showed. It was a victory nonetheless. The skins got revenge about a week later by breaking my friend's arm with a bat.

WALTER SCHREIFELS: I guess the main resistance we received would be from the drunk crowd; older punks thinking we were fucking assholes. But we were so sure of our message and what we were doing that we didn't give a shit about that. We played the whole country. Some of these people didn't know the story, but we knew the story—and we were spreading it.

TONY ERBA (FACE VALUE, CHEAP TRAGEDIES, FUCK YOU PAY ME, UPSTAB): I'm not sure if it was the first time Youth of Today played around Cleveland, but I saw them at JB's Down Under in Kent, Ohio. A lot of people liked them, but there was some pushback from the freakers who were into partying and being punk. This girl threw a bottle and hit Kelly Ulrich in the head and a big fight ensued.

The next time Youth of Today came to Cleveland, and their timing was perfect. The older Cleveland hardcore bands were long gone or had gone metal or rock. Younger bands like Confront and False Hope were the ones making things happen. That was really a high point for hardcore in Cleveland, a changing of the guard and the energy of youth. Confront took a lot of cues from Youth of Today; especially the jargon, dress sense, and mosh styles. I mean, we all did: That era of the new Youth Crew bands was pretty fired up and exciting.

STEVE REDDY: Albany had a big scene for the time, made up of about two hundred people. I moved in with Dave Stein and Pam Lockrow, who were booking bands like 7 Seconds, Youth of Today, and Underdog. Soon enough the part of our scene that was more punky and artsy fell by the wayside. People started going either straight-up skinhead or joining the "Youth Crew" that was growing around Youth of Today.

JOHN PORCELLY: By the time we toured for *We're Not in This Alone* a couple years later, there was a whole subgenre of hardcore that was straight edge and it was *big*. It was bizarre to us. We were just some dumb kids in Connecticut people made fun of; fast-forward three years, and straight edge was so popular.

CHRIS BRATTON: When Nirvana broke big in the 1990s, they instantly swept away and made irrelevant all the hair metal bands and all the other shit. Even Michael Jackson was infamously bumped from the number one position. When Youth of Today broke big in 1987, they also hit that same reset button, stripping shit all the way down to the basics, and also instantly swept away all that had become bloated and irrelevant in hardcore.

RON GUARDIPEE (BROTHERHOOD, RESOLUTION): I pretty much fell in love with Youth of Today when I saw them live on that tour. Ray sounded like my favorite singer, Blaine Cook from the Accüsed. There was nothing cool or positive about what I was doing. I was just getting fucked up and screwing up all the time. Then I saw Youth of Today for the first time and I came to a realization. I had already been cutting a lot of things out of my life, but seeing them just made me say, "Screw it, I'm done with all that shit." After many days of listening to Youth of Today while nursing raging hangovers or just getting out of jail, I thought, "You know, maybe straight edge is something I should do." I started hanging out with everyone who was straight edge in Seattle. Shortly after that, I was asked to join Brotherhood, and there was my support group right there.

STEVE REDDY: I ended up becoming the roadie for Youth of Today on the summer tour in '88 because they bought a used van, never checked the oil, and it blew up on their first trip to Rhode Island right before leaving on tour. I had a van and they knew that, so they called me up. I was supposed to go out on tour as a roadie for Underdog, but the Youth of Today was a month and a half longer and I was looking to get out of Albany.

We went to places where they'd been a bunch of times where there were Youth Crew kids with the sneakers and the uniforms and everything. But when we got into the South, there was still a lot of racist stuff going on down there. One of the things I love about Ray Cappo is he'll never back down. He's going to say his thing whether or not there's six or seven skinheads *Sieg Heiling* right in front of the stage. And when he got into real trouble, he'd scream, "Steve, come up here!" But that's what I lived for!

RICH LABBATE: When Insted went on our first tour in the fall of '88, it was a few months after Youth of Today's tour. There were these pockets of kids in the middle of America that were there because Youth of Today had already gone across the country a few times and planted the seeds. It definitely helped.

GREG ANDERSON (FALSE LIBERTY, BROTHERHOOD, ENGINE KID, SUNN O)))): Brotherhood toured in the spring of '89 and at that point, the only straight edge bands that did any touring were Youth of Today or Insted. So for a straight edge hardcore band like us to come and play Omaha, Nebraska, kids lost their minds. I mean, some nights it was just four dudes losing their minds, but it was the biggest deal in the world to them, because all they had seen by that point was Youth of Today. It felt to us like some real pioneer shit!

RON GUARDIPEE: Even though Brotherhood obviously really embraced the look of the straight edge scene, we went out of our way to distance ourselves from the trappings of the scene. We were all guys who had been in bands for a long time before Brotherhood. We had strong opinions on music, and there was a lot of stuff that I thought was total shit in the straight edge scene. We always wanted people to know that we had history; we weren't kids who just showed up in a Champion hoodie out of nowhere. That's why we went on tour with the Accüsed in '89. We had been friends with the Accüsed guys for years. On the first Accüsed LP, there's a picture of our guitarist Greg at thirteen years old singing along. The Accüsed weren't stupid. They saw the writing on the wall of the state of the hardcore scene at the time. They knew they could get new kids on the East Coast to come out to see them if they brought a straight edge band with them. It was a no-brainer for them. They got to go on tour with their friends, and they got a whole new crowd of kids to check them out.

MARK STARR: When Insight and Chain of Strength went on tour in the summer of 1989, long before the Internet, neither band had a tour booker. So Ryan Hoffman from Chain of Strength and I had to do it ourselves. We organized everything through phone calls. I'm not sure how we came up with the idea that we could fit two bands in one van. That to me was so hilarious, but we made it work—at least for the short time before the van broke down. The kids who helped us when we broke down, I won't ever forget them. We have photos of us pulling our van with this huge U-Haul with all of us in the back.

ROB FISH: In the summer of 1989, our friends in the band Vision asked Release to go on a monthlong tour across the U.S. with them. Many of the bigger straight edge bands were touring at the same time, and our paths were supposed to crisscross all over the U.S. I was fifteen, and I was pretty stoked. We were told we would be playing a big final show with Youth of Today at Fender's Ballroom in Southern California.

A week before we were supposed to leave, we learned Johnny Stiff had only gotten around to booking two of the tour's thirty scheduled shows. We were devastated. We only had shows in Syracuse and Buffalo. Vision were older and wiser; they cut their losses and played the two shows. We were not going to be deterred. We played two shows with Vision, then headed out to Cleveland, Chicago, Memphis, and some other random cities before ending up in Miami.

In Chicago, we were supposed to get on a show with Gorilla Biscuits, Judge, and Chain of Strength. When we arrived, the band Insight wanted to jump on the bill as well. The show had two promoters; one had said yes to us, the other had said yes to Insight. Somehow, neither of us got to play. I got into some trouble with a group of white pride skinheads. I was outnumbered and not much of a match for the gathering crowd. Mike Judge and Porcell walked up and essentially told them to fuck off.

In Memphis, we stayed with the Raid kids, who had yet to become a hardline band. A drunken college party was raging a floor below them, and I relieved myself in the ice machine outside of the party. That turned out to be a bit of a bummer to the partygoers. We also hopped trains, which led to a police chase, and we did other mischievous things. All in all, we ended up making a shitty situation into a fun summer.

SAMMY SIEGLER (SIDE BY SIDE, PROJECT X, YOUTH OF TODAY, JUDGE): We were going around the country, staying up all night talking to kids. Ray would be talking to the kids' parents, telling them about straight edge and vegetarianism. Yeah, he was a man on a mission. And, you know, the only reason my parents let me go on those Youth of Today tours was because they knew they were all good people and they weren't drinking. My mother knew I would get in more trouble playing on the football team then I would being in a van with Ray Cappo and John Porcelly.

From top: *Uniform Choice shows off its new look and sound, City Gardens, Trenton, NJ, August 2, 1987. News had not hit the East Coast yet of the band's switch from bald and burly to long-haired and nuanced. Singer Pat Dubar appeared on stage, decked out in black, without X's on his hands, and announced a new song titled, "Long Drink Of Silence." I rolled my eyes in defeat and made a beeline to the back of the club to sulk.* KEN SALERNO; *U.C. enjoys a fine pizza pie during their 1987 U.S. tour.* COURTESY OF PAT LONGRIE

UNIFORM CHOICE: STARING INTO THE SUN

PAT DUBAR: When Uniform Choice transitioned into a different sound, everyone was so shocked, and I didn't understand. To me, punk rock was always about being who you are. That's what first attracted me to punk rock. When we made our shift, it was natural thing. I was still straight edge and nothing had changed, so I didn't get what was the big deal.

PAT LONGRIE: There came a point in 1987 where Pat Dubar, Vic Maynez, and I didn't want to keep writing the same stuff over and over again. So we tried writing some new material. We just wanted to try something different. We saw what 7 Seconds had gone through in 1986 with *New Wind*, and the shit they got from that, but we were not people who gave a fuck what anybody thought. Getting our feelings hurt was never in the equation.

MIKE GITTER: Pat Dubar always tried to maintain that punk rock was always about challenging yourself.

BILLY RUBIN: I don't think Uniform Choice was trying to be separate. I think they were just simply growing up. I think the idea of having shaved heads and emulating Minor Threat wasn't as interesting anymore. They were going to college and were trying to fit into that part of their life without trashing their music.

JOHN PORCELLY: When we were done with the Break Down the Walls tour in 1987, I hung out in California for a while, staying with Ryan Hoffman from Justice League. Dubar and Longrie started coming to shows wearing frilly jackets. They were going in a different direction. If they wanted to play rock music, that was fine—just don't try to use the hardcore scene as a stepping stone.

STEVE LARSON: People were bumming out at Uniform Choice's transition.

They were still a good live band, but Dubar had long hair and was wearing these pointy boots. He was super into the Cult. It affected us, because we were huge Uniform Choice fans. They asked Insted to do an LP with them on Wishingwell, so we jumped in headfirst. Shortly after we agreed to do it, the label and Uniform Choice went through a huge transition. They went from putting out a band like Bl'ast! to putting out a solo acoustic album by Vic Bondi from Articles of Faith. Then a weird feud erupted between Uniform Choice and Youth of Today.

MIKE GITTER: When Uniform Choice went through their transition, Youth of Today seized the opening to step in there and say, "Hey, we're what you really want to see!" Youth of Today had an innate idea of how to market themselves and win over people's hearts and minds.

JOE NELSON: Youth of Today were huge Uniform Choice fans. The first couple times they came to the West Coast were special times, because everyone was so close. That's when Youth of Today was on Wishingwell. Then something happened between Youth of Today and Uniform Choice. Guys like Dan O'Mahony from No for an Answer took the Youth of Today side, and guys like me and the Sloth Crew kids went on the Pat Dubar side. Then there was a division in Orange County straight edge.

PAT LONGRIE: When Youth of Today had a problem with us, that was just funny to me. It just seemed like a pissing contest for those guys. This isn't Aerosmith or Whitesnake. We had the mind-set that these were all guys in bands with like minds. All of a sudden, they were telling people in interviews that we were assholes. Then bands in their fold started saying bad things about us, too. Why? Because we slowed down some of our songs?

CHRIS BRATTON: Look, you've gotta understand that Minor Threat was getting huge right as they were breaking up; like Black Flag huge, and possibly even beyond that size huge. The world wanted and really needed what Minor Threat was giving but then suddenly took away. For a short window, Uniform Choice tried very hard to fill that Minor Threat need. They were succeeding big-time at that goal in Southern California, but they abruptly changed direction at exactly the wrong moment. That's when Youth of

Today swooped in and gave all of those people worldwide exactly what they had been wanting and needing.

ALEX BROWN (SIDE BY SIDE, PROJECT X, GORILLA BISCUITS, *SCHISM* ZINE): I am definitely a purist. If you're a hardcore band, be a hardcore band. Don't try and challenge me with interesting vests and poses. I think there was also some bad blood between Uniform Choice and Youth of Today over the master tapes of *Break Down the Walls*.

JOHN PORCELLY: When Youth of Today put out our *Break Down the Walls* record on Wishingwell, Dubar and Longrie told us the label was a nonprofit thing, and that we'd get every dime we made on that record. They said they'd take money out for promotion, but that was it. Of course, we never, ever, ever got paid! It's no big deal to me in the here and now. I don't give a fuck about the money. It was just a bad vibe at the time. If I saw those guys today, I'd shake their hands and tell them how great a record they made with *Screaming for Change*.

BILLY RUBIN: With both Uniform Choice and Youth of Today, everyone's egos got so gigantic, and so intoxicated with their own personalities, that it was all destined to fail.

STEVE LARSON: Ray Cappo asked us to do a seven-inch on Revelation Records back when the label was just a concept. We said something to Pat Dubar about how Revelation wanted to do a seven-inch, and he said, "If you do a seven-inch with them, you're not doing a full-length with us." We identified Uniform Choice as "our guys," but there was all this weird tension. We weren't choosing sides, and it put us in an odd position.

MIKE GITTER: I was the road manager for Uniform Choice when they went on their first tour of America in the summer of 1987. At the time, everyone in Uniform Choice had long hair. I had long hair at that point, too, and I looked more like I should have been roadying for Black Flag than Uniform Choice. The two big questions on that tour were, "Where are the bald dudes?" and "Who are the longhairs?"

PAT LONGRIE: That tour was tough. It's hard enough to get up in front of people, let alone to go three thousand miles away from home and get up in front of a crowd that expects you to be bald. We were very well aware of that.

PAT DUBAR: Halfway through the summer of 1987, I christened it the Where Are the Bald Guys? tour. I've always been a defiant little fuck. If you tell me to do something, I'm going to tell you to fuck off. When Black Flag put out their slow, dirgy album *My War*, I was one of those guys who said, "Fuck Yeah!" I saw the brilliance as it was happening. I'm of the mind-set that if people don't hate you, you're not doing it right. If you're just in the middle, you're not going to inspire anyone. We would laugh and say, "If we just make *Screaming for Change, Part Two*, will all be forgiven?" Did they just want us to make the same record ten times in a row? I wondered a lot on that tour if I just shaved my head, would it make this all go away? But I knew if I did that, none of what we ever did would be real.

GENTLEMAN JIM NORTON (CRUCIAL YOUTH): The guitarist of Crucial Youth went away to college in Long Beach, California. He told us that when Uniform Choice would play their song "Screaming for Change" out there, everyone started throwing coins at them. So when we found out we were opening for them at the Anthrax in August of 1987, we thought it would be really funny to do the same thing.

The day of the show, everyone else in Crucial Youth showed up with twelve-ounce cups of pennies. I brought a giant peanut jar—maybe a two-liter container—filled with quarters, nickels, and pennies. We got to the show, and Ian MacKaye was there for some reason. He introduced himself to our guitar player, who he knew from corresponding with him for his college radio show. Our guitar player was flattered, as you would be when your rock hero recognizes you.

So the rest of the band got together and everybody decided that they wouldn't throw change at Uniform Choice. Nobody wanted to do anything goofy in front of Ian. When they flagged me down in the crowd and told me, I was like, "What? Come on! Seriously? We're not going to do this because *he's* here? I love Minor Threat as much as anybody else, but he's just some guy!"

I was very annoyed, standing in the back of the room while Uniform Choice was onstage. They started playing "Screaming for Change," and I just started whipping all the change I had in my two-liter container over-hand at the band. Ian MacKaye saw this and asked our guitarist, "Isn't that one of the guys in your band?" The guitarist sheepishly said, "Uh, yeah." Ian MacKaye just shook his head. "What an idiot!"

STEVE LARSON: When Uniform Choice came back from that tour, there was another weird feud between them and Dan O'Mahony from No for an Answer.

DAN O'MAHONY: For a good three years, Uniform Choice were our standard-bearers. Then I reached the age where someone else's voice wasn't enough. I started to see the cracks, and things slipped between us. I wrote the song "About Face," because I felt the band that inspired me and gave me strength for years was turning to nonsense.

RICH LABBATE: I remember Dan O'Mahony writing the lyrics to "About Face" at the No for an Answer practice space. A lot of us looked up to Uniform Choice, and to have them come back with their hair grown out and wearing pointy boots was such a letdown. I think O'Mahony formed No for an Answer thinking he was going to carry the torch, since Uniform Choice was turning into the Cult.

PAT DUBAR: When people started to get lippy and write songs about me, I didn't say anything. I knew these were dudes who didn't fight their own battles. But when you stay silent, others get brave; and when they know no one is going to check them, they get louder.

These people are still around today, but I avoid them. I don't go out of my way to avoid them; I just have nothing to say to them. I don't want an apology, but I would like those people to reflect on the situation from back then. I understand when you're young and in the moment, you say things without thinking. But as you get older and start connecting all those memories, you must sit back and think: "I remember that time when three guys were going to beat the shit out of me, and that dude stepped in and fought all three of them. So why did I go and write a nasty song about him?" If that's what they needed to do to get to where they wanted to be in the scene, then cool. But all you did was talk shit. You didn't slay any dragons.

DAN O'MAHONY: I wouldn't write "About Face" now, at least not with such vitriol. We were so young. Today, I think I would see I was overreaching my station a bit. Thirty years after the fact, you put me and Pat Longrie in the same room and it's all smiles and good fun.

PAT LONGRIE: Dan was not happy with Uniform Choice at the time, but we all laugh about it now. I don't hold any grudges. It was just boys being boys.

STEVE LARSON: Insted was working on *Bonds of Friendship* in Radio Tokyo studio, because that's where Pat wanted us to go. Uniform Choice was recording their second album, *Staring into the Sun*, there. It's not where we belonged, but we were naive, and went along with him. Pat was trying to be helpful, but he was clearly in a different headspace. He was making these weird suggestions on the chorus of our song "Proud Youth," and we wondered what the hell this guy was talking about. Our heroes were bumming us out. It wasn't malicious. There was a lot of backlash coming Uniform Choice's way. We were trying to be cool, because we liked the guys and they were putting out our record.

JON ROA: Pat Dubar played me a tape of their second record, *Staring into the Sun*, before it came out. I wasn't into it at all. He said, "Well, you're just a hardcore kid, so of course you're not going to like it." At the time, I was really into the Sensational Alex Harvey Band. I grew up on so many rock bands because of my older brothers. I probably knew more about rock music than he did. If you picked up *Staring into the Sun*, not knowing anything of Uniform Choice, you wouldn't know they were hardcore. You'd just think they were some random college rock band. I wasn't "just a hardcore kid," but *Staring into the Sun* was just another normal, bad rock record.

PAT LONGRIE: Listen to "Cut of a Different Cause" and "I Am You Are" on *Staring into the Sun* and tell me they're pussy songs. If those songs were on *Screaming for Change*, people would have loved them. I probably would have changed a few things with *Staring into the Sun*, but so what? Who gives a shit? I look back and laugh. I was probably wrong more than I was ever right as a kid, and I don't give a fuck. That's just a process of growing up. You make mistakes and you learn from them. That's how you progress as a person.

MIKE GITTER: Whether there were creative missteps or not, Pat Dubar insisted that what they were doing was challenging and pushing boundaries. Perhaps they were just becoming a rock band, but at least it was done in a challenging way.

PAT LONGRIE: Around that time, we tried to have some fun. We reformed my pre–Uniform Choice band Unity in 1989 to do the *Blood Days* LP.

JOE NELSON: The lineup of Unity that recorded *Blood Days* was jamming under the name Winds of Promise, or WOP—as us smart-asses liked to call it. Unity became like a project band or something for those guys. They had weird practices with strobe lights and flying hair. They rerecorded the songs from the 1985 seven-inch for the album, which wasn't a smart idea. I understand the argument of trying to keep everything sounding somewhat cohesive on a record, but I just wouldn't have done that. I think they figured it would be easier to just release those songs as Unity instead of as Winds of Promise. Looking back, it would have been smarter to just call it Winds of Promise and leave it as a standalone project.

PAT LONGRIE: That record wasn't for anyone else but us. If it was negative toward us, but made someone more self-assured and self-aware, then I guess it was a good thing. I never took any of that stuff personally.

PAT DUBAR: When Uniform Choice started, we didn't even consider that straight edge wouldn't be accepted out here. Punk rock to me always meant just doing what you wanted to do. If you wanted to wear a fucking popcorn bucket on your head, just do it. Who gives a shit, you know? To me, punk rock was freedom of expression. We thought punk rock was something where everyone was accepted, but we were wrong. Ironically, that naive notion haunted us until the end of Uniform Choice in 1989.

PAT LONGRIE: Pat wanted to pursue more of a rock thing. Our friend Mike Gitter from *xXx* fanzine had some connections, and helped Pat get into the band Mind Funk with guys from M.O.D. and Celtic Frost. But that was it. There wasn't any bombastic fistfight. We all knew it was time to move on.

BILLY RUBIN: I don't think Uniform Choice was making a conscious effort to sell out or anything like that. I just think fifteen-year-olds pumping their *X*'ed up fists weren't doing it for them anymore.

PAT DUBAR: When I left California to go join Mind Funk in New York, these kids called me a sellout. Before I left, I was trying to get our second label, Power House Records, off the ground. I was sleeping on the floor in our warehouse, budgeting myself to a $1.50 a day for food, trying to make it happen. These kids were living at home, wearing nice new Nikes on their feet.

From top: *Original Youth Crew mainstays styling in front of the Anthrax, March 1986.* From left: *John "Zulu" Zuluaga (Crippled Youth/Bold), Ray Cappo, Dave Stein (Albany Style), Tim Brooks (Crippled Youth/Bold), O.P. Callahan (Albany Style), John Porcelly, unknown, Drew Thomas (Crippled Youth/Bold), Steven Schneider, Eric Boofish, Matt Warnke (Crippled Youth/Bold), Dave Zukauskas (Run It! zine), Gavin Van Vlack (Absolution, Burn), Drew Keriazes (Albany Style), Glynis Hull, and Aura.* CHRIS SCHNEIDER; *Unit Pride vocalist Eric Ozone has the Youth Crew look down solid, complete with camo shorts over his sweatpants.* TRENT NELSON

YOUTH CREW STYLE: MORE THAN FASHION

JORDAN COOPER: I'd say that Youth of Today had a deliberate look, message, and sound, and they wanted to promote those things. Ray and Porcell have talked about it before, but they took elements of punk, hardcore, and jock fashion, and they wore it proudly. At the same time, they were promoting straightforward, positive hardcore and straight edge. The fact that it was a persuasive message that a lot of people were already into helped, but Youth of Today was also great at promoting those things. The band was good, the message was one to which a lot of people were receptive. Plus the people in and around the band were charismatic and funny, so I think people were drawn to them and the message.

JEFF TERRANOVA: If you look at any subgenre of music, there's always a look. If you look at footage from a Blue Öyster Cult concert from 1977, everybody looks the same. The same goes for any music genre, either underground or mainstream. Madonna made that really apparent in the '80s. Every girl in high school dressed like Madonna. I think people just take to what makes them feel comfortable. And if you're buying all these straight edge records, you're going to start looking like a straight edge kid. That just comes with the territory; it's nonconformity through conformity.

WALTER SCHREIFELS: I liked the suburban fashion of the straight edge thing. We weren't going to have Mohawks and wear leather jackets, we were going to dress in Champion sweatshirts and look like kids from the suburbs! I thought that was cool.

MIKE GITTER: From Malcolm McLaren and Vivienne Westwood onward, punk rock always had a uniform and fashion sense. Whether through Slapshot with their varsity jackets, or via Youth of Today and Chain of Strength using the back cover of DYS's *Brotherhood* as sort of a fashion guide, the image of straight edge took hold. Those moments formed the straight edge contour.

TIM MCMAHON (MOUTHPIECE, HANDS TIED, FACE THE ENEMY, SEARCH): Personally, I could never relate to the punk aesthetic. Combat boots, ripped-up bleached jeans, leather studded jackets, Mohawks; that kind of look was not something that spoke to me or that I felt comfortable wearing. It looked more like a costume than a practical way of dress.

PETER STRANDELL (SVART PARAD): In Sweden, we initially set up our own straight edge dress code with black pants, black shirts, bullet belts, and black hair. It had to be in unity and had to be clean. Much of the style came from Colin Abrahall in G.B.H. The idea was that we should look clean and proper.

JACK "CHOKE" KELLY: I credit DYS for the whole Youth Crew look—that uniform with the hoodies and the skater shorts. Look at the back cover of *Brotherhood*, that's what they're all wearing. There's no question.

DAVE SMALLEY: One thing definitely characterized the Boston Crew; we didn't feel we had to dress like Sid Vicious to be who we were. We wore leather jackets, but they look badass, and it was fucking cold in the winter in Boston. It wasn't a fashion thing. But I would wear a hoodie with shorts because it fit for skateboarding; a look came from that.

CHRIS BRATTON: The Youth Crew look landed fully formed in front of us on the back covers of Boston's SS Decontrol and DYS records. We all meticulously scrutinized the gear they were sporting: white and black Nike high-tops; athletic sweatbands; grown-out shaved heads bleached blond; even Jaime SSD's perfectly razor-crisp, symmetrically rolled cuffs on his jeans. That in particular was a big deal for me—so much so that I was super bummed at Jon Anastas' jean rolling. It was too sloppy, wrinkled, and uneven on the *Brotherhood* insert.

TIM MONROE: Before, to be recognized as a punk, the look was specific. You needed a leather jacket, ripped jeans, and orange hair. I was just a kid that liked the music, but I liked sports, too. So the straight edge look was just cool to me. I didn't have to look punk; I could just be myself. I didn't need to stand out or wear a Halloween costume every day.

CHRIS BRATTON: The holy grail of this brand-new look was the hooded sweatshirt. Dead center on the back cover of the DYS *Brotherhood* LP is an *X*'d

Clockwise from top left: *Dave Franklin of Vision shows the hip hop influence on Youth Crew style. Not pictured: his four-finger ring spelling out V-I-S-I-O-N.* JOE SNOW; *The First Step guitarist Aaron Chrietzberg takes Youth Crew style into the 2000s.* COURTESY OF AARON CHRIETZBERG; *A Chorus of Disapproval vocalist Isaac Golub spinning the Youth Crew look into the 1990s.* LENNY ZIMKUS; *Long sleeve Unit Pride shirt with a sleeve print, Spirit of Youth sweatpants and Vans: Up Front's Jeff Terranova has Youth Crew style down pat!* JOE SNOW up Dave Smalley wearing the entire ensemble that would launch the Youth Crew style as we know it today.

CAINE ROSE: I'll speak personally. I stole my look from Dave Smalley on the *Brotherhood* album cover. I bleached my already blond hair white and donned sweatshirts, jeans, and basketball shoes. I pretty much traded in my Doc Martens for Nikes after that album found its way into my hands.

JON ROA: DYS and SSD defined the look and aesthetic. Look at a Minor Threat record from back then. You didn't see people trying to lay out their records like that. No one was using the cover of *Out of Step* as a template. No one was doing studio headshots or just having a plain black background on their back cover. But to this day, you see hardcore records with live shots on the back cover like *Get it Away* or *Brotherhood*. You see people still wearing high-tops. More people were trying to look like Al Barile than like Ian MacKaye. I remember everyone getting Bermuda shorts after they saw Springa wearing them. Everyone starting rolling up their jeans the way Al had them on the back cover of *Get It Away*.

MIKE FERRARO (DEATH BEFORE DISHONOR, YOUTH OF TODAY, JUDGE): When I was a freshman in high school, I still wasn't down with the punk rockers in school. Pete Karlen, who played bass in Sand in the Face, was my closest friend. We were influenced by the older punk rock guys but we were at the same younger stage in our lives. We would listen to records at each other's houses. His mom had to go to Boston for work, and he asked me to come along so we could go record shopping. In New York, record stores looked like Bleecker Bob's, with flyers everywhere and shit. Newbury Comics in Boston was clean, very well-organized, and nice. We went to the punk section, and this kid with a shaved head, Hobie shirt, jeans rolled up, and Adidas high-tops, sitting on a huge stepladder, says, "That record just came out, and has some good Boston bands on it." It was the *Unsafe at Any Speed* seven-inch compilation with Gang Green, the Proletariat, Jerry's Kids, the F.U.'s, and the Freeze. Then he says, "Check that record out too, it's been out awhile but it has good Boston bands on it." That was the *This Is Boston, Not L.A.* compilation, with way more tracks by all of those bands. He pointed out the DYS *Brotherhood* record and said, "That's my band." I bought the record, and we were sitting in the car, just studying. I would always study the shit out of records and look at everything, "Wow, that guy that sold us the record is *that* guy"—I pointed out Jon Anastas. Right when I got home, I went to the mall and bought those

Adidas high-tops. Everyone had Nikes, because Al SSD had them on, but I had the Adidas because I was just tripped out that the guy that sold us the record was in DYS.

We started wearing hoodies, because there was a point where the guys from the metal band Anthrax would come to hardcore matinees every weekend. They would go on the dance floor and just act stupid. They had no class. It drove me fucking nuts. It was bothering me, so I came up with this thing I called "dance floor justice." When these guys would go out and do this stupid shit and throw punches, because they thought that's what we were doing, I would go and I would hurt them. I would be wearing my hoodie, and I'd fuckin' pull it up and tie it down, so they couldn't tell who hit them. Soon we all started wearing them. At first we bought these cheap blue hoodies at Port Authority for like ten dollars; they said "USA" and were these totally stupid tourist things. We wrote "Dance Floor Justice" on the back, fuckin' pulled the hoods over tight, and we went out on the dance floor and stopped that shit. That was dance floor justice.

JEFF TERRANOVA: In the '80s, to be a straight edge kid, you had to have an oversize T-shirt. I don't know why, but all the shirts were huge back then. On your feet you wore high-tops or Vans, and if you had jeans on, you pegged them. You wore cutoff army shorts. You were probably clean-cut and had a crew cut. That became the look of straight edge. It was just like tying a flannel shirt around your waist and being the Circle Jerks guy if you were a punk rocker.

TIM MCMAHON: The look just made sense and was practical. Anyone could wear it anytime, anywhere. A sweatshirt, a T-shirt, jeans or army pants, basketball sneakers; it wasn't outlandish or uncomfortable. You could buy it at any mall. It wasn't exclusive. For me, it just felt natural and looked damn cool.

JOHN PORCELLY: I always half joke about it, but I kind of invented camo shorts. Ask anyone in the '80s scene, I was the first person to wear them. I saw Agnostic Front in head-to-toe camo in the early days at CBGB and I thought it was way friggin' cool; but I was so into shorts that I would wear them even in winter with thermals underneath. So I got a pair of camos and cut them off. It was sort of a skinhead/Youth Crew hybrid of my own invention. Abercrombie & Fitch can send me a royalty check any time, *you're welcome.*

CAINE ROSE: The athletic look distinguished the straight edge kids from other punks. Hardcore had already set itself apart from the outlandish costuming of punk rock by the use of jeans or khakis, T-shirts, hoodies, and sneakers. Straight edge just took the dress code to a new level with sports jerseys, high-dollar basketball shoes, peg-legged pants, bleached or shaved heads, and varsity jackets.

GREG BENNICK (TRIAL, BETWEEN EARTH AND SKY, LES GANTS): If I started walking around today wearing a particular pair of shorts or a particular type of shirt or jacket, would it catch on? If twelve of my friends and I did, would it eventually catch on? I don't think it would. So why is it then that Porcell and Cappo came together with this aesthetic, kids went crazy for it? It's incredible to me. You saw it every night at the Anthrax shows in Connecticut.

JOHN SCHARBACH: I'm into visuals, and the look absolutely made it appealing. I think a lot of people create these intricate reasons for why they are straight edge, but the bottom line is that an X looks fucking cool on the back of a hand. There isn't anything wrong with that. If the layout of a record keeps someone from doing cocaine, then more power to that.

JOHN PORCELLY: We figured it was more authentic to just dress the way we always dressed. That meant varsity jackets instead of leather jackets; rolled-up jeans instead of bondage pants; crew cuts instead of liberty spikes; and Nikes instead of Doc Martens. It was a cool look. It was different from everyone else, which actually made it more punk and rebellious than just looking like every other Wattie wannabe. Every revolution needs a uniform, and eventually that outfit became the straight edge fashion statement.

DAVE ZUKAUSKAS: I will tell you that Ray Cappo was looking at the photos on the back of the DYS *Brotherhood* record. We were all knocked out by the early Boston Crew photos. We all intentionally modeled ourselves after that look. Even to the point of going to play the Rat in Boston and having Bruce Rhodes take photos, because SSD and DYS had played the Rat and Bruce Rhodes had taken their pictures. These things were all done intentionally and planned out for maximum visual effect, right down to the last detail. Making sure that you were jumping in the air in pictures with your fist out, that sort of thing.

ARTHUR SMILIOS: Fashion played a huge role, which is funny for a scene so vocally anti-fashion. For better or worse, my friends and I created the Youth Crew look. I remember going down to Orchard Street on the Lower East Side in Manhattan with Walter Schreifels and Porcell, because we had found a wholesaler who sold letterman jackets with fake leather sleeves; we were all vegetarian and trying not to wear leather.

RICHIE BIRKENHEAD: I had the first *X* Swatch in New York City. I know that, because I lived around the corner from the Swatch flagship store and I saw some piece of literature about it coming out. Of course, it wasn't intended to be a straight edge thing by them. I said to the girl in the shop, "Let me know when that's going to become available." I will say this—it was many months to a year before I saw anyone else on the scene rocking it, either. I will go to my grave swearing I owned the first *X* Swatch out of the whole New York scene!

TOBY MORSE: When I moved to New York from Virginia and lived in Queens with Walter, Civ, and Alan Cage, the whole look came together for me. I had bleached hair, and I wore tapered army pants, Swatch watches, Vans, varsity jackets, and all that. That was the look, and I was a part of it. You got fucked with in high school by the jocks and then you looked like them. I never liked sports but I wore Champion hoodies and Nike Air Force Ones. It's weird that we appropriated a look from people that inspired us to not be like them.

JOEY VELA: The funny thing is, a few years before, I never would've even considered dressing the way I did in the late '80s. Some of it was no different—shorts and a T-shirt; but then came the whole jock look, and the jocks were the ones we hated the most when we first got into punk rock and hardcore in the first place. I think at some point, we kind of let our guard down and felt like we didn't need to look so punk rock to be a part of the scene.

ADAM NATHANSON (LIFE'S BLOOD, BORN AGAINST): I thought Youth of Today was a great band, and I was always really into being straight edge. The only thing I didn't like about the whole Youth Crew thing was just the visual aesthetic. The whole jock look didn't flow with me.

JOHN PORCELLY: Something was happening in the scene. The old guard was being replaced and something new was taking hold. You could feel it.

That's when I first started noticing kids with *X*'s on both hands, Champion sweatshirts, and low -top Vans. It was kind of strange, but kind of cool at the same time. Like I said, I think the whole thing was bigger than just the band—it was the dawning of a new era and kids just used our clothes as a symbol of that.

SAMMY SIEGLER: Straight edge became a powerful culture and look, like hip-hop, in that there was an identifiable look.

CHRIS BRATTON: Interestingly, in an old Run-DMC interview, Run spoke about the same casual-wear revolution saying they were turned off by the glam, S&M, and disco look of Grandmaster Flash and the Furious Five. Run-DMC wanted to walk right onstage with the same look they sported in the street. That was perfectly in sync with the Youth Crew ideals.

TOBY MORSE: I don't want to say it was like a gang, but you had people wearing these varsity jackets that had the name of their town with "Straight Edge" underneath. Everybody was representing straight edge and where they came from, and that was pretty cool.

CHRIS BRATTON: Wearing Nikes and camos and a hoodie was like throwing hand signs. Those in the know quickly got it and latched onto your band. People would introduce themselves and often become instant friends and valuable allies. We were creating an entire community from fucking scratch, and the visual clues were an extremely helpful tool that we all used to maximum efficiency.

RON GUARDIPEE: I have to admit, I was really into the look. I thought it was so cool. I had been wearing white high-tops my whole life, because I was a metalhead, but instead of wearing Levi's, I started wearing camo shorts. I got every Champion sweatshirt. I moved all my Metallica and Slayer shirts to the back of the closet and starting wearing Wide Awake shirts. To me, the look went along with that feeling of camaraderie—that feeling of brotherhood.

MATT WARNKE: I was very much into sneakers and basketball and brand names and street culture. That, coupled with a Northeast aesthetic and the burgeoning hip-hop scene, informed how I looked and carried myself.

JOEY VELA: I remember being at a show at Gilman Street Project in Berkeley, and this skinhead asked us if we were even into punk rock at all. We kind of clowned him a bit and asked him shit like, "Do you mean, do we hate our parents, like that kind of punk rock?" We just hit him with every lame punk rock cliché and the guy seemed so confused.

DAN O'MAHONY: Slapshot had their letterman jackets. No for an Answer switched to all black. Judge had their construction gloves. Everybody seemed to be hoisting some kind of a flag for a while. I think to a certain extent that's just part of enjoying a shared interest, but it can grow out of hand and toxic pretty quick.

ARI KATZ: When it got to a point where straight edge became a uniform, that's when certain people started to separate themselves. I started to look around at my friends and think, "This is just conformity going on now. I thought this was what we were against." It felt weird.

STEVE REDDY: There was a dude from Virginia Beach who was a real disciple of Ray Cappo. Porcell, Walter, and I were joking that we should call this dude up and tell him Ray had become a Hasidic Jew, because we knew if we could get that rumor out there, this guy would be curling his hair behind his ears in no time.

HOWIE ABRAMS (IN-EFFECT RECORDS): There really was this look—the Champion sweatshirts with the cuffed jeans and the brand-new kicks. I didn't get what that had to do with hardcore. I wasn't adopting that uniform. Good for them, they looked great. It wasn't me, and wasn't what I recognize as the New York hardcore scene.

TOBY MORSE: I don't think the look took away from the sincerity of the philosophy. Punk rockers have their own look. Skinheads have their own look. Does that take away from the sincerity of their cause?

KENT MCCLARD: There's no doubt those bands associated with that look were great. Chain of Strength was a good band. Youth of Today were a great band and so was Gorilla Biscuits. Good bands attract people; that's just a fact. It's just unfortunate with attracting all those people that straight edge became so much about the visual identity and not so much the philosophy.

IAN MACKAYE: While it might be true straight edge as a brand or a look or aesthetic or philosophy was taken from the Boston model, I also think it's true that the idea I had to sing about my own life and the right to make my own decisions resonated with far more people. Some may call what we did straight edge and some may not. But it's not something you can get out of a box. You gotta make it yourself.

KENT MCCLARD: When straight edge became associated with this visual thing that was associated with Revelation Records, it hurt the philosophy and the concept and I think fewer people became involved in straight edge because of that. Straight edge was codified into this silly youth movement and lost its significance as a rebellious punk concept. This interesting philosophical movement in punk that was saying, "Let's try to figure out these problems in our society," was lost.

RAY CAPPO: When you think about it, we were figuring out the concept of branding before we even knew what it was. I remember being in a club in East Germany and seeing all these kids wearing Revelation Records T-shirts. They looked they could have been from New York City circa 1986, but this was in 1995! That's when I realized, "Oh my God! We created a whole fashion and culture." We never thought it was going to become that. It wasn't that sophisticated. It was very grassroots and homegrown. We did it because it was a cool time with cool music and cool people.

GREG W (MENTAL, LOCKIN' OUT RECORDS): If you're into hardcore punk, some part of you wants to play dress-up. If a kid dresses a certain way, it's because he's attracted to the message of that part of hardcore. I just think it's a statement to show what genre of the subculture you align yourself with. It's stupid, but I'm guilty of it. When I was in a band. I worshipped the fuck out of New York hardcore, to the point where I wore a chain as a belt. I wanted to be the dudes in the old videos I got in the mail. You want to emulate your heroes. It was badass to have a flattop and an X Swatch. I studied the mosh moves and everything. So if I was doing that then, there have got to be kids doing it today.

GREG BENNICK: I wasn't really excited to jump into calling myself straight edge. I saw this homogenized scene with the bands often sounding exactly alike. One of the reasons I wanted to get into punk rock was how different every band was compared to the music on mainstream radio. So I was a little wary of this homogenization of a social culture. At the same time, I was highly attracted to the basic idea that I didn't have to drink to be accepted. In the context of how I had been drinking, I was drinking to be like everyone else. For that same reason, I was afraid I was jumping into straight edge just to be accepted on the hardcore scene in Connecticut. What if I bleached my hair and wore camo shorts and put on Nike high-tops for the same reasons I drank beer at a party? What if I just replaced the social structure, but I hadn't done the internal work?

PAT FLYNN (HAVE HEART, CLEAR, FREE, SWEET JESUS): When I rocked that look in the early 2000s, I wanted to represent my affinity for the late-'80s hardcore scene. I'm sure people thought I was like some weird *Back to the Future* case when I'd roll off to shows wearing a Crippled Youth shirt or something. Invariably, fashion does play its role in everything. So I'm sure the ever-changing understanding of what it means to look straight edge has played its role in its continued existence. But I hope to hell that straight edge has not continued to exist because of its look. That'd be just about the saddest reality for something that I personally perceived had virtually nothing to do with aesthetics at all.

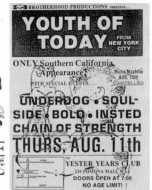

Kevin Hernandez of Insted provokes a reaction from the proud youth of California. KENT MCCLARD

ORANGE COUNTY: WE'LL MAKE THE DIFFERENCE

KEVIN HERNANDEZ (INSTED): I was going to shows, buying records, and trying to be involved in the hardcore scene as much as possible. It became my entire life. Everything revolved around straight edge and the hardcore scene. I always thought it would be cool to get a band going, so I formed Insted with a couple buddies. I think our first official show was playing with Doggy Style at a pool hall in Anaheim.

JOE NELSON: Though their first record, *Bonds of Friendship*, came out in 1988, Insted started in 1986. The first demo tape, *Be Someone*, was fantastic. They became huge in California, and then rode the straight edge wave just as it was peaking in the state to the point where they could draw a couple thousand kids. In their prime in the late '80s, they were probably the biggest straight edge band on the West Coast. They earned everything they got.

KEVIN HERNANDEZ: We sold our *Be Someone* demo out of our trunks at parties or shows just to get the word out. We tried to replicate what Uniform Choice did with their demo by putting ours in a small manila envelope with a lyric sheet and a sticker.

RICH LABBATE: Insted would play with D.I. or Agnostic Front or the Adolescents. Kevin came from a punk rock background listening to Subhumans and G.B.H. We weren't a bunch of guys whose first show was Uniform Choice. We played with anyone. We saw it still as a scene full of outcasts.

KEVIN HERNANDEZ: You would build your name playing parties in Orange County. Most of the time you'd get more people at a party than at a show. Most importantly, you'd get this diverse crowd of skaters and punk people and jocks and high schoolers—a very wide range of people. That's the way a lot of people in Southern California got into straight edge or hardcore.

STEVE LARSON: After Insted's first show with Doggy Style and Final Conflict, we would play on the same bill as the Weirdos, MDC, and Bad Religion. In our minds, we weren't trying to do anything but be in a punk band.

KEVIN HERNANDEZ: Insted loaded up the van with about a hundred shirts and left on our first tour of America. We were gone for three months. The shows in the middle of the week were great. We'd play Denver to fifty people during a blizzard, or Omaha on a Wednesday night with SNFU. Those shows were the best because you knew those people wanted to be there. We stayed for a month in New York at Roger Miret from Agnostic Front's house. He would come to shows with us, and I remember people being like, "Wow, why is Roger at an Insted show?" He had all these pit bulls, and I'd never seen a damn pit bull in my life. He had some word he'd say that would make the dog attack a person. It was nuts! I knew I was far away from Orange County.

STEVE LARSON: Orange County had more than one straight edge zine at the time: Billy Rubin did *Think*, and then Dan O'Mahony had his zine, *S.I.C. Press*.

DAN O'MAHONY: There were only two issues of *S.I.C. Press*. I always had a thing for the written word. Unlike a lot of zines at the time, each issue contained three or four editorials for that reason. Looking back, I suspect a big part of my motivation was the simple fact that doing a zine gave me the chance to pick the minds of people who were having a very real impact on my thinking and values. In a very short time, I found myself across the table from people like Shawn Stern from Youth Brigade and Kevin from 7 Seconds, something a lot of other teens in 1985 might not have done.

RICH LABBATE: Dan O'Mahony got going with No for an Answer quickly after his zine took off. Soon after that, you had Hard Stance. Everything happened really quickly; within six months a full-on Orange County straight edge universe was in place.

DAN O'MAHONY: No for an Answer came together in 1987, actually as an off-shoot of my original band, Carry Nation. Gavin Oglesby and I got in touch with the fact that we were pretty much creatively in lockstep with each other, and we just wanted to run wild with it. We were pulling from a very specific pool of influences, namely the early D.C. stuff and Stalag 13.

From top: No for an Answer. MURRAY BOWLES; *No for an Answer at CBGB in New York.* KEN SALERNO; *Orange County scene fixture Mikey Garceau of* Fast Break *zine tackles the pit head-first—but not without proper protective gear.* COURTESY OF MIKEY GARCEAU

From top: Hard Stance faces reality at the Gilman Street Project, Berkeley. TRENT NELSON; *Zach de la Rocha of Hard Stance raging.* MIKEY GARCEAU

ROB HAWORTH: I played second guitar in No for an Answer for about a year and a half before Hard Stance and Farside. If you look at the label of the B side of their *You Laugh* seven-inch, that's me playing guitar in the picture.

CHRIS BRATTON: I was in No for an Answer for a short time and played on their *A Thought Crusade* LP. Gavin was really great with his total graphics vision for the band, and Dan was a good front man with a lot of confidence when talking to audiences. As a big dude, he wasn't afraid to wade right into pits and stop fights during the shows, which was great and always entertaining to watch. Dan and I both liked to think and project ideas in big, cinematic terms.

DAN O'MAHONY: Hard Stance was younger than all of us, and they came from Irvine, a very affluent part of Orange County. I met their guitarist, Zack de la Rocha, in junior college. We shared a ton of interests; for a while, we really clicked, talking hardcore, shooting pool, and strategizing the future of the scene as we saw it.

CHRIS BRATTON: Hard Stance had a good live show and featured five very handsome dudes. Four of them, at various times, were in the different lineups of Inside Out.

ROB HAWORTH: Hard Stance was a mixture of friendship and that power of trying to figure out your identity as a kid and getting pissed off at the world beyond the suburban wasteland we lived in. We thought hardcore was a way to move things forward and do something, as opposed to other avenues of doing absolutely nothing with your life. Hard Stance never really got a lot of recognition. We didn't have the notoriety of No for an Answer or Insted, because we didn't brand ourselves like those bands did. We weren't afraid to cruise around in different facets of hardcore. Hard Stance would play with different bands, and people would be confused, asking why we were playing with Infest or Excel.

CHRIS BRATTON: No for an Answer was really rising high in Orange County, when Dan suddenly threw in the towel and folded the band in 1989.

DAN O'MAHONY: At the end of the 1980s, I think that in Southern California and all across the country, hardcore kind of lapsed into its most derivative phase ever. My own way of rebelling against was to start throwing curves, with bands like Voicebox, 411, and God Forgot. I developed a real distaste for templates.

ROB HAWORTH: When bands like Against the Wall or Pushed Aside started to come out of Orange County, it felt like an aftereffect where there was a template already there to follow. We wanted to be more organic and just have a chance to take this cool journey. The people in those bands were all nice guys, but they didn't do the heavy lifting of playing in Northern California and Arizona like us or No for an Answer or Insted. I think Southern California hit a point where some people were using a strategic element to what they were doing. There was this thought of, "I'm going to go this route to get to this space."

JOE NELSON: No for an Answer, Hard Stance, and Insted were bands that had to put out demos and work on their craft. But around 1989 or so, there were bands that just showed up and were like, "We're straight edge, here's my membership card." They walked into getting records released and going on tour.

KEVIN HERNANDEZ: At the time, I didn't think the scene in Southern California was oversaturated with straight edge bands. When Pushed Aside and Against the Wall were opening up for us, I thought they were good bands. My attitude was always, The more the better.

ROB HAWORTH: Somewhere there was a divide. The bands in Southern California all had very different perspectives on what we believed hardcore could do. For us, we wanted to put on benefit shows, and make things happen through music. You can see that after Inside Out with what Zack went on to do with Rage Against the Machine. He still understands it's not about him; it's about fucking shit up.

JOE NELSON: Chain of Strength was the first band where I was like, "Holy shit, this is so contrived." They got the straight edge starter-kit box from Toys "R" Us, full of riffs and lyrics, costumes, and yelling, "Let's go!"

JOHN ROA (CHAIN OF STRENGTH, JUSTICE LEAGUE, END ON END): I started Chain of Strength with the best of intentions; whatever happened after that isn't my issue. People from Orange County were into them at first. I remember Kevin from Insted invited them along to play a show in Arizona. I rode to the show with Vic from Beyond and 108; he was hyped on Chain of Strength, too. Then, all of a sudden, Chain were not cool, and there was a backlash against them from the Sloth Crew guys. Honestly, I think the hatred all stems from the fact that the guys in Chain are genuine weirdos. Chris Brat-

Southern California straight edge stage invasion at Gilman Street Project, Berkeley, CA. MURRAY BOWLES

Clockwise from top: *Against the Wall identified at Spanky's, Riverside, CA.* MIKEY GARCEAU; *Alex Barreto from Chain of Strength.* BOILING POINT ZINE; *Guitarist Jeff Carlyle of Pushed Aside, Whisky a Go Go, Hollywood, May 17, 1989.* DAVID SINE

ton was this guy who didn't know how to throw a ball. They didn't fit the jock mold the Sloth Crew guys loved about Pat Dubar and Ray Cappo.

CHRIS BRATTON: After our band Justice League broke up in 1988 and feeling unsatisfied with the results, this time around Ryan and I were both extremely focused. We set out with a goal to be nothing less than *the* definitive, pure, uncut Southern California straight edge hardcore band: Chain of Strength. Sonically, the songs would be brutally simple, stripped down, rabid, and lean for maximum stage demolition, yet still retain enough just enough melody to remain catchy, which I think was key for Chain. Visually, we would utilize at will the history of straight edge hardcore key items; East Coast inspiration blended with our strong Southern California personas. We wanted an image that jumped right out of the record.

JOE NELSON: I like all those dudes in the band, they're good guys. I have to say that first seven-inch of theirs, *True Till Death*, is fantastic; a total classic. But back then, all of us who hung around together in what we called the Sloth Crew thought that record was cheesy and the beginning of the end.

KEVIN HERNANDEZ: Chain of Strength was the beginning of the end for me in that era of straight edge hardcore. They were a manufactured band. When I look back on them, I consider them almost a fraud. They set up a show just to take pictures for the first seven-inch. They stopped in the middle of one song and told people to stage dive on another side of the stage so the photographer could get better pictures. This isn't secondhand information; I was at that show. You can see me in the pictures on the record. They were as fake as you can get. Five years prior, that would not have been accepted. Word would have got out about them, and no one would have wanted them to play shows. They probably would have gotten their asses kicked.

CHRIS BRATTON: We didn't give a fuck what anybody thought except ourselves. We sure laughed at all the old men that whined and tried to give us shit while we quickly took over the Southern California scene. First we put out Chain's *True Till Death* seven-inch on Revelation Records, then we created our own Foundation Records label to put out and support other new Inland Empire hardcore bands. We released former Justice League singer Jon Roa's new band, End to End; our other band, Statue; plus our own second Chain of Strength seven-inch, *What Holds Us Apart*. Simultaneously, we talked a restaurant owner in Riverside into hosting CBGB-style Sunday afternoon hardcore matinees. That helped him become the premier Southern California hardcore venue, Spanky's Cafe.

JOHN ROA: If anyone wants to say Chain of Strength jumped on a bandwagon, then Ryan and I built the first wheel of that wagon five years beforehand when we were in Justice League. Let's just say this: The best bands are either hated or loved. And the fact that anyone has anything positive or negative to say about Chain of Strength almost thirty years later must say something about the band.

TIM MCMAHON: People often called Chain Of Strength "contrived" because they appeared to have put too much thought into everything they did. People thought it came off too calculated and manufactured. I think all of the calculation was a byproduct of what big fans of hardcore they were. They studied those records that came before them, and they applied all that they saw to their own band in an attempt to create the perfect band. Some people felt it was phony and forced, but I saw the other side and appreciated it.

DENNIS LYXZÉN (STEP FORWARD, REFUSED, INTERNATIONAL NOISE CONSPIRACY): I'm going to say something nice about Chain of Strength, because I love them myself. Refused used to cover "True Till Death." When I was a kid, I went to a hairdresser with a Chain of Strength seven-inch, and I told the hairdresser I wanted my hair cut like the members of the band.

ROB HAWORTH: After playing in Hard Stance and the original lineup of Inside Out, I formed Farside. We started playing with all kinds of bands, like Down by Law, Scream, Big Drill Car, Pitchfork, and Gameface. From there, you started to see a scene built within the scene in Southern California representing a broader aspect of music. It felt like a natural growth. It was great.

I look back on that as such a vibrant time in my life. We were serious that we could fuck up the programming of the world and do something different. That got me amped and hopeful in a way to build a solid foundation to live differently. To this day, I try to figure out ways to have autonomy over my life as opposed working forty or fifty hours for some asshole boss—and it all came from that scene in Orange County.

From top: *Chain of Strength exuding energy in a live setting.* MIKEY GARCEAU; *Chain of Strength guitarist Ryan Hoffman steals the scene from vocalist Curtis Canales at Spanky's Cafe. Note blown-up condom at his feet, hurled by someone mocking the Chain Crew's sexual prowess.* DAVID SINE

Billy Rubin of Half Off spouting the truth. Young Zack de la Rocha soaks it in. FRED HAMMER

HALF OFF & THE SLOTH CREW

CHRIS BRATTON: Brian Baker, when he was in Dag Nasty, famously insulted Youth of Today by referring to them as "big-nose hardcore," which was an uncalled-for slam on Ray and Porcell being Italian-Americans. Brian later received a banana cream pie in the face at the Country Club in L.A. courtesy of Orange County's Sloth Crew, who were fanatical supporters of Youth of Today.

JOE NELSON: Orange County guys like Billy Rubin, Dan O'Mahony, Pat Dubar, Pat Longrie, and Gavin Oglesby were the first wave of straight edge dudes in the area. Then you had us: the Sloth Crew. We were about fifteen dudes and we were a second generation of straight edge in Orange County. We were in high school and we were very tribal. We were dealing with a lot of gang culture at the punk shows in California, so that vibe resonated with us, whether we knew it or not.

The Sloth Crew—we were just a bunch of fucking assholes! We were always breaking shit and blowing stuff up. We would go to parties and blow up a cooler full of beer with a pipe bomb. I remember one of our guys, Jim Brown, going to a party with a can of gasoline and lighting someone's entire backyard on fire. Our thing was to show up at a party, steal the stereo, piss in the underwear drawer, write "Sloth Crew" in lipstick in the hallway, and then leave. We would have gone to jail for this stuff today.

DREW THOMAS: We had a lot of fun out in Southern California, staying in the Huntington Beach area while on tour. There was a really good scene; everyone would stay at each other's houses, these big houses with tons of people hanging out. We'd also drive around and just have an awesome time. We would go out in vans with fire extinguishers, ransack places, all sorts of crazy mischief and not-nice stuff! It was like the show *Jackass*.

STEVE REDDY: The Southern California scene was unbelievable. Being out there on tour with Youth of Today was one of the best times of my life. The Sloth Crew was a huge crew there. Lukie Luke Abbey from Gorilla Biscuits and I slept on a yacht on a dock on the Pacific Ocean.

JOE NELSON: The Sloth Crew might have been straight edge, and Uniform Choice might have bonded us together, but we were all damaged. We came from a place where Jack Grisham of TSOL and Pat Brown—the guy immortalized in the Vandals song "The Legend of Pat Brown"—were our heroes. These guys were punk rock pirates. So we were listening to 7 Seconds and Minor Threat, but our real heroes were fuckups.

ALEX BROWN: I went out to California with Youth of Today in early '88 and we ended up staying at the *Maximum Rocknroll* house. We met all the guys from the Sloth Crew down in Orange County, and then we drove to San Francisco to play at the Stone. We all went out one night to see a movie. There must have been ten of us. We took the bus. On the way back, some homeless guy was trying to scam money aggressively. One of the Sloth Crew guys shoved the guy down and we split. We got back to the *Maximum Rocknroll* house and told this story about the bum. Those people were super bummed—pun intended—that we used that word. I think we all had to get in a circle and have a heart-to-heart about it. What a joke.

JON ROA: When those Sloth Crew guys were growing up, they were some mean dudes. They would start fights and ruin shows and act like jerks. They threw water balloons at people out of cars, and would jump out and scare old ladies. You don't drink or smoke but, so what? I couldn't picture Ian MacKaye or Al Barile driving up to a drive-through window at a fast food place and blowing a fire extinguisher into it.

CHRIS BRATTON: Orange County always had this weird pride and a super-competitive streak that was always kind of a turnoff. They were sort of like the guys in the '80s John Hughes movies or the bad Cobra Kai dudes in *The Karate Kid*. Being from the uncool Inland Empire, we were more like Daniel-san, the Ralph Macchio character.

KENT MCCLARD: Orange County is a weird place. Where else could you be socially pressured into being straight edge? When I first moved there and went to Fender's Ballroom to see No for an Answer and Hard Stance, there was this group of pretend thugs who called themselves the Sloth Crew. I got the impression they were into straight edge just because their friends were. It seemed like the dumb choice you made in Orange County wasn't taking drugs, it was being a part of the straight edge scene for the wrong reasons. I thought it was laughable, because I had already made the transition from high school to college. I understood being straight edge was a huge burden. Before I was into punk, I hung out with Dungeons & Dragons nerds. I already understood what it was like to be on the outside. I don't think these kids understood what being straight edge was going to be in the long term. So, when I moved to California and saw these kids in Orange County, I was like, "'True till death, my ass!"

STEVE LARSON: We kept pushing for big straight edge shows in L.A. and I think that idea might have backfired. I think that's where people like Billy Rubin and his band Half Off started to sour on straight edge. Billy Rubin definitely noticed where the straight edge thing was going right away, and he tried to distance himself from it quickly.

JOE NELSON: Billy Rubin was one of the original players in the Orange County straight edge game. He had a fanzine called *Think*, and he worked at Zed Records before he joined Half Off as the singer. He was the John the Baptist of that scene.

KEVIN HERNANDEZ: I was never a fan of Half Off, but those guys were at every show and very involved in the scene one hundred percent. Billy Rubin probably doesn't get enough credit. He was involved whether it was his zine *Think*, Half Off, or putting on shows.

BILLY RUBIN: I got into straight edge the way a lot of other people do, but the herd mentality turned me off quicker than it did a lot of other people.

RAY CAPPO: Billy Rubin from Half Off at first was one of the biggest straight edge clones. He did one of the first straight edge fanzines, called *Think*, full of drawings of guys in hooded sweatshirts. He really pushed that image, and then, all of a sudden, he got out of it and said, "All these people are jerks." He had been pumping us up with all these drawings of guys in Youth of Today sweatshirts screaming with shaved heads.

JOHN PORCELLY: One thing I've learned in life is that the people who are your biggest supporters in the beginning are usually the ones who end up being the first people to rip you down.

BILLY RUBIN: Straight edge became a strange cult, and I thought that was lame. It wasn't punk rock to me any more. Ray Cappo became the center of the universe there, destroying any semblance of diversity in the hardcore scene.

STEVE REDDY: Billy Rubin wanted to be in the crew, and would have done anything to be in the crew. So when he didn't get to be in the crew, he decided he was going to tear it all down.

BILLY RUBIN: Half Off did a song called "What Seems Right" that talked about being obsessed with anti-obsession. When that song came out, I think we became targeted because we weren't playing along. It was almost like social media! If you "liked" something and wore the T-shirt, everything would be okay; but if you weren't doing that, you weren't going to fit. We fell out with some people, but, luckily, the scene was big enough that we were still okay to play shows. I heard that the band Project X had a song about me. I can honestly say I've never heard a single song by Project X, so I don't know.

JOHN PORCELLY: No one caught more shit for being straight edge than Ray or me. I had more beer bottles thrown at me than anybody. I've had beer poured on my head and I've been threatened. When there was a huge backlash against straight edge in the scene, we formed bands like Judge and Project X; that was sort of the backlash against the backlash.

Project X as a band was just that feeling where you just can't take any more and you say, "Fuck you!" As much as Project X was a little tongue-in-cheek, our song "Straight Edge Revenge" still strikes a chord in anyone who ever tried to be straight edge in an American high school, especially in the 1980s.

ALEX BROWN: Project X was a direct response to the people who were talking shit. I don't know if it was actually tongue-in-cheek, but it was really fun to put something so polemical out there and wait for people to take the bait.

WALTER SCHREIFELS: There was definitely a sense of humor to Project X. We wanted to give these people the monster that they actually thought we were. We created that monster for them.

JOHN PORCELLY: At the last Project X practice before recording our seven-inch in 1987, someone said, "Hey, did you hear what Half Off said about

Photos from top: *Billy Rubin and Ray Cappo in a reflective moment.* BESSIE OAKLEY; *Despite his disdain for the Youth Crew, Billy Rubin sure looked the part.* MURRAY BOWLES; *The official T-shirt, unironed, of the Orange County Sloth Crew. Accept no substitutes.* LUKE ABBEY; *"Slam" (aka John Porcelly) dares you to cross him at the Anthrax during Project X's set on June 4, 1988.* JIM NARGISO

you?" We were like, "Fuck, how are gonna get even with Half Off?" So we wrote "Cross Me" in like five seconds.

ALEX BROWN: I have no idea who lobbed the first grenade between Project X and Half Off. It was total bullshit. Billy would talk shit, then we talked shit. Whatever. I always thought that he was jealous of the New York bands because Half Off sucked so bad, but maybe that's just me being a dick. I always enjoyed stirring the pot, as did Porcell. It made life that much more interesting.

JOE NELSON: The way the songs went back and forth between Half Off and Youth of Today, and all the shit-talking that went on in fanzines, was almost like rap beef. But the Youth of Today guys were like Jay-Z, and Billy Rubin and Half Off were like a rapper out of Omaha, Nebraska. Billy had no way of winning that battle!

RAY CAPPO: It was a simple mathematic formula. Some people are God-centered. Some are family-centered. Some are pet-centered. Billy Rubin was enemy-centered. His only existence became hating Youth of Today—which only made Youth of Today bigger.

BILLY RUBIN: I regret that it consumed so much of my time and effort. My opposition ended up alienating me from the scene that I loved. I gave my enemies control over me. Some of these people were demonizing me, the person that had brought East Coast hardcore out to Southern California. That sounds egotistical, but I think it is accurate.

JOHN PORCELLY: Youth of Today were not perfect people; we may have made mistakes. But we were putting our asses on the line, getting into fights with Nazi skinheads and drunk assholes show after show. We have people coming up to us years later saying how we changed their lives for the better. We slugged it out for our beliefs. What the fuck did that guy do?

JOE NELSON: The Sloth Crew kids had major issues with Billy because he was such a shit-talker. But so were we! Now I look back and I love that dude, because we were obviously cut from the same cloth. We both wanted to make it interesting. He wasn't going with the herd. He was truly out of step with being out of step.

DAN O'MAHONY: Half Off and specifically Billy were outliers. He was a contrarian by nature. As I've gotten older, my appreciation for that has really grown. Billy was often crass and childishly abrasive, but the guy said what needed to be said. He had a bullshit detector like no other.

BILLY RUBIN: It became very obvious to me straight edge was becoming more about intolerance than anything else. The Youth Crew movement was about hooded sweatshirts, sneakers, and total intolerance of people that were different. That was the opposite of punk, and I was always a punk before I was straight edge. How cool would it have been if the straight edge movement could be about rehabilitating drunk kids?

MIKE GITTER: People tend to get into this kind of music because they don't want to go along with status quo, or be dictated to. The problem when you have super-charismatic figures like Ray of Today, who set themselves up to be held up to an ideological magnifying glass—well, people find out that nobody's perfect. He couldn't have lived up to the image he had created for himself; nor should he have.

STEVE LARSON: When guys like Billy Rubin from Half Off started turning on me, I didn't get it. But the reality is that Billy noticed things that were fucked and lame. Maybe I couldn't see beyond the microcosm of success Insted was having. After a few years, I realized what was happening. For me, I was probably responsible for influencing some of those people. Since I was making records and touring, I never really stopped and thought about it.

DAN O'MAIIONY: Youth of Today definitely captured the attention of a new breed of slightly better-off suburban youngsters out here on the West Coast. We were close friends to be sure, but they represented a departure from the punk vibe of my youth. At times it rubbed me the wrong way. I remember dyeing my hair black and wearing my Final Conflict T-shirt just to make a point once when No for an Answer and Youth of Today made a road trip together to Gilman Street in Berkeley. Make no mistake, I have never thought of Youth of Today as enemies. I just tired of certain aspects of the association.

JEFF TERRANOVA: Straight edge also started rubbing *Maximum Rocknroll* editor Tim Yohannan and his people the wrong way. After that, any straight edge record they would review, they'd just make fun of it and call it generic. It reached a point where I went out and bought anything they called cheesy or generic, because I knew it would be for me. Thanks for the buying guide, guys!

JOEY VELA: *Maximum Rocknroll* hated all of the East Bay straight edge kids. Well, not *us* exactly, but they hated that straight edge had become a trend. I think they figured that all of these newfound straight edge kids would be here today, gone tomorrow. In most cases, they were right.

MIKE FERRARO: *Maximum Rocknroll* had made Youth of Today out to be like borderline Nazis and militant, which is so ridiculous because you couldn't be more of a pacifist than Ray.

JOEY VELA: Brotherhood came down from Seattle in 1988 or 1989 to play Gilman Street and they were selling their "Fuck Racism" shirts. We all showed up to a 7 Seconds show at Gilman, and the *Maximum Rocknroll* people had made shirts mocking the Brotherhood shirts that said "Fuck Straight Edge." I think they thought it would bum out all of the straight edge kids. Instead, we all thought they were great! We all bought the shirts and wore them all the time, which, in turn, I think bummed out the people that made the shirts. I remember Kevin Seconds saying how great it was that we were wearing the shirts, and how he would love to wear one, but he knew that people would think he was serious and it would start a bunch of crazy rumors.

At first, it seemed a little weird because a lot of the bands we were into before the big straight edge boom hit were all about unity. All of a sudden, scene unity flew out the door. Everything had kind of come back around. When we first got into punk rock, there was a definite us-versus-them attitude, and when the straight edge scene took off, it really divided a lot of people. People hated us for no other reason other than that we were straight edge—the usual shit. People wanted to fight us because we didn't drink, so they would call us straight edge pussies. There were actually people that lived near us that were self-proclaimed ""straighter haters." It's all so stupid, but back then, we were like, "Okay, fuck you!" It was us versus them, all over again.

INSTED THE Proud Youth

HALF OFF Long Beach's MOSH MASTERS

WALK PROUD AND FATAL BELIEF

MOSH ITUP!

MOSH KREW

$4   ALL AGES   APRIL 17   Starts At 7:30 p.m

3437 ANAHIEM st   LONG BEACH

NO FIGHTS · NO FUCK UPS · JUST GOOD CLEAN FUN!

Up Front vocalist Roger Lambert keeps the spirit alive at the legendary Anthrax. JOE SNOW

THE ANTHRAX: HOLD TRUE

JOHN PORCELLY: As far as being a landmark place that changed the face of punk or hardcore, the Anthrax is definitely an overlooked club. When the Anthrax started having shows in Stamford in 1983, there was pretty much no straight edge scene in Connecticut. Then in 1985 and into 1986, things caught on. The situation went from being afraid to show *X*'s on your hands at a show, to Youth of Today playing for six hundred straight edge kids wearing *X*'s on their hands. It was phenomenal. The Anthrax single-handedly spearheaded straight edge as a youth movement.

STEVE REDDY: At first, the Anthrax was this scary punk club in a basement, and then when it moved to Norwalk in 1986, the shows became like going to a straight edge pep rally. There was a crew there that kept growing in Connecticut and it was unbelievable. The shows there were so much fun, and the stage diving was frickin' next level!

JEFF TERRANOVA: The Anthrax was run by first-generation Connecticut hardcore punk rockers, Brian and Shaun Sheridan. You also had Jeff R. from Contraband and Bill Knapp from C.I.A. and 76% Uncertain doing sound. They were members of the first generation of Connecticut hardcore bands. John Sex Bomb from Seizure ran the door every night.

CAINE ROSE: I think Minor Threat, the Faith, SSD, DYS and a few West Coast bands already heralded the turn of the philosophy into a movement in the early to mid-'80s. The late '80s saw a new and more powerful revival of straight edge by these amazing New York, Connecticut, and mid-Atlantic bands. It wasn't necessarily new, but it was more dynamic and even supercharged. It was the right time and place for a music revolution. And straight edge hardcore was undoubtedly one of the most formidable champions of musical zealotry.

JOHN MCLOUGHLIN (WIDE AWAKE): I grew up right outside of Danbury, Connecticut. There were no punks, skateboarders, or crews in our little town before us, but nearby at Western Connecticut State University we had Darryl Ohrt and his WXCI radio show, *Adventure Jukebox*. On Sunday nights, he played the Sex Pistols, Dead Kennedys, Black Flag, and a local band called Violent Children.

RAY CAPPO: Before Youth of Today, my earlier band Violent Children made this really shitty demo tape, and we took it to the radio station at midnight. We threw pebbles against the window. When the guy opened the window, we were like, "Hey! We're in a hardcore band!" The guy was so psyched that Danbury, Connecticut, had a hardcore band. He actually played our demo, saying, "We have Danbury, Connecticut's, only hardcore band, Violent Children, in the studio!" It was so cool.

JOHN MCLOUGHLIN: Before long we began bumping into Ray Cappo at skate jams, along with other people that would later start bands in Connecticut. Skating was the catalyst that brought us all together, and the glue that many bands from that era shared.

SEAN MARCUS: Connecticut had lots of ramps scattered all over the place; some in backyards or in the middle of the woods. I built a ramp in my backyard. I would come home with my parents from some family dinner and Ray Cappo would be skating my ramp. Once we pulled up and the ambulance was leaving because Rob Anderson from Wide Awake broke his collarbone. Ray taught me how to drop in on a half-pipe. All I have to say is, I hope he's a better yoga teacher these days than he is a fucking skateboard teacher, because he was really poor at teaching people to drop in. It took me a while to get it right.

I met Tom Kennedy, who became the singer for Wide Awake, while skating at the Danbury library. Tom went to a private school, so he was wearing a sweater-vest or something like that. He had a ramp, so we became fast friends. Through him we met this guy Tom Bussmann, and we started going to hardcore shows with him because he could drive.

JOHN MCLOUGHLIN: One day, we all wound up a ramp jam at the house of Tom Kennedy, with whom I formed Wide Awake. That day I met Tom; Sean Marcus and Mike Feinson, who would form Aware; Ray and Porcell of Youth of Today; Chris Daily, who did *Smorgasbord* fanzine; Todd Ransick

Clockwise from top: *A crowd gathers in front of the Anthrax.* CHRIS SCHNEIDER; *Wide Awake vocalist Tom Kennedy doles out some insight.* JOE SNOW; *New York City's Supertouch were an Anthrax favorite, despite not aligning themselves with straight edge.* JOE SNOW

of the D.C. band TouchXDown; legendary photographer Joe Snow; and Roger Lambert, who later on sang in Up Front. Ray and Porcell talked about their "new" band Youth of Today. They played a tape of the mixdown from the *Can't Close My Eyes* EP, and told us about going on tour with 7 Seconds.

All these guys were good people, sick skaters, and driven to be different. I could relate. It just clicked. I felt like I had found my tribe. We all found hardcore through our own individuality, but I think we all were witnessing the power of a new scene as it was forming in real time. The bands Wide Awake and Aware were simultaneously formed from the same skate crew basically. We all hung together as skaters already. But when we decided to form a band there were just too many dudes, unless we were starting a polka band. We basically split into two bands depending on proximity.

SEAN MARCUS: Aware started when the guitarist Mike Feinstein and I got together with Mike Eddy, who knew already how to play both bass and drums. For a young kid, he could play anything. We kicked around various basements in our neighborhood. At one point, we were using a drum machine.

The first show Aware and Wide Awake played was at Chatham Oaks Hall with Youth of Today, Bold, and No Milk on Tuesday on January 2, 1987. Mike Eddy's mother was the manager, so we got to book the hall. We flipped a coin with Wide Awake and we had to open up. All our parents were there even though there was a huge snowstorm going on.

JEFF TERRANOVA: My friends Jon Field, Steve Keeley, and I ended up going to a show at Chatham Oaks in Danbury that has now become infamous. The lineup was Youth of Today, Bold, No Milk on Tuesday, Wide Awake, and Aware. There was an ice storm going on. I stormed out of the house against my mother's wishes, and she didn't talk to me for two weeks after that. That was probably the first time in my teenage life that I disobeyed my mom. I don't know how we even got there, because we were literally driving on sheets of ice.

JOE SNOW: It was a harrowing experience just getting there, but Wide Awake and Aware were already my buddies, so I had to make it to the show.

JEFF TERRANOVA: That night changed my entire life, because at that show I met the kids in Wide Awake and Aware. We met the guys that would form Pressure Release a few years later. I met Malcolm Tent from Bunnybrains and his wife Kathy, who were just opening up their store, Trash American Style, in the area.

JOHN MCLOUGHLIN: The Chatham Oaks show was the start of the Connecticut straight edge scene as far as I know it. Wide Awake and Aware both played our first official shows that night. We met Jeff, Jon, and the guys who would form the band Up Front. They become like brothers to us soon after. When we had a room full of people show up in a blizzard that night in Danbury, and we didn't get shut down or arrested, it felt like we were changing the world.

JEFF TERRANOVA: Steve, Jon, and I talked about starting a band, but couldn't find a drummer. That night, Trenton Sicola, the drummer for Aware, offered to jam with us. He ended up playing the first Up Front show with us at this club called Images in Brewster, New York. That night in Danbury was a big catalyst for us.

Up Front was made up of lower-middle-class kids from Mahopac, New York, who got into metal first and then crossed over to hardcore in '84 or '85, after seeing Metallica and Slayer wearing Discharge, G.B.H., and Dead Kennedys T-shirts. That was our gateway into hardcore. Uniform Choice's *Screaming for Change* came out in 1985, and that same year Youth of Today put out their first seven inch on Positive Force. They were local guys who put out their first record on a label run by the guy who was in 7 Seconds, so that was a huge deal.

We gravitated to the uplifting lyrics of these bands. Mercyful Fate was great, but I couldn't personally relate to being born in a cemetery or worshipping Satan. And I couldn't relate to a song like "Holiday in Cambodia" by the Dead Kennedys; that was above my head. I didn't know enough to defend what that song was about. But I could defend the lyrics of Uniform Choice and Youth of Today. As a teenager, those messages were monumental to me. It was fast, loud, and fucking obnoxious, but the lyrics were positive as hell. We wanted to have a band with a positive message and be a part of it.

JOE SNOW: The next thing you know, we had Aware, Wide Awake, Up Front, and Pressure Release forming. Then the Anthrax venue moved from Stamford to Norwalk, Connecticut, and they all started playing there. Before you knew it, Connecticut was on fire with straight edge bands. Chris Daily was covering that in his zine *Smorgasbord*.

SEAN MARCUS: We met Chris like we met everyone else, through skating. There was a ramp in Stamford where he lived, so we would skate it once in a while. His zine was an influence and he was a presence.

CHRIS DAILY (*SMORGASBORD* ZINE, SMORGASBORD RECORDS): Seeing the straight edge scene explode around me just lit a fire to do my zine, *Smorgasbord*. Then meeting Up Front made me want to start a record label. So I released the *X Marks the Spot* seven-inch compilation, and then the Up Front LP, *Spirit*.

CAINE ROSE: TouchXDown came up from D.C. and played the Anthrax with Supertouch, Up Front, and Wide Awake at the very start of that iconic year 1988. That show was the pinnacle of our performance experience. Arriving at the Anthrax was like journey's end of a hallowed pilgrimage. We felt like we were now on the map. We were really honored to be there.

JOHN MCLOUGHLIN: The Anthrax was our home, and the Connecticut straight edge scene would never have existed and thrived if not for Shaun and Brian Sheridan. They were the salt of the earth. They let Wide Awake and Aware record our demos there at the club on Sunday afternoons for no charge; just some Burger King sacks and a six-pack. Those guys didn't have to do shit for us, but they did, because they were the keepers of the hardcore flame.

JOE SNOW: I definitely felt some tension when the straight edge thing started to take off in Connecticut. I was definitely aware that these older punk rockers on the scene weren't always down with what was happening. I think they felt pushed out in some ways. Anytime Wide Awake or any of those bands were on a bill at the Anthrax, the attendance was huge. The next night, Lost Generation or 76% Uncertain would play, and the attendance would be half of that. I thought they were great bands that I loved just every bit as much as Wide Awake or Aware, but I think they had some resentment.

JOHN PORCELLY: I have nothing but love for Connecticut and that whole early Connecticut scene. Before I found the Anthrax, I felt like such an outsider and such a loser. I couldn't connect with anybody. There might have been three punks in my school, but I was the hardcore punk. I was obsessed

Clockwise from top: *Up Front carries the Anthrax vibe to the Gilman Street Project, Berkeley, summer 1989.* MIKEY GARCEAU; *Pressure Release fighting for disenfranchised Connecticut youth.* JOE SNOW; *Wide Awake guitarist John McLoughlin, vocalist Tom Kennedy, and the infamous zebra-striped walls of the Anthrax.* JOE SNOW

Clockwise from top: *Wide Awake elicits a typically enthusiastic response at the Anthrax.* JOE SNOW; *Beyond and Pressure Release matinee flyer;* Smorgasbord, *the bible of the Connecticut straight edge scene*

with it. It was my whole life. I couldn't think of anything else. So when I found all those other guys in Connecticut, it was such a refreshing connection to be able to go to a show and talk about bands that I loved and to trade tapes. Vatican Commandos, No Milk on Tuesday, C.I.A.; I love those guys!

JEFF TERRANOVA: A lot of the guys who helped out at the Anthrax had been there and done that by that point. So a band like us or Pressure Release or Wide Awake was rehashing what they saw before with SSD, DYS, or Minor Threat. They would poke fun at us, but not in a vicious way. They would just bust balls and say things like, "Have any of you guys even *had* a drink?" I didn't think at all that there was any disconnect. To me, the second generation was sprouting, and the first generation was mentoring the new generation. Mentors shouldn't give you false hope or aspirations.

DAVE ZUKAUSKAS: Wide Awake and Aware and Chris Daily and his zine *Smorgasbord* were nice, because they kept the Anthrax club strong. I don't think the Anthrax club would've flourished even half as much if not for the Youth Crew scene helping to pull it along financially and popularity-wise. But hardcore to me was about the unpopular kids who no one liked in high school. After a while, it turned into conservative yuppie jocks, with their Swatches and expensive sneakers and polo shirts. I have nothing in common with people like that. So it was kind of discouraging.

SEAN MARCUS: I'd say Aware was the band that didn't play every show with Youth of Today, Bold, or Gorilla Biscuits. We weren't trying to roll with that clique. We were would play outside of that realm, and weren't afraid to play shows with Token Entry, Verbal Assault, Dag Nasty, or D.O.A.

JEFF TERRANOVA: Up Front was too far from New York City to be considered a New York band, but being just over the state border from Danbury, we gravitated to the Connecticut scene very quickly. Up Front was never accepted or initiated into the Youth Crew scene in New York. We were always known as a Connecticut band. I don't know if we weren't invited because we weren't part of their jock culture. Maybe the Youth Crew wasn't into us because we didn't show up wearing basketball jerseys? I don't know.

SEAN MARCUS: Maybe straight edge in Connecticut was just going along with what the cool kids were doing. Ray Cappo was really cool and very charismatic and had a big influence on everyone I guess in some ways. I have a brother two years older than me who started smoking pot in eighth grade. When we got to high school, he would be driving us to school while smoking a bowl. I'd have to grab the wheel and steer down these winding Connecticut roads in his diesel Rabbit that had something like two hundred thousands miles on it.

One day, when we were getting ready to go home from school, he lit a bowl and said, "You know, Sean, this is the twenty-second bowl I've smoked today." I was like, "What? It's only two thirty in the afternoon! How the fuck did you get that done?" He went down the list. "Before first period, then after first period, before and after second period then I skipped third period," and he just went on and on. Eventually, my brother ended up smoking crack. He's fine now and we talk every day. Back then, I knew I didn't want to be him. Straight edge seemed like the better way.

GREG BENNICK: I think the Anthrax and that entire time of the late '80s had a something truly magical going on. In retrospect, it would have been amazing for me to have the social wherewithal to say, "You know, everyone here does look alike," and from there find out what was the underlying idea that is bringing out this external manifestation. But I was seventeen. I didn't have the brain in my head to think that way. All I knew was there would be nights at the Anthrax where there was a feeling in the air and all you could think was: "We are going to win!"

JOE NELSON: No for an Answer played a show at the Anthrax one night with Gorilla Biscuits and maybe Chain of Strength. A couple of the Sloth Crew dudes, including me, were out in New York, so we went to the show. All the trains stopped running, so nobody from California, except for Chain of Strength, had a way back into New York City. This was like in late November, and I remember it was snowing. Our situation really seemed pretty bleak. None of us ever entertained the idea of pooling our money for a motel room, of course. That would have made too much sense.

The owner of the Anthrax eventually said we could crash inside the club, then catch the morning train. I remember Porcell's last words to me as he pulled out of the parking lot with Walter Schreifels, Lukie Luke, Alex Brown, and Nicole Straight Edge: "Hey guys, I see a soda can over there you can curl up next to!" What a fucker.

Anyway, the Anthrax was pretty warm inside, so it wasn't the worst thing in the world—so we all thought. What we discovered in horror was it was only warm because of the body heat that collected during the show. About forty-five minutes into the sleepover, it became freezing inside. The cold was unreal. People were running laps around the inside of the club in a feeble attempt to stay warm. Everybody curled up next to one another on the stage, trying to collect our body heat to prevent what we all thought for sure would be a major hypothermia problem. A couple dudes even broke down and cried. I don't remember what he said exactly, but Dan O'Mahony from No for an Answer said something pretty fucking funny that busted everyone up, which at the time was my only real criteria for making a person okay in my book. Obviously, everyone survived. The next morning we all ate breakfast together and took the train back into the city.

GREG BENNICK: In 1990, the Anthrax closed. The people next door started to complain that it was too noisy, and that too many people were gathering in the parking lot. So the club closed. I think it was a reality check for some people. I know it shook me up. "How are these people's complaints more powerful than straight edge?"

SEAN MARCUS: The Anthrax was a special place, but it could have happened anywhere. Out of a couple cans of paint, a shitty P.A., and a ten-thousand-square-foot warehouse, the Sheridan brothers created a place for something to grow.

JEFF TERRANOVA: The closing of The Anthrax was one of the many factors in the straight edge thing dying off in Connecticut. There were a handful of kids who went to all the straight edge shows regularly. Once the Anthrax shut down, they disappeared. But I don't care what it is in life—you're always going to get that. There are always going to be people doing something for the wrong reasons.

SEAN MARCUS: Without the Anthrax as the glue to hold the scene together, people scattered. The whole scene seemed to stop. There wasn't even anywhere to go in New York City, because CBGB wasn't really doing hardcore matinees anymore, either. That whole period was lightning in a bottle.

JOE SNOW: The Anthrax was home base. We were forced to disperse to New York or New Jersey to see music when the Anthrax closed, and things weren't the same. Everyone had to find something new musically.

Judge's first visit to City Gardens, Trenton, NJ, March 11, 1990 was quite an event. The band was shooting a video for "Where It Went" from the Bringin' It Down *LP, and many locals shaved X's into the backs of their heads for the occasion. Note the foam "We're #1" Philadelphia Flyers fan hand, modified with a huge X!* KEN SALERNO

JUDGE: FED UP!

JEFF TERRANOVA: When people starting saying that other people were becoming straight edge just to be accepted—I didn't get that. You're not getting laid with a big *X* on your hand and a crew cut. I was going to high school wearing two different-color Converse high-tops, army pants, a hardcore shirt, and a shaved head with big *X*'s on my hands. I was making a statement. I was taking a stand and showing my support of the concept. I put myself out there to have rocks thrown at me in the parking lot of my high school. But I was okay with that, because it was my rebellion against those people. I didn't like them anyway. The thing I didn't understand as a kid was this: by not fitting in and by dressing the way I did, I actually drew more attention to myself. If I had known that, I just would have dressed normal, because maybe then people would have left me the fuck alone.

RYAN DOWNEY (HARDBALL): My interpretation of straight edge was that it was something positive, healthy, optimistic, and kind. We were drug-free for the animals. We were drug-free to help create a better world. We were drug-free to reject the dumbing-down of America; the drug epidemics thrust upon the poor, people forced into prostitution, the illegal and immoral dealings of the U.S. government in places like Latin America. Like animal rights, I figured this was just something people would either embrace wholeheartedly, as we had, or at the very least respect. Even if they didn't feel the same or didn't choose to live the same way, people would generally understand the good intentions behind straight edge, right?

At my friend John Johnson's high school, a group of jocks beat him up in the locker room, threw his Death Angel T-shirt in a garbage can, and pissed on it. When he got out to his car, he found they'd decapitated a squirrel and impaled it on his antenna. John dropped out of high school after that and got his G.E.D. at night school because of all this.

MIKE FERRARO: I went on a tour of the whole country playing drums with Youth of Today. I didn't know about the preconceptions of the band people had. All I knew about them was that I dug them. I knew nothing about the whole PMA and positive thing. I was from more of a violent background. I was always getting reprimanded in the beginning, especially by Ray Cappo. That's why I wound up wanting to quit Youth of Today. I couldn't deal with having to turn the other cheek.

I was pissed off at the people coming down on Youth of Today and Ray for the positive message of the band. But I also wanted to lash out at Youth of Today for not knowing when their positivity wasn't going to work to get through to people. What good is a positive message when people are just laughing in your face about it?

Youth of Today's van broke down in Florida, and we had to park it in a junkyard while it was getting repaired. We talked these girls into letting us stay in their apartment, but someone had to sleep in the van with the equipment. We'd take turns. On my night to watch the van, I was in the middle of this Florida junkyard, and I got these ideas in my head while lying there. I started writing down words for a band that I didn't even have yet. Looking at these words, it was painfully obvious that they would never be in a Youth of Today song. So I thought when I got back to New York I would start my own band. I couldn't keep muzzling myself.

CAINE ROSE: There was renewed drive to take this expression to a new level. A more militant straight edge movement came out of a place of discontent with what was becoming status quo in the scene. Youth of Today had a generally positive and uniting message in their lyrics; bands like Judge, Project X, and TouchXDown sought to step apart and be noticed for more extreme passion and righteous intensity.

JOHN PORCELLY: Mike Judge lived in an apartment with Al Brown of Gorilla Biscuits and me. In 1987 Mike told me, "I really want to do a band and I want to sing." At first, I was very skeptical. Mike can be a hothead, but he's pretty shy, an antisocial kind of dude. I couldn't picture him as a front man whatsoever. I could picture him getting onstage and staring at his shoes. I didn't think he had it in him to be any kind of front man, but we started working on songs.

MIKE FERRARO: I wanted to say to *Maximum Rocknroll*, "You think *that* earlier approach to straight edge is bad? Oh, just wait. Just wait until you see what I have in mind." I wanted to be as confrontational and over the top as I could.

JEFF TERRANOVA: The vibe of Judge was summed up with the title of a song on their debut *New York Crew* seven-inch in 1988: "Fed Up." Porcell and Cappo and the other straight edge kids got made fun of for being positive and trying to push a positive message. This was revenge.

MIKE FERRARO: Calling the band Judge was about the band being an authority figure; everything that you're not supposed to be in this music. I wanted to show and force on people that authority voice, that cop attitude, and that hard stance. I wanted that. I wanted something like SSD; something you saw in big, block letters that was right there in your face. Something that would look good as a tattoo, that's what I had in mind. Once I said the name of the band was Judge, Porcell called me Mike Judge.

JOHN PORCELLY: Mike's original lyrics were way more militant and violent than what's on that EP, let me tell you! Those are the "edited by Porcell" versions! There was stuff in there about killing motherfuckers or something. I forget the actual line.

MIKE FERRARO: Porcell would call me up, and I would read him some lyrics as I was writing them. One night, I read him the lyrics to "New York Crew" over the phone, and he was like, "Great song but you've got to change the words. You can't fucking say that shit! You're copping to crimes in some of this shit." When I got off the phone with him and sat back and read it, I was like, "Yeah, I think I know where he's coming from."

In my mind, I was writing those lyrics to get that reaction, but when the *New York Crew* seven-inch came out and I got that reaction, I was kind of like, "Whoa, I can't believe I got that reaction!" I couldn't believe it fucking worked!

JOHN PORCELLY: Youth of Today championed a higher cause. It was more positive, and we pushed vegetarianism and people probably thought we were into lifting weights or something. But Mike was troubled, and he sang about it in a very sincere way. Consequently, Judge attracted a very troubled crowd. People could connect with the songs because they had fucked-up lives, fucked-up families, and fucked-up childhoods.

MIKE FERRARO: People took quickly to the message of Judge. In fact, they liked it so much that I started seeing people acting on these words that I wrote. I thought maybe I had fucked up, and that I started some bad shit. Maybe it was the beginning of a bad thing.

RYAN DOWNEY: I started reading about militant straight edge bands in *Maximum Rocknroll*. These bands turned the tables. They were outcasts among the outcasts, and they wore it like a badge of honor. After I discovered the first Judge seven-inch and later their full-length, *Bringin' It Down*, I found a drummer named Keith Steele, and we formed a band called Hardball in Indianapolis. We adopted larger-than-life, hip-hop-style names for ourselves, both in deference to the revolutionary-minded ideas of keeping real names off of government watch lists and in defiant opposition to our foes. I became "Ryan Hardball." Keith went by "I. K. Steele," his actual first initials and last name. Our guitarist John Johnson went by "John Terminator AK-47." We generally called our bassist Matt by his last name, Reece. This was all one hundred percent a response to the way we had been treated in the local scene. The first song we ever wrote, "Payback," was about the rivals who bullied us in the local scene. In 1990, we released our demo, *My Fist Your Face*.

JOHN PORCELLY: Unfortunately, I would say Judge probably did influence a lot of backward thinking in the straight edge scene. But to Mike's credit, he made an attempt with our 1989 LP *Bringin' It Down* to not be so reactionary with his lyrics. He wrote some really deep, well-rounded stuff on that record. But it didn't matter; we still had people coming to shows, beating the fuck out of people in the name of Judge. Things did get way out of control. I realized how powerful music is. When you take music and put a real negative message behind it, that can really drive people into a bad place.

ROGER MIRET (AGNOSTIC FRONT): When the Youth Crew early on started to flex their muscles and say, "We don't want any metal kids around," that was just stupid. Later on, all those bands did metal records. Every single one of them talked shit, and then they just ended up going that route. I remember when our *Cause for Alarm* record came out, I got shit from the Youth Crew. But go and listen to the second or third records by some of those bands. Listen to Judge! *Bringin' It Down* is *more* metal than *Cause for Alarm*!

CAINE ROSE: Ultimately, the harder-edged bands that followed the original pioneers probably rose to popularity because of a need for innovation. It was an unconscious rebranding of a fading product. The concept of being the hardest band was soon the high bar, which we all fought to attain. I honestly believe it's what put an end to the Youth Crew movement. The focus changed from unity to isolationism—from good clean fun to "Fuck you, I'm better than you." The end was imminent.

Civ of Gorilla Biscuits front and center for Judge. Directly above him is Tim Singer, editor of Boiling Point *zine.* BOILING POINT ZINE

YOUTH OF TODAY support the vegetarian philosophy and diet. If you'd like to learn more about the dangers and problems with meat eating, check out your local library or health food store for the following books:

Animal Liberation
by Peter Singer

Food for the Spirit
by Steven Rosen

For for Life
by Harvey and Marilyn Diamond

Survival into the 21st Century
by Viktoras Ku vinskas

The Higher Taste
by Prabhupada

The Yoga of Nutrition
by Omraam Mikhael Aivanhov

Poisons in Your Body
by Gary Null and Steven Null

Clockwise from top left: *Pillsbury Hardcore vocalist Bill Tuck was a huge influence on members of Insted becoming vegetarians.* CASEY JONES; *Insted flyer promoting vegetarianism, distributed during their summer tour in 1989; Strife drummer Sid Nielsen in a vegetarian shirt made by New Age Records sings along to Outspoken.* MIKEY GARCEAU; *Youth of Today included a vegetarian reading list on the lyric sheet of their final LP,* We're Not In This Alone; *Flyers for the New York hardcore animal rights benefit featuring the cream of the crop of the Youth Crew.*

VEGETARIANISM: NO MORE!

KENT MCCLARD: Sometime in 1984, I became a vegetarian for the same reason that I became straight edge: I wanted to make my own choices. I looked around and saw everyone doing what they were being told to do. Everybody got drunk. Everyone ate meat. There was no decision making. I didn't want to buy food in chain supermarkets. I was connecting all of that in regard to eating meat and being straight edge. At that point, I realized the things you consume funds all these different organizations and institutions. I lived in a small town in Idaho at the time, and I saw how all these big chains were coming in and taking all the money out of our community off to some other rich city.

MARK STARR: I was in a punk band called Censored Reality in 1984. We were very into political and animal rights. So I was already a vegetarian when Insight was active. What appalled me was just how cruelly people treat animals for the world to consume. It's amazing we have pets, yet we eat other animals without blinking an eye.

RAY CAPPO: I always had this pull toward spirituality. I got a calling to be a vegetarian. I wanted to be very careful about what I put in my mouth, and if I was harming other beings. I made the public statement that I was a vegetarian and decided we were going to preach that as a part of being straight edge. I told Porcell, and he was like, "Oh man! We've already stirred up so much stuff with straight edge, now we're really going to piss people off!" And it did!

WALTER SCHREIFELS: I think people thought of us as a weird band to do the vegetarian thing. When you think of vegetarian punk bands, you think of Crass and all those heavily political old British bands. It threw people for a loop, so that was cool.

JOHN PORCELLY: Cappo and I became vegetarian at the same time, and we started working at a health food store. We really got into it. We would have these conversations wondering if we should sing about vegetarianism and animal rights. We thought it was an evolution of straight edge. We didn't know if people were ready for this, and they weren't! People thought it was completely off the wall.

KARL BUECHNER (EARTH CRISIS): My grandfather worked in a slaughterhouse. My grandmother went there one day, and that made her stop eating meat. That's how I got exposed to the concept of vegetarianism. When I was thirteen, I got into hardcore punk through my cousin; stuff like Angry Samoans was the soundtrack to us skateboarding. As I explored further, I got around to hearing DYS and Minor Threat. I thought, "This is exactly who I am." I never wanted to expand my mind with drugs or smoke cigarettes or drink alcohol or any of that stuff. I really fell in love with Conflict, because they were reflecting, magnifying, and pushing the same ideas. When Youth of Today came out with their vegetarian song "No More" in 1988, the timing was perfect for me.

TIM MCMAHON: I can credit Youth of Today one hundred percent with introducing me to and enlightening me on the subject of vegetarianism. They brought vegetarianism to light on the *We're Not in This Alone* album. Once I looked into it myself and made the decision to go vegetarian, I never looked back.

RICH LABBATE: I was vegetarian already, so I was psyched when Youth of Today came out with "No More." I have to give credit to Bill Tuck and Eric Wood from Pillsbury Hardcore, because they were hard-core with that stuff. Eric Wood would say, "Don't eat fucking meat, they're grinding up pigs." He showed me a video of how hot dogs were made, and I said, "I don't want to be a part of that."

SEAN MARCUS: We played with Youth of Today at Lupo's in Rhode Island. I was standing outside with Ray and asking what the fuck was up with all this Krishna and vegetarian stuff. He was like, "You've got to get into it, man," and I was like, "Fuck that shit!"

JOHN PORCELLY: When Youth of Today put out *Break Down the Walls* on Wishingwell, Pat Dubar and Pat Longrie edited the lyrics to our song "Free at Last" on purpose. They took out the line "From the animals in the slaughterhouse to the drugs on the street." They actually censored the lyric sheet. They thought it was too weird, and we were taking straight edge to some other place. To me, it seemed if you were in straight edge and taking care of your body and the world around you, if that is your value system, vegetarianism fits right in. I wrote an article in *Schism* called "Straight in '88" and really pushed it because I thought it was important.

PAT DUBAR: Whenever it got vegetarian and vegan and all that, straight edge was in the rearview mirror for me. By then, I saw not drinking or smoking as a personal decision. So don't tell me I'm not straight edge if I have on a leather belt.

JACK "CHOKE" KELLY: Straight edge is a good thing in my mind. Not doing all those things is good. If you got some thirteen-year-old kid who's on the fence and you want him to come to your side, don't throw things in like vegetarianism or veganism, because he's just going to be like, "Oh fuck that!" Now *that's* a bad thing. Straight edge should be easy to adopt. The harder you make straight edge for people, the less likely they'll get into it. These kids thought if they added more things onto straight edge, it made them more hard-core. Everyone wants to be more hard-core than everyone else, and be into mixed martial arts, and have tattoos all over their neck and hands. That's cool, but if you want people to more accepting of your opinion, you have to make it easier. In their zeal, they made it more unlikely for people to join. For a few years, I didn't even call myself straight edge, because people would say to me, "But you eat meat!" I came back with the term "I'm MacKaye edge."

JOE SNOW: When the vegetarian thing became such an issue, I saw all these kids that were new in the scene looking at me as an old guy who wasn't really straight edge because I wasn't a vegetarian. That really bummed me out. I felt like I was being pushed out of the scene. All of a sudden, it seemed like I wasn't straight edge enough.

AL BARILE: To me, the choice was using alcohol or drugs—straight edge didn't involve sex or the food you eat or whatever. The choice I was talking about was drugs and alcohol. That's it. Obviously there are other choices in life, too, but those were things that I was not concerned with.

JEFF TERRANOVA: When I found out about vegetarianism, it was like discovering straight edge again for me. It was something I didn't know existed.

Once I did, I reached a conclusion about who I wanted to be. But vegetarianism was almost harder to explain than straight edge. People would say, "You cheat, right? You eventually eat some meat, right?" I was like, "You don't get it, dude." That seems to be something that has forever followed me—people not getting what I do.

TOBY MORSE: I was living with Walter Schreifels and Civ from Gorilla Biscuits in Queens and they got me into animal rights. Then I sang backup on Gorilla Biscuits' *Start Today* album on the song "Cats and Dogs." I got to scream, "Thou shalt not kill!" Then I heard the rap MC KRS-One talk about being vegetarian on his song "My Philosophy." Soulside had a song called "Name in Mind" about vegetarianism. These were the things happening that put it all together. Animal rights in straight edge came together because the whole straight edge thing was about mind, body, and soul.

TIM MCMAHON: I don't think you have to be a vegetarian to be straight edge, but it is a natural extension of straight edge and to me it made sense. I have plenty of friends that are straight edge and aren't vegetarian. In my eyes, they're no more or no less straight edge than me. It's a personal decision, one that I will always support, but a personal decision nevertheless.

JEFF TERRANOVA: I never considered vegetarianism a part of straight edge, and I never will. Straight edge to me is straight edge; don't drink, don't smoke, and don't do drugs. I can understand how vegetarianism would be seen in the same light, but to me straight edge isn't all-encompassing.

JOHN PORCELLY: The weird thing was that, for the most part, the vegetarian thing caught on like wildfire, when we thought it was going to backfire!

DJ ROSE: These days, you see people drinking soy milk to reduce their blood pressure. I have no doubt that the reason these products are now readily available in supermarkets is because twenty-five years ago there was an army of fifteen-year-old straight edge kids demanding it from their parents.

JOHN PORCELLY: Being a vegetarian in 1988 was like being Lewis and Clark. You couldn't find a brick of tofu even in New York City. It was weird and unheard of. Now, the general populace has opened its eyes to this thing. You have all these documentaries coming out like *Forks over Knives*, where people are finally waking up and saying, "Holy shit! My food choices affect the world."

DEMIAN JOHNSTON (UNDERTOW): You can't help but think that straight edge or hardcore helped make things so you can go to any city in the country and get something vegan off a menu. As the straight edge kids became the grown-ups, we changed the world. We gained those morals and insight from groupthink. We came together and said, "This matters to us all."

MARK STARR: I don't think vegetarianism is part of any scene anymore, simply because now it's a part of many people's lifestyles. I think Youth of Today helped a lot to generate that movement. If you can have that impact on people to start a movement, then bring it on. As I got older, I backed away from jamming my ideals down people's throats. To each their own—but I still believe in animal rights and always will.

JOHN PORCELLY: There were a few milestone choices I made in my life that incredibly improved my life. Straight edge is one of them. Vegetarianism was the other huge one. Those were two of the best decisions I ever made. I'm fifty years old, and I'm in super good shape. I can do all the same stuff I did when I was eighteen, and it's all because of those two choices.

Youth of Today's final West Coast show, Fender's Ballroom, Long Beach, August 4, 1989. Gorilla Biscuits, Bold, Judge, Insted, Up Front, and Chain of Strength also appeared. PHOTOS BY MIKEY GARCEAU

DISENGAGE

JOHN PORCELLY: By 1988 or '89, I could see why people got pissed off with straight edge. There were kids coming in who were just into straight edge, and they shit on every other band. For the first time, a lot of bands on the scene started to get cookie-cutter to me. In Youth of Today, we loved Minor Threat, we loved SSD, we loved DYS, but I don't think we sounded like any of those bands. There was this punk mentality that you would find your own style and sound.

PAT DUBAR: Eventually, our band created a little bit of a monster. We made it safe for a lot of kids to come to shows—all the kids that ended up in these influential Orange County straight edge bands that came after us—but I didn't like where it went. I had to fight a lot of their physical fights for them. They weren't stepping out there and putting up their dukes. They were hiding while we fought for them. We fought this fight to eradicate all these guys so they could feel safe, and they just walked in and said, "Is it safe? Are they all gone?" Then they set up camp and became just as bad as or worse than the people we got rid of. If some kid came to a show with a G. G. Allin shirt on, he would get his ass kicked. These guys who were shaving their heads and professing to be positive youth were isolating and pushing out people that weren't wearing the right Vans on their feet, or that didn't have an X on their hand. I joined punk so I wouldn't be associated with the people I went to school with; straight edge was looking a lot like a high school clique I hated.

RICHIE BIRKENHEAD: In the straight edge scene, it became like once you got your membership card, you were better than anybody else. It's such bullshit, especially for a bunch of bourgeois fucking white kids. There are people in the world scrounging for their next meal. I was always on the fringes. I loved straight edge bands, but I've always been turned off by the attitude.

PAT LONGRIE: We never pointed at a guy who paid his eight dollars to see Uniform Choice and said, "Fuck that guy because he doesn't look like us." I never understood when it morphed into that thing. It just made me think, "I don't want to get lumped into this pool." I made that crystal clear. When straight edge became a code that you could put in your pocket, then look at someone and say, "You're not fitting the commandments of straight edge," that was something we didn't embrace at all.

JOHN BELLO (HAWKER RECORDS): Back when the straight edge scene started, it was saying, "Be tolerant of me, I'm just like you." But when it got bigger, they started dictating everything. It became, "If you're not straight edge, you're not getting a gig," or, "I'm not gonna lend you my drum kit." Even bands like Token Entry were having trouble getting gigs. With all due respect, these straight edge kids were guys coming from wealthy New England, wearing two-hundred-dollar Air Jordans. Meanwhile, there were bands here in New York who had been playing for ten years that were living on the streets, hanging out and kind of struggling for the next gig.

JOHN PORCELLY: Very early on, Ray Cappo saw kids becoming straight edge and looking down on other people. We came from the punk scene, where we went to CBGB and heard Agnostic Front sing, "United and strong! Punks and skins!" We were into unity. Look at the *New York City Hardcore* compilation Revelation Records put out; there's Nausea and Y.D.L., not just straight edge bands. It was all of us against the world. When the straight edge thing took that turn where everyone got too proud, Cappo wrote the song "Break Down the Walls," and took a stance early on.

CHRIS BRATTON: By the peak of the later Youth Crew era, the initial interpretation of straight edge seemed lost, abandoned, or straight-up removed. Straight edge became a huge worldwide movement that uncontrollably morphed away from individualism to something more resembling large group fascism. That same old intense group peer pressure flipped and refocused, so instead of drinking everyone had to be straight edge. Everyone had to look, act, and be the same. It was no longer "the straight edge"; it became "the straitjacket." Fuck that.

PETE KOLLER (SICK OF IT ALL): I stopped drinking a long time ago, but I don't consider myself straight edge. I didn't like having to label myself in a scene where there was supposed to be no labels. Hence, we wrote the song "No Labels, No Lies." I'm sure it was written about that movement coming in.

GREG BENNICK: Every week, it seemed like fifteen new straight edge bands had demo cassettes available at stores and shows. As soon as you saw the cassette, you knew it was straight edge by the font or the drawing on the front.

TOBY MORSE: Straight edge got really big and became very cliquey. I identified myself as a punk rocker, so I didn't like the separation that was going on in the scene. I never thought I was better than anyone else. All my friends drank and partied, and I still have friends who do that.

SAMMY SIEGLER: I loved the hardcore scene in 1987, when we had Nausea, Y.D.L., and Youth of Today all together in a big melting pot, and everyone could hang together. When straight edge got more popular, it seemed everybody divided into factions.

RAY CAPPO: The straight edge scene became too much of this thing where kids thought they were perfect. They didn't realize it was a stepping stone to do greater things with your life. I felt that the straight edge scene was limiting itself. An arrogance appeared that you find in religion, or anything where you do something for your self-betterment. Instead of doing it for yourself, you do it to lord over other people and you end up hating other people. It defeats the whole idea of self-betterment. I was watching this happen and it was super bumming me out.

TIM MONROE: Around 1987, there started to be straight edge bills that had just one style of music. It was definitely cool at first; we got to play with bands we were into and that had similar views as us. I remember one show at Gilman Street in Berkeley, we played with Verbal Assault, No for an Answer, Insted, Hard Stance, and Breakaway. That was great. But in the grand scheme of things, there is something to be said about having a different variety of bands on the bill. In the long run, the sameness ended up bumming me out.

STEVE LARSON: When Insted came through the country in 1988, things still seemed very punk rock, and by that I mean very loose and open. When we came back in the spring of 1989 to tour with Vision, I noticed a change. All of a sudden, everyone looked the same, with just a sprinkling of punkers. Everyone had Nikes and their pants were cuffed and rolled. They were wearing Champion sweatshirts and their hair was bleached.

Clockwise from top left: *Walter Schreifels expands his sonic horizons in Quicksand.* JUSTIN MOULDER; *Crucial Youth vocalist Joe Crucial brandishes the "Youth Brush."* KEN SALERNO; *Crucial Youth's Gentleman Jim Norton.* KEN SALERNO

JOE NELSON: On that first tour I did with Insted, you'd still get a show where you were playing a show in the middle of nowhere with a band who wore pantyhose on their heads while wearing nothing else but jockstraps or something like that. But on the later tours, it was just bills stacked with straight edge bands.

RICH LABBATE: By the time Youth of Today started touring, there were enough straight edge bands to put on a full bill of them—and enough of an audience who wanted to see that.

GENTLEMAN JIM NORTON (CRUCIAL YOUTH): The genesis of Crucial Youth was our singer Joe "Crucial" Madsen seeing this Youth of Today show with a few other straight edge bands that was just band after band preaching to the choir. There were a hundred and fifty people at the show, and twenty of them were in bands and everyone knew each other. It was like, "We all agree with each other, now let's scream in each other's faces about why we agree with each other!" What was that? There was nothing challenging about that.

A guy who was not in the band, Roger Giner-Sorolla, drew all our record covers and he collaborated with us on the lyrics. He just had a great knack for taking a song by another band to its most ridiculous conclusion. If Ian MacKaye said, "Don't drink, don't smoke, don't fuck," what could come after that? How about, "Be straight, don't be late, bench your weight, don't masturbate." What else could be ridiculous? How about adding that you can't *curse* to the rules of straight edge? How about making a rule that you have to mosh in a counterclockwise direction to keep everyone safe? We just kept taking the idea of straight edge and expanding it to a point where we thought people had to get the joke.

RAY CAPPO: Straight edge created a bubble, a scene within a scene, that wasn't really interested in anything that wasn't straight edge. That made me sad. I loved the Buzzcocks, P.I.L., and other things. Newer kids were only getting into Youth of Today or Uniform Choice. They would buy any record that was straight edge by these bands like Wide Awake and Aware.

SAMMY SIEGLER: Those shows at the Anthrax in Connecticut with Wide Awake and Side by Side and Youth of Today with all the kids looking the same, wearing Air Revolutions and Champion sweatshirts, were really cool in one sense. It was nice to have all that energy in one room. That's why those shows were so magical. But eventually, it started to get bland. All the records and T-shirts started to look the same.

WALTER SCHREIFELS: Our dream sort of backfired. We would go to shows and everyone would look the same. I started feeling like maybe this wasn't that cool. It just became so much about the T-shirts, and the Swatch watches with the *X*'s on them.

MARK MCKAY: As you move forward with a counterculture, and you are attracting more people, the counterculture becomes less dangerous and less edgy. It became a thing where it was like, "I don't have to fight for my choices anymore. I saw a kid wearing a Champion sweatshirt, so I guess I'll wear one too."

MARK STARR: When we toured, we would really notice how generic things had gotten. Even with the demos we would get were the same. I feel bad saying that, because everyone was always very cool, but, honestly, being cool doesn't mean your band is any good.

RICH LABBATE: That period of the late '80s, with a lot of bands into straight edge with the look of the hooded sweatshirts and sneakers, is almost parallel with the grunge thing a few years later where tons of bands were buying flannels and trying to fit in. Still, I think if you looked close enough, you could figure out what bands were the real deal, and which ones weren't.

JOHN PORCELLY: After Youth of Today's last LP, *We're Not in This Alone*, we felt we had said everything we wanted to say. We had taken straight-up hardcore to its limit. We were all going in different directions. Walter wanted to get serious about Gorilla Biscuits. I was totally into Judge. Ray was on his spiritual trip.

RAY CAPPO: In the straight edge scene, everybody was looking up to me. Truthfully, I didn't know what I was talking about. There were tenets of the straight edge thing; like you should strive to be a better person and be forgiving and not kill animals. But, you know, my mom could tell you that! It's not like I was some Dalai Lama for saying something as simple as that. I began to read books by yogis and Buddhists and Christian mystics. All the things about the material world that all these great yogis and mystics wrote about, I felt like I was over that shit. I didn't feel greedy, or envious, or competitive, and I knew the material world would be temporary.

But I was immersed in the success of this micro-world, filled with greed, envy, lust, and ignorance. I thought I was above it, but I was immersed in it. I got to thinking about what I really wanted. Did I want to become ten times bigger in hardcore? Would that make me happier?' I wanted to know how to become a happier person. I always had this pull toward spirituality and a quest for truth. I came to realize nothing would make me happy except for some sort of God quest.

STEVE REDDY: Before I went out on tour with Youth of Today in the summer of 1988, I was flopping around philosophically. I got a couple of books. The first was *The Higher Taste* by A. C. Bhaktivedanta Swami Prabhupada, which Dave Stein from Combined Effort Records gave to me. After that, I wrote away for some other books on Krishna consciousness. When I showed up to go on the tour, I either had a bead bag or some Krishna books on me. Porcell and Walter were like, "Oh my God!" I wasn't that close to Cappo at the time, so I didn't know how far he was into Krishna then, but he was pretty deep. He was giving out books pretty much throughout the whole tour that summer.

SAMMY SIEGLER: Youth of Today's final U.S. tour in the summer of '88 was a mission. No doubt about it.

JOHN PORCELLY: One of our first shows on that tour was in Miami, and we found a Krishna temple right there on the beach. We went there and ate the food. Ray and Steve chanted a round or two, and, from there, those two really got into it.

STEVE REDDY: When I got back from that tour, I moved to a Krishna farm in Pennsylvania and stayed there until 1992.

RAY CAPPO: I quit music. When I recorded the first Shelter record in 1990, it was supposed to be my final record ever. Shelter was a project I did with Tom Capone from Beyond and Quicksand, and some older guys I knew from Connecticut. They helped me record this music that I wrote and that was supposed to be my goodbye to hardcore. Then I became a monk.

JOHN PORCELLY: Judge broke up in 1990 and it was a very hard time for me. I was going through a real spiritual crisis. I was always wondering what life was about. People kind of looked up to me, and I had an easy life. I had all these things that people were knocking themselves out to get, yet I was completely unsatisfied with them. What could I do in my life to find true

friday, aug. 18 · 6pm

shelter
shift
Ubisunt

UPSTAIRS AT NICK'S
16 SOUTH 2ND STREET

SCREAM
shelter

HEAD FIRST
ONE STEP AHEAD
DOWNCAST
REALITY CONTROL

free

shelter
Farside
OUTFACE
gallowstree

TO WATCH THESE BANDS PLAY MUSIC:

·**shelter**·
RORSCHACH
LINCOLN
108 Assück

MONDAY, JUNE 2
ECUMENIA WAREHOUSE
926 N st. NW (rear)
enter thru Blagden Alley
6:30 pm ALL AGES
info ... (703) 908-939
$5 plus canned ge

SOLITUDE®
PRODUZIONI   PRESENTA:
·**shelter**·
FROM USA

HARE KRISHNA HARE KRISHNA KRISHNA KRISHNA HARE HARE RAMA HARE RAMA

CREATED BY: R.KING "SIDEBURNS" '92

-C.I.P. VIA PANCIATICHI 70 -

BAND SUPPORTO HARE BABA FROM FIRENZE

MARTEDI 8 SETTEMBRE
ALLA JUNGLA VIA PANCIATI 70 FIRENZE
ZONA FIRENZE NUOVA DI FRONTE
ALLA "NUOVA PIGNONE"

·ORE 22.30·

☸ SHELTER ☸
·With special guests·

108
HOLYNAME
AND
Worlds
Collide

FRIDAY
JUNE 25

CLUB DETROIT
16 2ND ST
DOWNTOWN
ST. PETE
INFO (813) 921-7271

TICKETS
$8 ADV
$10 DAY OF SHOW

CREEPY CRAWL PRODUCTIONS PRESENTS

·shelter· ☸

special guests

SHIFT H₂O

THURSDAY August 17
Doors 7pm $7   ALL AGES
Coney Island High
15 St. Marks Place   212 - 674 - 7959

satisfaction and happiness? What was the secret? Please, somebody tell me! It was a dark, soul-searching time for me, and I spent a lot of it alone.

RAY CAPPO: The more I studied Indian philosophy, I noticed a big part of that philosophy is you don't quit what you were born to do. You take what you do, and do it in a spiritual way, instead of the material way. That's how Shelter was born again as full-fledged band.

JOHN PORCELLY: I always had a lot of respect for Krishnas. Way back when we would get food from the Krishna temple on Avenue A, these Hare Krishnas were out on the street in orange robes—they were the real deal. I was always the type of guy who didn't do things halfway. If I was going to reject the world, I was going to reject the world completely! It was attractive to me to drop out of mainstream society and go off. I sold everything that I owned, except for my guitar and my amp. I put them in storage and moved into the Krishna farm in upstate New York with nothing.

WALTER SCHREIFELS: There were things going on in the scene at the time that I wasn't into. I didn't like the Krishna consciousness thing that was coming into it. Maybe it's just being from Queens, but I think my root reaction to Hare Krishna was that it was a cult. Not to discredit the people that get a lot out of it. In the end, Ray and Porcell did get a lot out of it; I'm just describing my impression at the time.

JOE NELSON: Ray was the pied piper and everyone was behind Ray drinking his Kool-Aid until the Kool-Aid became *prasadam*. That's when the Sloth Crew guys in Orange County were like, "Ray's cool, but we're not going to some farm in Pennsylvania to shovel shit!"

JOE SNOW: Some of the people involved were looking for something more out of straight edge. The vegetarian thing became big, and some expanded into animal liberation. Some got into the Hare Krishna thing, which I personally thought was fucked up. This is punk rock and you want people to go to church? I just saw droves of kids follow Ray Cappo off a cliff, and I didn't like it. Then there were people like me who didn't want to go in either direction. We started checking out other music. That's when I think the straight edge scene for that period died.

RON GUARDIPEE: I booked a bunch of Shelter shows in Seattle. One was at an actual temple. I think about that, and to this day I feel bad. I allowed these children to go to this temple, and four or five of them got real into it. I hope I didn't screw these kids' lives up by introducing them to Krishna-core.

ROB FISH: I got interested in Krishna consciousness through the Cro-Mags, and later Ray and Youth of Today. I was pretty fucked up mentally and emotionally. I needed something, anything, to explain and give me relief from things I experienced as a kid. Krishna consciousness, and specifically karma, was something I needed to survive until I got to a point where I could confront some fucked-up experiences. It was that simple. I needed an escape, and it provided easy answers. I gained something to focus on that explained away my experiences and provided temporary relief and a purpose when I needed one the most.

ROB HAWORTH: As much as I disagreed with the Krishna stuff, people were trying to find themselves spiritually. I can totally understand that. It probably helped folks figure themselves out instead of doing stupid shit.

JOHN PORCELLY: I had very little contact with Ray for that whole time period between Youth of Today and my joining him in Shelter. He didn't know that I was going to the Brooklyn temple every week, and that I eventually moved to the farm. Vic DiCara, the guitarist for Shelter, quit the band after a couple years, and someone suggested to Ray that he get me to play guitar. He didn't know I had become a Hare Krishna. Ray was in India and he came back and went right to the farm to talk me into joining Shelter. I was like, "No way." I was happy at the farm. But eventually I gave in and joined Shelter.

By the time our *Attaining the Supreme* album came out in 1993, all of us in the band were monks. We were going to bed at nine o'clock and waking up at three in the morning. We had enough control to sit there for two hours straight and chant. It was no joke. We would go to India. It was incredible. That was the potency of Shelter. We were all fully into it. Hare Krishna wasn't an act or a gimmick. People got into it. In Europe, people picketed our shows, thinking we were in a cult; but overall being monks worked in our favor, because in the '90s, weird was cool! Who was weirder than Shelter, a punk band made up of four Krishna devotees who all lived together in a temple? The press practically wrote itself.

Despite the shift in sound, Shelter still summoned the live mayhem of Youth of Today. PHOTOS BY KEN SALERNO

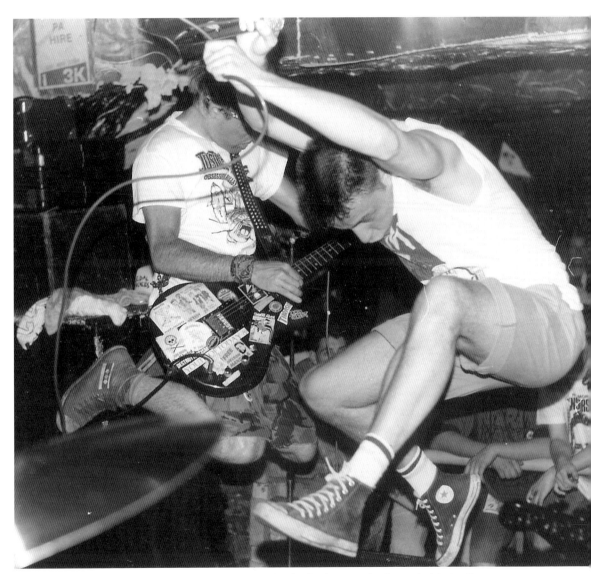

Lärm leading its campaign for musical destruction. PETER HOEREN

NO ONE CAN BE THAT DUMB: THE U.K. & EUROPE

PETER HOEREN (CRUCIAL RESPONSE RECORDS): The first band from Europe I was into was the Dutch band Lärm, a political hardcore punk band that played really fast parts with mosh parts in between. As far as I know, they labeled themselves not as a straight edge band, though they were all straight edge and addressed straight edge in their lyrics and interviews. They came from a radical left-wing background.

PAUL VAN DEN BERG (LÄRM, SEEIN' RED, MAN LIFTING BANNER): My brother Olav and I first heard punk in early 1977 when the Dutch radio station started to broadcast a fifteen-minute radio show of proto-punk like MC5, Dr. Feelgood, or the Stooges. A character named Doctor Punkenstein started calling into the show to tell the DJ to play real punk stuff like the Sex Pistols, Ramones, the Clash, Blondie, and the Damned. Although it was just fifteen fucking minutes, it made a big impact on my brother and me. When one of the local record shops finally put three punk records in their bins, we put all our pocket money together and bought the Sex Pistols' *Never Mind the Bollocks* LP; the Clash's self-titled LP; and the Damned's *Damned Damned Damned* LP. We had heard punk only from a small transistor radio; now we finally could play it loud! From then on, we considered ourselves punks.

We started to get into graffiti and with our huge black markers we wrote the names of punk bands, and our tags, A'FOORT PUNX and PUNX '79, on as many toilet doors, walls, lampposts and trash cans as possible. One day we saw that someone had written a reply to our writings on the wall: A'VELD PUNX GREETS A'FOORT PUNX. Achterveld was a small village near Amersfoort, so that gave us some hope that there were more punks in the area.

'SEE THEM SUFFER' BENEFIT GIGS

SPRING'S IN THE AIR

29 APRIL 1990
J.H. C'EST FOU
TE MOL

AANVANG 15.00 U.
ENTREE 200 BFR

COURAGE
RISE ABOVE
PROJECT HOPE
PROFOUND
BETRAY

| STATION | RETIE |
| G. GEZELLESTRAAT |
| GB |
| GEEL | RIJKSWACHT | 20A | J.H. C'EST FOU |

ANTI-VIVISECTIE BENEFIET

VENERDI 29 SETTEMBRE
DA NEW YORK CITY

GORILLA BISCUITS

ORE 22.00
ISOLA nel CANTIERE
via S. Giuseppe 8

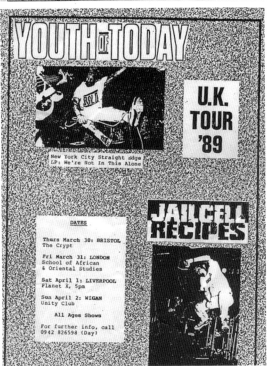

YOUTH OF TODAY

U.K.
TOUR
'89

New York City Straight Edge
LP: We're Not In This Alone

JAILCELL
RECIPES

DATES

Thurs March 30: BRISTOL
The Crypt

Fri March 31: LONDON
School of African
& Oriental Studies

Sat April 1: LIVERPOOL
Planet X, 5pm

Sun April 2: WIGAN
Unity Club

All Ages Shows

For further info, call
0942 826598 (Day)

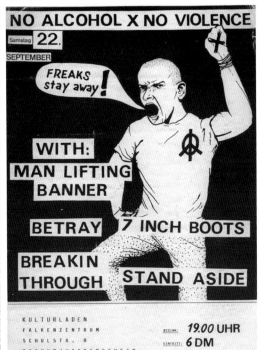

NO ALCOHOL X NO VIOLENCE

Samstag 22.
SEPTEMBER

FREAKS
stay away!

WITH:
MAN LIFTING
BANNER

BETRAY   7 INCH BOOTS

BREAKIN
THROUGH   STAND ASIDE

KULTURLADEN
FALKENZENTRUM
SCHULSTR. 8
BOCHUM/WATTENSCHEID

BEGINN: 19.00 UHR
EINTRITT: 6 DM

At the end of 1979 we went to a local snack bar and saw this young kid at the counter wearing punk buttons on his jacket. He was Jos Houtveen, one of the two punk kids that came from Achterveld. We soon having our first practice as a punk band called the Sextons. At first, the guitar, the bass, and the microphone were all plugged in one amp. Olav played drums on a chair and some washing-powder cardboard boxes. All of it was very primitive, but that was our first fucking step into what would become an amazing journey of playing in punk and hardcore bands for more than three decades.

OLAV VAN DEN BERG (LÄRM, SEEIN' RED, MAN LIFTING BANNER): There is an old phrase: "A worker who drinks doesn't think, and a worker who thinks doesn't drink." The founders of the Dutch social movement—Ferdinand Domela Nieuwenhuis and Pieter Jelles Troelstra—used that phrase.

PAUL VAN DEN BERG: I pretty much was straight edge before I got to know straight edge as a concept. The Rotterdam-based punk band the Rondos were already rallying against the whole alcohol and drugs culture in the punk scene by 1980, long before I heard of Minor Threat. The Rondos wrote pretty fierce anti-alcohol and drugs articles in their zine, *Raket.* Their song "We Don't Need No Speed" says: "We get our kicks making noise. We don't want those stupid toys." What the Rondos had to say spoke a lot to me.

PETER HOEREN: The Rondos were an awesome band. I think they were Maoists and came from Rotterdam, Netherlands. They reminded me a bit of the Proletariat from Boston. Punk with post-punk mixed in, very minimalistic.

PAUL VAN DEN BERG: After we had the bands the Sextons, the Disturbers, and Total Chaos, Lärm started halfway through 1982. Straight edge became an important part of the band. That was a conscious effort of Olav and mine, because we could no longer turn a blind eye to the self-destructive, punker-than-you kind of attitude of the time, seeing what it did to some of our friends.

PETER STRANDELL: The rumor that Svart Parad was the first straight edge band in Sweden is really strange, actually. I guess we can only blame ourselves. We did know fairly well what straight edge was, considering we were a bunch of fifteen-year olds in the middle of nowhere in 1984. Jörgen did that thing with the crosses on his hands and such—mainly because it looked tough, though he was actually one hundred percent straight edge at that time. This mainly had to do with the fact that he was thirteen years old. He simply hadn't had the chance yet to indulge in sins like sex, alcohol, and tobacco!

TOMAS ANDERSSON (SVART PARAD): I was kind of sober for almost a year, I guess, quite some time. I guess the others were, too. We had the straight edge ambition, but it was on a very shaky foundation.

PETER STRANDELL: So briefly, the entire band was more or less straight edge. It was mainly to break fixed patterns, it wasn't really political in our eyes. It wasn't about being a vegetarian or left-wing, even if we were. We just wanted to have hard codes. The sexual abstinence part wasn't by our choice, though. The fact was that no girls even looked at us. We found other things to do. We skateboarded a lot, and hung out in the forest doing barbecues alone. We talked about how we wanted to change the world, while standing under some park shelters in the middle of nowhere.

TOMAS ANDERSSON: I was very interested in politics during that time, and straight edge was in line with other ideas I liked. The problem was that I already back then was battling an addiction, and that addiction destroyed the noblest of intentions.

PETER STRANDELL: I guess much of it was a revolt against the Scandinavian punk scene, which had always been about drinking and boozing as hard as possible. To say that you didn't drink was very extreme at that point. People were shocked. We wanted to challenge everybody in everything. We wanted people to react. Many punks did get very anxious when we said we didn't drink. Later we didn't follow our own rules, but I guess that was just even more punk!

In all honesty, for some time we drank way too much. The rumors about our drinking habits soon erased any straight edge connotations. Tomas especially never slowed down, even though he had previously been kicked out of Asocial because of his wild antics. He was out of control, and Svart Parad partly crashed due to that in the end.

SIMON KELLY (*PUNCH IN THE FACE* ZINE): There were no straight edge bands in England, but starting around 1985 some bands appeared that flirted with straight edge in their approach. I guess those bands would be the Stupids, Heresy, and A.Y.S.

IAN LECK (STEADFAST, VOORHEES): The only people I knew who were straight edge at that time in England were either in a band with me called the MacDonalds, or some friends in another Durham City band called False Face. Prior to that, the only sign of anyone being straight edge was Tommy Withers from the Stupids wearing a baseball cap with "XXX" on it, but he wasn't actually straight edge. A.Y.S. covered Minor Threat's "In My Eyes" on their seven-inch that came out at the end of 1985, but they weren't straight edge, either; their singer, John Cato, was just against *excessive* drug and alcohol use.

PETER HOEREN: The northwest part of Germany only had a handful of straight edge kids before 1987. Two friends of mine, Andreas Grüter and Georg Opora, were the prototypes of straight edge kids in our area by 1985. They both had big mouths and were troublemakers in a good sense. Marc Zeyen, my best friend, became straight edge around 1987. A few others were straight edge for a very short period. Down in southern Germany, a few kids were straight edge, too. Yvonne Ducksworth, who sang for Manson Youth and Combat Not Conform, both bands from Berlin, was and is still straight edge to my knowledge. Basically, before 1987 Germany was pretty much the land of no straight edge kids and no straight edge bands, aside from a few kids in bands who were straight edge.

When bands like Suicidal Tendencies and D.R.I. became metal around 1986, the attitude within the scene changed a lot. Lärm wrote a song which reflected the situation, called "Metal Attitudes Suck." Another of their songs was "Drunk Freak." Those two songs pretty much summed it up. Kids became less active, and drinking beer became the dominant force within the scene. Straight edge people were being attacked by non–straight edge kids, and a lot of discussion was going on. Kids felt threatened, because they couldn't handle their own alcohol consumption, I assume.

LINS CUSCANI (VENGEANCE OF GAIA, THIRTY SECONDS TO ARMAGEDDON, BREAK IT UP): I can categorically say that the majority of non–straight edge punks did not welcome those who were straight with open arms in the U.K. In some instances, the opposing ideals brought about conflict and violence. Instead of punks fighting the establishment and norms, they fought each other! I can recall going to crusty punk shows even in the early '90s and being stared at and verbally abused for being into the straight edge scene. Also, from the reverse angle, I recall seeing straight edge people freaked out on those who dared drink or smoke at straight edge gigs! It wasn't a massive issue, but it did raise its ugly head every so often. For the most part, the shit-talking from both sides was mostly done in fanzines or on records.

SIMON KELLY: In late 1985, I stopped wearing Doc Marten boots and motorbike jackets, and I started wearing flannel shirts and Converse sneakers. I'd get older punks calling me a "Yankee clown!" So when we started to put X's on our hands, we knew it would piss off certain punks.

PETER HOEREN: By 1987, a new breed of hardcore kids came into the European scene and things changed drastically. Straight edge became a force on the scene, and a lot of non–straight edge people got really pissed off about it. I remember Armin Hofmann from X-Mist Records in southwestern Germany handing out anti–straight edge pamphlets. People got really hysterical about straight edge, and we fired back. We were a force to reckon with.

We put X's on our hands and we got more militant about things. Andreas Grüter from *Vengeance* fanzine got pulled to the ground by five people during a Circle Jerks and Gang Green show, and they tried to fill him up with beer. I was threatened a couple of times by some druggies at a show, and I was threatened by a friend with whom I used to go to shows. Somehow he couldn't take that I was straight edge. I was pretty mellow in the beginning, but when stuff like that happened we got pretty ballistic. The straight edge kids split from the regular punk crowd. Before, I thought we were all lumped in this together—punks, crusties, straight edge kids, or whatever. You have to bear in mind that the punk scene was pretty small in a way, so it was strange when you got attacked. Straight edge kids were hanging out more together and taking care of each other. It was all about camaraderie. We started our own bands, fanzines, and shows. It was not like a conscious thing, but that's what happened.

IAN LECK: In the northeast of England we weren't welcome at all; we would end up fighting with crust punks when we went to see U.S. hardcore bands in Newcastle. They didn't like the way we looked, as we skated and wore flannel shirts, baseball caps, hoodies, blue jeans, and basketball sneakers. Their uniform was all-black clothes covered in patches, combat boots, dreadlocks, spiced up with a bottle of cider and bad hygiene. The way we danced caused the most problems. We would start moshing in a circle pit, and they would try to trip us as we went past them. Punches would be

Man Lifting Banner ends the fear. PETER HOEREN

MANLIFTINGBANNER
UTRECHT

FEEDING THE FIRE
KERKRADE X WEST

inner X circle
MÜLHEIM

FREITAG 4. SEPT. 92
19.30 UHR
JZ HELENENSTR.
433 MÜLHEIM-DÜMPTEN

#1

YOUTH OF TODAY

COLT TURKEY

Se-Hc
SUNDAY-MATINÉ WITH:

ONWARD
(OSLO)
RECTIFY
(OSLO)
CLOSE CALL
(PORSGRUNN)
AND
SPORTSWEAR
(OSLO)

XXX

PICTURE: RECTIFY

HVELVET (NEDRE SLOTTSGATE 4)
19. MAI KL. 16.30
35 KR ALL AGES

CONNECTION X
FANZINE

MANLIFTINGBANNER
GORILLA BISCUITS
LAST
STRAW
...FUCK
YEAH!
+MORE...

COUNTER
CLOCKWISE
FANZINE

2
MAN LIFTING BANNER
STRONG EVENT
POLITICS
50% PHOTOZINE

thrown in retaliation, and people would jump in to defend their friends. Sometimes it was a bit of a mess.

LINS CUSCANI: I would definitely say that out of all bands, Youth of Today was the one that really got people into doing their own straight edge bands. Yes, Minor Threat laid the foundations as to what the straight edge message and ethics were, but Youth of Today took it to an altogether different level. I really think the main catalyst for kids forming straight edge bands on this side of the Atlantic was when Youth of Today toured England and Europe in the start of 1989. Kids who were straight edge then realized that they could have a scene like that of their peers in the United States. The most important aspect became forming bands with other straight edge kids and laying down a foundation.

PAUL VAN DEN BERG: Around 1984, I was one of the first European hardcore kids to mail-order the Violent Children EP; at least that's what they wrote on a note that accompanied my order! I kept in touch with Ray Cappo, and found out about Youth of Today and Crippled Youth. I really liked the bands, because they brought a youthful energy and enthusiasm back into the scene. Hardcore at that time needed the spirit of youth kicking the asses of the old guard. So I felt kinship with them. I was already an old guy of twenty-five, but it was no reason for me not to be buying their records and enjoying their music and message. My brother and I and other members of the Lärm crew did a fanzine called *Definite Choice*. We always gave Youth of Today good reviews and put interviews with them and other bands in the zine. In 1988, I started to play in Profound, a band that took a lot of influences from Youth of Today, Chain of Strength, and Crippled Youth. We brought a strong message of left-wing politics combined with a straight edge attitude. To our surprise, the record did really well.

VIQUE MARTIN (*SIMBA* ZINE): I first started going to shows in the summer of 1989 in Brighton, England, seeing bands like Firehose, Shudder to Think, Rollins Band, and Verbal Assault. In the autumn of 1989 I moved to London to go to university, and a whole new scene opened up to me. I don't remember how I found the first London straight edge zine, *Positive Dislike*, but I soon became friends with Mike Wilson, the kid who did it, and he started taking me to small shows. There were only three straight bands in London at the time: Long Cold Stare, Insight, and Harmony as One. I remember those three bands playing a show together. Apart from the people in the bands, only two other people were there—me and Tony Sylvester. It seems crazy to me in retrospect that the London straight edge scene was so small. The scene in the North seemed like it was much bigger, with more bands and more straight edge kids. As far as I remember, I was the only straight edge girl in the U.K. until around 1993, when some others started getting into it. It was mostly boys and me.

IAN LECK: The first U.S. straight edge band to come to the U.K. was Youth of Today in March of 1989. I organized a fifty-two-seat bus to go from Durham to Liverpool to see them. It was easy to fill the seats, as that was the closest they came to the Northeast. We must have made up about a third of the crowd in the club Planet X that day; we certainly made our presence felt when the crust punks started heckling. There were threats getting thrown around between every song.

JOHN PORCELLY: The European scene in 1989 reminded me of the U.S. scene when straight edge was just coming back. It reminded me of being on the Break Down the Walls tour in 1987.

WALTER SCHREIFELS: It seemed like nothing had really happened in Europe since the last wave of bands like G.B.H. at the beginning of the 1980s. A lot of times they didn't know what hardcore was. Hardcore was an American thing, a new thing to them. It was cool to meet people who didn't know what the hell we were about.

JORDAN COOPER: When Youth of Today went to Europe in early 1989, they were nice enough to invite me along. Europe seemed to be a lot less receptive to straight edge, and that showed occasionally with spit, beer, and maybe a bottle being thrown Youth of Today's way.

JOHN PORCELLY: For seventy-five percent of the tour, people were open-minded toward straight edge and vegetarianism. But another twenty-five percent of people stood by the bar with Mohawks, going, "Fuck you!" and throwing beers at us.

WALTER SCHREIFELS: We were facing some misconceptions when we hit Europe; Ray had a shaved head on the cover of the first Youth of Today seven-inch, so people thought we had a skinhead in the group. That didn't matter, because Ray was pretty fearless. There was a straight-up riot in Belgium, with everybody fighting, and Ray taking on all these Nazi skinheads. The next night we almost got into another fight, which I think we would have lost badly.

We finally expanded into Europe. We were the first band from New York that toured there. The Cro-Mags had been there opening for Motörhead, but that was not the same. We played squats every day for two months on five dollars a day, eating whatever the club gave us. I didn't even bring a sleeping bag and it was winter. I remember wrapping band T-shirts around myself every night to keep warm.

SAMMY SIEGLER: We were on tour for two and a half months in a van with Lethal Aggression, this New Jersey band who called themselves "drug core" and played songs about drinking vodka and ripple wine. We were playing to audiences that were not straight edge. There was a straight edge scene in Belgium, but, aside from that, there wasn't a straight edge scene in Europe. Whether it was ten kids or a bunch of U.S. military dudes or an angry punk crowd who just wanted to drink and party, Ray Cappo was getting in their faces. He was preaching the message.

PETER HOEREN: The Youth of Today show in Namur in Belgium was great. Lethal Aggression had to break off the tour because someone from the band had threatened the tour manager with a knife. When Youth of Today hit the stage, people were throwing bottles from the back. Ray Cappo was jumping around onstage like a maniac, and the whole stage cracked. There are pictures from the show of Ray crawling out of a cracked hole in the stage.

JORDAN COOPER: Everyone in Youth of Today was vegetarian. Even though a lot of the punk venues in Europe were run in community centers or squats and had vegan food, plenty of the shows were in clubs or bars that didn't seem to know what to do for vegetarians. There would usually be a nice deli spread, but the only thing for vegetarians was bread and cheese. Youth of Today and company were grateful for it, and the bread and cheese there are actually really good, but after a few weeks it started to feel like there were some things missing from our collective diet. We had to make an effort to find other stuff to eat to supplement those fine staples.

By the time the band was in Berlin, everyone was pretty used to the routine, and wasn't thinking about it anymore. At one point we were somewhere near the Berlin Wall, which at that point was in its final days, and we saw some graffiti that made everyone realize that we really were not in this alone. "Verbal Assault: Bread and Cheese tour '89." Rhode Island hardcore had already made the rounds!

From top: *Youth of Today in Italy in the spring of 1989.* FREDDY TWICE; *Youth of Today airborne in Italy, 1989.* FREDDY TWICE; *European straight edge crew in full effect, 1989.* PETER HOEREN

PETER HOEREN: After Youth of Today came to Europe, the scene started to change drastically. More straight edge bands started to pop up. Profound had just formed with Bart Griffioen on bass and Michiel Bakker singing, plus they added Paul and Olav van den Berg from Lärm. Betray from Netherlands started around 1989, and Marc Hanou from Betray also did Revelation Records Europe for a while. Youth of Today was totally outspoken when it came to straight edge. When they came over to Europe, they were pushing it hard.

SAMMY SIEGLER: When I went back to Europe in 1991 with Gorilla Biscuits, we saw the change within two years. In '89 we planted the seeds, and in '91 we were looking at the flowers.

ALEX BROWN: Gorilla Biscuits first played in Europe at the end of 1989 in some big community hall in Holland. I was watching the opening bands, and people were whipping full cups of beers on them while they played. I had never experienced that sort of crowd dynamic. It was much more of an old punk scene than in the U.S. at the time. We were touring in the wake of Youth of Today, who had preceded us by about six months. I think they really laid the groundwork for New York bands touring in Europe. There *were* lots of kids who knew all our music, wore Champion hooded sweatshirts, Nikes, had crew cuts, and really looked the part. Holland, Belgium, and England were the most receptive to the music and message. Yet the Youth of Today–inspired kids were definitely still the minority. There were lots of drunk and drugged punks, skins, and random rock guys that would watch us play.

PAUL VAN DEN BERG: Profound did a gig in Apeldoorn, Netherlands, with a band called Changing Systems. Together we launched a five-piece secret project kind of inside-joke band called Colt Turkey. We released the *Christmas Sucks* EP in 1990, and soon after that the band became Man Lifting Banner. We made the decision to change gears and put politics before straight edge. Not that we were getting rid of straight edge, but the political message became far more important and in your face.

DENNIS LYXZÉN: As much as I loved New York hardcore, one of the most important things that existed at that time for me was the European hardcore like Man Lifting Banner. They were very political. When we first started Step Forward, I wrote a letter to the band and they sent me all these pamphlets of leftist radical ideas. That really influenced us in Sweden a lot in regard to what straight edge meant.

PAUL VAN DEN BERG: Man Lifting Banner took politics to an extreme. The Marxist stance and the Lenin quotes on the *Ten Inches That Shook the World* record puzzled people in 1992. We were not welcomed with open arms, to say the least. Some people from the hardcore scene reacted with hostility toward the band. U.S. customs returned shipments of our ten-inch because of the sleeve. Anti-communist sentiments even led to calls to boycott our shows and to super bad reviews in fanzines. At the same time, there was appreciation and support.

PAUL VAN DEN BERG: After taking off the blindfold of intoxication of alcohol, smoking, and drugs, it makes sense that your interests venture toward class and social issues, or the oppressive conditions and bullshit you run into in your daily life. Within socialist, communist, and anarchist movements, there were factions that advocated a life free of intoxication, so there was some connection. For us, it was more like coming to terms with what we considered most important in our lives: straight edge and communism. It worked for us. For some time, the "straight edge commie" image appealed to quite a lot of people. But it was never a natural union, because moralism and materialism just don't mix.

From top: *Tim McMahon of Mouthpiece rides the wild crowd at "the place where everyone was friends," the Unisound, Reading, PA.* COURTESY OF TIM MCMAHON; *Mouthpiece's apparel leaving an impression.* TRACI MCMAHON

THE NEW BREED

ANDREW KLINE (STRIFE): The start of the 1990s saw all the Youth Crew bands like Youth of Today, Bold, Gorilla Biscuits, and Judge breaking up. We got involved in hardcore at the very tail end of that. We saw Gorilla Biscuits, Judge, and Insted for the first times at some of their last shows. After that, the whole straight edge scene died down quite a bit.

TIM MCMAHON: Coming into 1990, the straight edge scene that had been so huge seemed to be falling apart rapidly. You had all the popular straight edge bands of the late '80s breaking up, going away to college, getting out of straight edge, going more the rock route, and moving on to other things.

WALTER SCHREIFELS: I remember touring with Gorilla Biscuits in Europe and someone gave me Nirvana's *Bleach*, and I was, like, "Wow." Fugazi was happening at the same time, and that was interesting to me. Something there seemed more adult to me, and I wanted to grab onto that. I wanted to write lyrics that were more inwardly focused. I wanted to do something scary, but also poppy—and that was kind of a step on the way to Quicksand. Forming Quicksand was my reaction to the monster I helped create in hardcore.

TOM CAPONE (BEYOND, QUICKSAND): We were trying to step away from hardcore, but not in a snotty way. We definitely weren't trying to push the people we knew from hardcore away from us, not at all. We were just trying to create a new sound for ourselves.

CHRIS BRATTON: That Gorilla Biscuits dis song "New Direction," about Uniform Choice, has lyrics that fucking rule: "Stage dives make me feel more alive than coded messages in slowed-down songs." What made it even radder was when Walter's post-hardcore band Quicksand then had coded messages in slowed-down songs the following year!

ROB MORAN (UNBROKEN): It felt like a lull for sure. The Revelation Records scene and bands like Gorilla Biscuits and Judge started to wind down just as kids my age were starting bands, so it was an odd time for straight edge. Everyone had their hands up in the air trying to figure out what to do next.

JEFF TERRANOVA: Straight edge had run its course. Up Front toured the country in 1991, and we certainly did not go over like during the tour we did in 1989. Quite frankly, no one cared. All the bands on Revelation became "post-core," including Farside, Into Another, Sense Field, and Quicksand. People were looking for something fresh.

MARK STARR: I know that Insight just really started to get better at playing. We were listening to other things. We met a lot of people who only listened to straight edge music, and I never understood that. Bands were breaking up, but music in general was just changing—and I was glad it was changing. Straight edge was getting to be sterile and saturated, with really bad bands. When Insight broke up in 1990, I needed a change. I wanted to do some of the shoegaze music that I was really digging at that time.

TIM MCMAHON: Although I was doing fanzines smack-dab in the middle of that high-point era of the late-'80s straight edge hardcore scene, I always wanted to be doing a band—not just covering the music, but doing it. Watching videos of bands playing places like the Anthrax in Connecticut and CBGB in NYC, I wanted to be opening up for those bands and be to fully immersed in that scene any way I could. Unfortunately, by the time we formed Mouthpiece in early 1990, things were on the downslide. Traditional hardcore just wasn't cool anymore. Everyone had outgrown playing fast, and wanted to do something different.

While most bands wanted to expand their musical styles and skills by experimenting with metal and rock, we wanted to stick with what we felt the most connected to and what spoke to us. At that point, we tried to play with as many of our favorite bands as we could that were still around. Before we knew it, we were in the minority. By 1991, there just weren't many bands playing anything that resembled that classic straight edge hardcore we grew up on. So we took it upon ourselves to push even harder and carry the torch. We weren't ready to move on. Soundgarden was cool, but, to us, Youth of Today was still cooler.

LINS CUSCANI: Hand on my heart, I thought Mouthpiece were the saviors of straight edge hardcore and hardcore in general in the early '90s. They were kids of our own age that still held onto the values and beliefs of the predecessors of the straight edge scene. They also sounded a lot like Chain of Strength, which was the most amazing thing ever. By that time, Chain was gone and rumors of their non–straight edge activities were starting to unfold. To me, Mouthpiece was as relevant to us as Youth of Today and the older bands. So we supported the new bearers of the straight edge torch.

KARL BUECHNER: Going into the '90s, a lot of the bands on Revelation Records would come out in interviews saying that straight edge was cool when they were younger, but they weren't into it anymore.

JORDAN COOPER: During the first year or two of Revelation starting in 1987, our goal was to document what was already happening with hardcore having a resurgence. Revelation became inextricably tied to the idea of hardcore and straight edge promoted by Youth of Today, and that was probably a conscious effort on Ray Cappo's part. While that profile might have been the posture Ray wanted the label to have, the funny thing is that there really weren't many bands on the label that perfectly fit that mold. I think the image mostly has to do with Ray, more than our bands. By 1989, though, Ray was disengaging and getting into Krishna, and a lot of the hardcore purist scene around Ray was having their own sort of revolution summer and going in new directions.

The label continued just documenting what was happening, never intentionally changing focus. Some of the bands pretty much signed themselves to Rev by just telling me, "This should be on Revelation," and me just saying okay. Shelter, Quicksand, Inside Out, Burn, and CIV were pretty much like that as far as I remember. If Ray, Walter, Alan Cage, Porcell, and a few others told me that they thought we should do something, I would just listen—thankfully.

DEMIAN JOHNSTON: Revelation was the quintessential hardcore label for us. But then they started putting out things like Into Another and Iceburn. Our band Undertow would cover "One Family" by Youth of Today because it was a blast, and a reaction toward that feeling slipping away. But Undertow was pretty far from what Youth of Today sounded like. We listened to a lot of Slayer, and were trying to rip off Integrity's *For Those Who Fear Tomorrow* more than anything.

GREG BENNICK: I remember walking around the streets of Seattle with two CDs in my hand—one by Quicksand and one by Rage Against The Machine. Both were on major labels, and both contained members of straight edge hardcore bands that were super influential on me: Youth of Today and Inside Out. I wondered what was happening. If Walter Schreifels and Zack de la Rocha went this route, what was my place and what should I be doing? These were guys we would have followed into the flames. This music was all coming from a very different mind-set than what it felt like at the Anthrax back in Connecticut, where it seemed like we were in it together and we were all going to win.

KARL BUECHNER: The Revelation bands were viewing straight edge more as a chapter in their lives than something that was a commitment. I guess that made sense for them. From what I understand, Ian MacKaye's original definition of straight edge was about moderation and anti-obsession. But in the small circle of friends that I had, we viewed straight edge as a life-long commitment.

SAMMY SIEGLER: At one point, I thought straight edge and hardcore were serious fucking business. If you were straight edge, you should stay straight edge; and if you get into hardcore, you should stay part of the scene. I respect that frame of thought, because I was once like that. At the same time, there's no rule manual. Nobody owns hardcore or straight edge to say who can stay and who can leave.

STEVE LARSON: With the direction hardcore was taking, Insted started to feel obsolete. Our favorite bands were breaking up and moving on.

KEVIN HERNANDEZ: The scene was changing. Bands were trying to one-up each other and make money. You started hearing bands asking for guarantees for shows. They were thinking they could pay their rent through hardcore. I always said, "Get a job if you need money so bad." Wouldn't you make more money at a job than playing hardcore? Come on! Why would you ruin what you worked so hard on to sell out for a few thousand dollars?

STEVE LARSON: When we were making the last Insted record, *What We Believe*, Goldenvoice Productions asked if we wanted to play with 7 Seconds. We said yes, of course, and they said, "Good, if you guys are playing we can book it at the Country Club. If not, we'd have to book them at the Whisky a Go Go. They don't draw as many people as they used to." That

From top: *San Diego's Unbroken living, loving, and hopefully not regretting; Strife from Thousand Oaks, CA, keeps the fire burning.* PHOTOS BY DAVE MANDEL

was a bum-out, because they were so influential to us. History was being lost on a newer generation. We saw it happening to our idols, and we could see it happening to us. So we said, "Fuck it, let's go out on a good note," and we played our final show. From that point, new bands like Strife appeared. They had the spirit, but their slower, Judge-inspired sound was the new sound of hardcore.

TOBY MORSE: Strife did make straight edge big in the '90s, but they had a different sound than the hardcore I listened to growing up.

TIM MCMAHON: I remember hearing about Strife, right around the time that they were signing with New Age Records. Dave Mandel from *Indecision* zine would give me little reports and updates on them. He told me that Strife was basically the West Coast version of Mouthpiece. Not that we necessarily sounded the same, but that we were both young, up-and-coming straight edge bands, made up of kids similar in age that had come from the late-'80s hardcore scene. We both loved the late-'80s Revelation Records catalog. We kinda went for a more West Coast, Chain of Strength–inspired sound, while Strife went for an East Coast, Judge type of sound.

ANDREW KLINE: When Strife came out, the only straight edge bands on the West Coast were Outspoken, A Chorus of Disapproval, Unbroken, and us. Then in Seattle you had Undertow. We weren't even trying to build anything; we just wanted to be a part of the hardcore scene. We were all straight edge kids who loved Youth of Today and Chain of Strength and all these other bands before us. We just thought we were doing a straight edge band to help spread this message that we felt was important. I don't think we were consciously thinking we were going to rebuild the scene. We weren't shit; we were little fourteen-year-old kids.

ISAAC GOLUB (A CHORUS OF DISAPPROVAL): Chorus of Disapproval got going during a changing of the guard, when California hardcore was in a low valley. A lot of the great clubs had closed, and a lot of the great bands were gone—or had gone straight pussy-core. The days of seeing Youth of Today, Cro-Mags, or Uniform Choice at Fender's were over.

ROB MORAN: Unbroken was part of a bastardization of straight edge, to say the least. We were young and didn't know what we were doing. We put out a couple of shit records that were horrible copies of what we thought people wanted to hear. It took us a few years to sort through things and become a better band. For most new bands from that '90 to '93 time frame, we all took a while to get in a comfortable place with our music.

DEMIAN JOHNSTON: Undertow didn't play shows in Seattle where there were four straight edge bands solid on a bill. We'd play with crust punk bands or Born Against or Bikini Kill. I felt we were more part of that world, because we all had dreadlocks and blue hair, and we'd play benefits for legalizing marijuana. It felt very different when we finally got to tour California and the Northeast, and we saw this completely different thing with bills of all straight edge bands. Undertow was definitely a band that came from straight edge, but I don't think we ever sat around and talked about it. Occasionally we'd hear something about Walter from Youth of Today not being straight edge anymore, and we'd joke around about it, but we honestly didn't give a shit.

ROB FISH: Once all the straight edge bands returned home from that summer of touring in 1989, everything changed. It seemed every band, including the bigger ones, all of a sudden had grown up and grown out of straight edge and that style of music. Within a year, most of those bands were gone, or existed as a shell of themselves. The straight edge scene on the East Coast fell off the face of the earth. From that, a new group of bands came to life, such as Mouthpiece, Lifetime, Resurrection, Encounter, and Flagman. Shows went back to being in basements and garages, with mostly just the bands there.

DAVE LARSON (*EXCURSION* ZINE): Undertow, Unbroken, Strife, and Mouthpiece were all different bands. They each had their own special thing. They weren't just New York hardcore style, or into the Washington, D.C., stuff. They were influenced by all of that, but separately they all had their own special thing.

ANDREW KLINE: All of a sudden, on the East Coast, you had bands like Mouthpiece, Lifetime, and Resurrection, who were doing the same exact thing that we were. They had similar influences, and they watched these bands from the late '80s fall apart. They wanted to keep this message alive, and they knew it could happen with a new breed of bands.

TIM MCMAHON: I think Mouthpiece stuck out from other hardcore in the '90s because we were five middle-class, suburban kids that rode skateboards. We weren't violent. We weren't from the streets. We weren't getting beaten

From top: *"Y'all ready for this?" Outspoken at Spanky's in Riverside, CA.* MIKEY GARCEAU; *Lifetime's Dan Yemin is not fading into the background.* ADAM TANNER

up or robbed. We weren't in any kind of serious pain. We were normal teenagers with typical teenage issues, and we never felt the need to fake anything or pretend to be something that we weren't. We had no interest in trying to be hard, and we weren't wrapped up in whatever trends were popping up in the early '90s. We just did what came natural and what felt right for us. That's one of the things that always appealed to me about bands like Youth of Today and Bold; they were who they were, normal suburban kids, nothing radical or outlandish.

ANDREW KLINE: None of our bands sounded alike, and every band had their own flavor. For the first time, straight edge hardcore didn't have to fit into this box and sound a certain way. Resurrection was really noisy and influenced by Bl'ast! and Black Flag. Lifetime was more melodic. Mouthpiece held onto the influences of Chain of Strength and Youth of Today.

TIM MCMAHON: Mouthpiece played one of the last Release shows. I remember talking to future Resurrection singer Rob Fish at that show about how so many kids had dropped out of straight edge. I guess Rob looked at me as one of the few Jersey guys that was still carrying the straight edge flag high, so we kept in touch. Around 1990, while Rob was wrapping things up with Release and living at the Philadelphia Krishna temple, he started talking about his plans to start a new band. Rob was still super fired up about straight edge. As a reactionary statement to everyone that was falling off, Rob wanted to scream the message even louder. Naturally, I was pretty stoked on what Rob wanted to do. Considering I was in an up-and-coming band, I wanted to help any way I could. At this point Resurrection came together.

ROB FISH: The whole movement had become so bland and devoid of individuality that when people started to grow out of it, you saw most people move on all at once. Straight edge needed to diversify in respect to not just the people, but the sounds and visuals. We weren't ready to do that. Despite having been a part of the whole scene that whitewashed itself out of existence, we felt it still had value and wanted to encourage it. Mouthpiece, sound-wise and visually, really continued to mirror the whole straight edge sound and look of the past. Resurrection and Lifetime definitely brought a different feel.

CHRIS ZUSI (RELEASE, RESURRECTION, FLOORPUNCH, SEARCH): With Resurrection, we purposely wanted to do something different musically and visually. We wanted to be a straight edge version of Black Flag or Bl'ast. At the time, most of the Youth Crew bands had died out or were dying a painful death. We wanted to provoke people—do a dirty, sloppy, straight edge band that felt like any song could fall apart at any minute. It was really meant to be a contrast to the tight punch of the late-'80s sound.

TIM MCMAHON: Maybe even slightly prior to Resurrection, Ari Katz from Enuf and Up Front was starting Lifetime. I remember talking to Ari at the first Middlesex, New Jersey, show Mouthpiece played. Like Rob, Ari was still pretty fired up about straight edge. Although Lifetime wasn't a straight edge band, many of the members were. Ari was eager to do what he could to keep straight edge and hardcore well represented in New Jersey.

ARI KATZ: Lifetime was definitely trying to build something back up. All the New York bands were gone, or they were playing halfheartedly with no original members. It was a weird time. Lifetime, Resurrection, and Mouthpiece all wanted to build something up together. But Lifetime was not a straight edge band; guitarist Dan Yemin was always a drinker. I would still X up when we played, just because hardcore was in such a strange place and floundering. No one knew what was going to happen next, so I was trying to keep my part in straight edge alive by doing that.

TIM MCMAHON: During the summer of 1991, Mouthpiece, Resurrection, and Lifetime started being asked to play a lot of shows together. Honestly, I couldn't have been more excited. I was coming from doing a fanzine that interviewed and supported New Jersey straight edge bands like Release and Enuf. Now I was doing a band that played shows with the new bands these guys were doing. We all became friends and there was a real sense of unity and togetherness. It definitely felt like something special was happening that was reflected in the growth that we saw in the New Jersey scene.

ROB FISH: For me, the return culminated with a weekend where we played on Friday with Sick of it All, Vision, Up Front, Lifetime, Mouthpiece, and Resurrection, followed by a show on Sunday at City Gardens in Trenton, New Jersey, with Gorilla Biscuits, NOFX, and Resurrection. All of a sudden, these new bands had really strong and enthusiastic followings.

ANDREW KLINE: Mike Hartsfield and his label New Age Records played a huge part in that early '90s resurgence of straight edge. He pretty much had every important band of the time on his roster: Mouthpiece, Lifetime, Resurrection, Strife, Unbroken, Mean Season, and Trial.

Rob Fish of Resurrection. DAVE MANDEL

THE UN(A)BOMBER PRESENTS:
SUNDAY JUNE 30, 1996

Strife
BATTERY
RAIN ON THE PARADE
TEN YARD FIGHT
EYELID

AT THE 1ST. UNITARIAN CHURCH AT 21ST AND CHESTNUT PHILADELPHIA
$5 YOU GREEDY BASTARD!
STARTS AT 3:00
CALL 215 575 0472 (ROB REDCHEEKS)

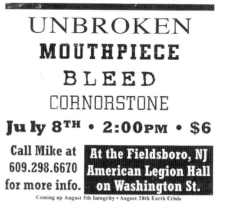

DOWN BUT NOT OUT
HARDCORE FANZINE
PRESENTS

XXX

UNBROKEN
MOUTHPIECE
BLEED
CORNORSTONE

July 8TH • 2:00PM • $6

Call Mike at
609.298.6670
for more info.

At the Fieldsboro, NJ
American Legion Hall
on Washington St.

Coming up August 5th Integrity • August 20th Earth Crisis

SAT NOV 17
STRIFE
WITNESS A REBIRTH REDDED RELEASE

"...and so we all painted the letter X on our hands to show our commitment."

"Grandpa, the 90's sound really weird"

BITTER END   PIECE BY PIECE

XIBALBA   SKINFATHER

7PM   ALADDIN JR $10
296 W 2ND ST
POMONA, CA

THE UN(A)BOMBER PRESENTS:

Strife
BATTERY
RAIN ON THE PARADE
TEN YARD FIGHT
EYELID

SUNDAY JUNE 30, 1996
"The TROC   CAN SUCK IT!"

AT THE 1ST. UNITARIAN CHURCH AT 21ST AND CHESTNUT PHILADELPHIA
$5 YOU GREEDY BASTARD!
STARTS AT 3:00
CALL 215 575 0472 (ROB REDCHEEKS)

TIM MCMAHON: Our friend Jason Bush, from York, Pennsylvania, did a label. He had just rereleased the Unit Pride seven-inch and he asked Mouthpiece to record a song for a seven-inch compilation. We booked Skylab Studios around Princeton, New Jersey, where Release had recorded their final seven-inch, *No Longer*. Not sure exactly what happened to Jason's plans, but we were left with a recorded song, so we took the opportunity to send it to labels and try to gain some interest. We definitely had our sights set on New Age Records, who had put out records by Pressure Release, Powerhouse, Turning Point, and Outspoken. Almost immediately, Mike Hartsfield called and told us he loved the song. He was smack-dab in the middle of putting together a seven-inch comp himself, *Words to Live By, Words to Die For*, with Turning Point, Outspoken, Drift Again, and Undertow. Mike said he had room on the compilation and would like to include us if we were interested. We were of course thrilled, honored, and immediately said yes.

DEMIAN JOHNSTON: I would say Chain of Strength *True Till Death* ended phase one of straight edge for me, and then phase two picked up when New Age Records started to put out a steady stream of releases. That *Words to Live By, Words to Die For* seven-inch compilation had Turning Point, Mouthpiece, and Outspoken; these bands still had something to say. Also, due to Mike Hartsfield and New Age Records, there was a pretty good straight edge community happening down in Southern California. We could go out there from Seattle; stay for a week at the house of someone like Dave Mandel, who did *Indecision* zine; play six shows; and not ever leave the immediate area.

TIM MCMAHON: Mike Hartsfield was the spark that connected us all. I think all our bands would have existed either way, but Mike brought us all together and helped unify us. Mike unintentionally recreated what Revelation had done a few years prior, showcasing straight edge hardcore bands from both coasts.

MIKE HARTFIELD (FREE WILL, AGAINST THE WALL, OUTSPOKEN, NEW AGE RECORDS): The best thing about New Age is that I actually listened to and liked everything I put out. I know many label owners that need to trust A&R people to tell them what's good and what sucks. I just put out what I liked and had fun with it. Since I am straight edge and gravitate toward straight edge music, that's just the way it happened for the most part.

ROB MORAN: While everyone was coming up and doing their own thing, Mike from New Age—to whom we owe just about everything—was part of capturing what was going on. Sure, other labels came around, some got bigger, some went away. New Age was a big deal in the '90s, and a lot of credit goes to Mike for recording what was the perfect storm of hardcore at that time, including us, Mean Season, Strife, A Chorus of Disapproval, Mouthpiece, Resurrection, and Lifetime. He helped revive straight edge hardcore.

TIM MCMAHON: After Mouthpiece got on New Age, I told Mike about Lifetime and Resurrection, and I heavily encouraged him to check both bands out. Simultaneously, I was suggesting to Lifetime and Resurrection that they get in touch with Mike and send him their music. I had visions of all three of our bands releasing records on New Age, all three being from New Jersey and sort of uniting and playing together and becoming a force. I wanted to re-create our own version of Youth of Today, Bold, Judge, and Gorilla Biscuits; bands that hung out together, played together, were on the same label together, and toured together. I felt like we had something special happening, and the combination of it all coming together on an up-and-coming label like New Age was very exciting.

Everything came together as hoped. New Age signed Lifetime and Resurrection and we all released seven-inches, one right after another. Mouthpiece was New Age 8, Lifetime was New Age 9, and Resurrection was New Age 10. Then came Strife, Unbroken, and Mean Season. There was definitely the feeling of a perfect storm. All the planets were aligning, as they say. The East Coast straight edge scene was thriving, shows were getting bigger and more consistent, and the West Coast appeared to be a mirror image of that. A new breed was born and people were taking notice. New Age became the destination for early-'90s straight edge hardcore and we were right in the thick of it all.

ARI KATZ: Lifetime and all the other bands on New Age Records seemed to be the ones trying to get the scene going again. It was pretty cool for the time, but it didn't last forever.

TIM MCMAHON: It felt like as the 90's moved on, a lot of the other bands we were playing with when we started, began to move in other directions. Lifetime seemed to latch on to the New Brunswick, New Jersey, punk rock scene. Lifetime was hanging and playing with bands like the Bouncing Souls, rather than the younger straight edge hardcore bands that were coming around.

ARI KATZ: Lifetime started changing. We felt like we were always getting dismissed as a New Age Records band. We started realizing there was a whole other world out there of cool bands and cool scenes that weren't based around New Age Records. It got to a point where we weren't going to play with Mouthpiece and Resurrection anymore, as a rule! I remember telling Tim that we didn't want to play with Mouthpiece anymore. That was really weird, and I don't know how he took it. We were really trying to break out and forge an identity.

TIM MCMAHON: With Resurrection, Rob had started singing for 108 at the same time, and 108 seemed to be taking the front seat. 108 were touring, recording, and Resurrection just seemed to fade away. Not sure if it was a conscious decision or just the natural flow of things. Either way, before we knew it, Resurrection was no more. Mouthpiece did continue to play a lot of shows with 108, but the feeling was a bit different. We all got along and there were no issues, but 108 was on an entirely different level. 108 was heavily into Krishna consciousness and spirituality, and they had a very serious tone.

Although the scenes splintered and everyone went deeper into different directions, Mouthpiece continued on the same path. Nothing drastically different ever came to our music, our identity, or what we were into. Some consider that stagnation; we just saw it as consistency. The members of Mouthpiece, Lifetime, and Resurrection still got along, but the days of us all hanging out, eating food, talking shit, and acting like goofballs seemed to be in the past.

A WARNING TO YOU WHO TRANS-
GRESS THE NATURAL ORDER -
INFRINGING ON THE RIGHTS OF THE
INNOCENT TO SATISFY YOUR
SELFISH DESIRE:
NO LONGER SHALL YOUR CRIMES
AGAINST THE PEOPLE, ANIMALS AND
THE ENVIRONMENT OF THIS PLANET
GO UNPUNISHED. JUDGEMENT DAY IS
AT HAND.
EITHER CHANGE YOUR EVIL WAYS OR
DIE IN YOUR MAN MADE HELL.
THE VEGAN REVOLUTION IS HERE AND
ONLY THE RIGHTEOUS SHALL LIVE ON.

A typically forceful public service announcement from the Hardline. COURTESY OF SEAN MUTTAQI

HARDLINE: THE WAY IT IS

REVEREND HANK PEIRCE: The "hardline" thing could be considered a reaction to the whole thing in the 1960s where everybody was thinking they'd change the world. The hardline kids were saying, "You didn't!"

STEVE LOVETT: At the close of the '80s, the straight edge scene was no longer interesting to me. The look and message of most straight edge bands was getting played. Simply saying, "I'm not going to drink, smoke, or do drugs," didn't really answer many of the questions of philosophy. We wanted something deeper than simply not using drugs. We wanted something new, active, and threatening.

SEAN MUTTAQI (VEGAN REICH): Straight edge was definitely not something I was into, living on the West Coast in the early '80s. My politics and vegetarian inclinations drew me into the anarchist punk movement. The Flux of Pink Indians *Neu Smell* seven-inch turned me vegetarian overnight, and Conflict's *To a Nation of Animal Lovers* made me militant about it. Rasta was always a cultural influence. I knew Jamaicans and Rastas growing up, and I had been into reggae before punk. Then the whole Two-Tone era of ska led me to discover skinhead culture.

RAT STATEMENT (STATEMENT): Even if they never actually listened to anarcho-punk music, many straight edge vegans today don't realize that anarcho-punk played a big part in them going vegan.

SEAN MUTTAQI: In the early days, general vegetarianism was being promoted. I didn't even hear about the concept of veganism until a couple years later. At some point, I got in touch with Jay Dinshah of the American Vegan Society, who sent me a bunch of literature and cookbooks. That was that. Once I saw the connection between the dairy industry and the exploitation of animals, there was no way I was going to continue eating eggs and using dairy products. I switched from vegetarianism to vegan at sixteen. From there, Rudimentary Peni influenced me not to do drugs. My friend Rat from England was a great motivator to stop drinking.

RAT STATEMENT: Sean and I started communicating in maybe 1985 or 1986. He wrote to me after seeing a demo for my band Statement advertised somewhere and it just went from there. I first visited Sean in 1987, and we did a big-ass road trip from Southern California to an anarchist gathering in Toronto.

SEAN MUTTAQI: I can definitely say that process of physically forming the "hardline" movement from a lifetime of influences and experiences began at the 1986 anarchist gathering. That was the starting point of our small group's discontent within the anarchist movement over the issue of animal liberation. Two years later, the excessive behavior we witnessed at the 1988 Toronto anarchist gathering was the nail in the coffin. We realized that we needed to form some new construct. Within the next few months, hardline was born.

Vegan Reich began as an idea and as a crew, before becoming a band. As militant animal-lib activists within the anarchist community, where the majority were carnivores, our ideas were constantly derided as being fascist. The label was applied albeit somewhat jokingly by those who felt we wanted to take away their rights to eat meat. We labeled ourselves Vegan Reich in response. At a certain point, we decided to further promote our ideas via music, and Vegan Reich recorded our first song in 1986.

The concept or ideology of hardline was really a cumulative process that happened over many years, and honestly had almost nothing to do with straight edge. In the mid-'80s, I had been involved at a trade school in using a printing press and old-school typesetting. My teacher was sympathetic, and for years let us use the facilities to print anarchist literature. After a couple years away, we dropped by to print some hardline pamphlets, and we ended up meeting a couple of straight edge kids. I heard that some of the guys in Youth of Today, Gorilla Biscuits, and Judge were vegetarian. I definitely thought that was cool, especially since they had arrived at some similar conclusions in an entirely different scene. Straight edge was the scene that later became most receptive to hardline ideas, enabling the ideas to grow into a movement.

From top: *Original label art for UK band Statement's* Prepare for Battle, *the second release on the Hardline label.* COURTESY OF SEAN MUTTAQI; *An advertisement for the early Hardline label releases.*

STEVE LOVETT: Hardline was essentially militant straight edge with an emphasis on radical veganism and environmentalism. Direct action was our chosen path to accomplish our goals. Hardline to me was built on the building block of straight edge. By contrast, straight edge was simply being straight, which was predictable and boring. We wanted to change the perception of vegans as wimpy hippies. I think we were successful.

SEAN MUTTAQI: At that stage, the straight edge scene was more vibrant and energetic than anarcho-punk. Anarcho-punk had seen better days even by the mid-'80s. Clearly, the latter part of that decade belonged to the straight edge scene. We started talking to these straight edge kids about veganism, and they were really receptive. In the beginning, we used "vegan straight edge" when talking to straight edge kids as a way to introduce them to hardline. As it grew, some became hardline, and others were always more comfortable with the "vegan straight edge" moniker.

STEVE LOVETT: Basically, Sean of Vegan Reich and I created the philosophy of the movement. As far as I'm concerned, the movement did not exist before the first three Hardline Records releases by Vegan Reich, Statement, and Raid.

SEAN MUTTAQI: With the birth of hardline, I decided to stop doing my old anarchist record label and form a new one with the sole intent of promoting hardline. In 1989 we put out an ad in *Maximum Rocknroll* announcing some planned record releases, largely in order to make connections with other like-minded people. The response was amazing.

STEVE LOVETT: We created Raid as an all-vegetarian straight edge band, and later we became a full vegan band. After a while, the rest of the members and most of our crew became vegan. Around this time we recorded a demo and wanted to shop it around. I saw an ad for Hardline Records in *Maximum Rocknroll*. At that time, Hardline didn't even have a record out yet, a scene, or certainly a developed ideology.

RON GUARDIPEE: I loved Vegan Reich; their music was great. At first, I thought it was a bunch of crusty punks making fun of straight edge. But everything they said and every interview they did and every letter they wrote into *Maximum Rocknroll* was ridiculous. So I went out of my way to make sure that people knew we had nothing to do with it. I just wanted to call them out on their shit.

RYAN DOWNEY: I discovered hardline via *Maximum Rocknroll* through an ad announcing upcoming releases from Hardline Records. That ad inspired responses from people all over the world, including myself. I was intrigued by the name Vegan Reich, as its mercilessly contrarian punk approach represented my band Hardball's same sort of pushback against the hippie-dippie characterization of veganism, and the ridicule that folks into animal liberation endured from mainstream types and many hardcore and punk kids alike.

SEAN MUTTAQI: We were not really expecting how much controversy our ad in *Maximum Rocknroll* would cause among straight edge kids. In the punk realm of Southern California, which had always had a huge gang influence, guns were never out of the ordinary. Even many of the anarcho-punks had guns. Circle One used guns in their band logo, as did the Apostles in England, among others. But our logo definitely freaked the fuck out of many people in the hardcore scene, especially the more posi-type kids.

We had contemplated using AK-47s in our logo, as that was the sort of more traditional revolutionary gun imagery. But starting up in America, we decided to use guns with ammo that would be more readily available in the States should stuff pop off, so to speak. Placing the rifles on the X both referenced a link to Malcolm X, as well as us purposely trying to co-opt straight edge imagery to get kids into the revolutionary struggle. As far as whether we believed in using weapons or violence, yes. We absolutely did.

DJ ROSE: When Sean put that ad in *Maximum Rocknroll* about kids getting dressed up every Sunday in puffy Nike sneakers and then doing nothing else the rest of the week, that spoke to me. I wanted to establish contact with the guy.

SEAN MUTTAQI: We were immediately getting letters from all over the world. From that initial seed, hardline started sprouting up around the country, notably in areas like Memphis and Indianapolis, followed later by Syracuse and Salt Lake City. After Vegan Reich, Raid and Hardball were probably the two earliest American bands with hardline members.

DJ ROSE: In hardcore, you learn there's reality and then there's perception. If you can make the world perceive you as bigger and better than you actually are, they're going to flock to you. Anyone could place a full-page ad in *Maximum Rocknroll* and make it look like their band or label was

SOBERING CONSEQUENCES

-AND-

RAID

HSEC

june 18

6:00

Antenna

1588 Maddison

IT'S TIME TO BREAK OUT, WALK APART, JOIN THE FEW!

RAID

$5.00

PURE BLOOD

DEMOS WILL BE ON SALE

Recoil

MONKEYWRENCH

FRI. MARCH 29TH
5:00 ANTENNA 1588 MADISON

MARCH 29TH

BROUGHT TO YOU BY THE

-Memphis HARDLINE Militia-

Memphis, TN's, Raid causing some crowd action. COURTESY OF STEVE LOVETT

this giant thing, when it was just a one-man band with maybe twelve kids worldwide supporting him. Illusion goes a long, long way.

RON GUARDIPEE: I might be wrong, but wasn't that band Statement just one guy? In that way, it's the same thing as Bathory or Burzum or any of those one-man black metal bands. Sure, he's got some good riffs. But it's just one fucking guy sitting in his fucking bedroom coming up with all these crazy ideas and theories who couldn't even get enough people together to play in a fucking band with him!

RYAN DOWNEY: As the hardline movement developed, I felt very connected to people like Sean Muttaqi. He got me into the Jamaican dub poet Muta-baruka and smarter anarcho-punk bands. Even back then, Sean knew a lot about multiple martial arts, meditation, Chinese medicines, and a wealth of other interesting subjects.

SEAN MUTTAQI: Memphis, Tennessee, was unique in terms of how quickly hardline came to dominate the whole scene. For a brief and vibrant period, Memphis definitely became the place where Hardline first transformed into a functional scene and a burgeoning movement. Raid was one of the key drivers of that Memphis scene. Being the first hardline band to have come from the straight edge movement, they certainly helped hardline ex-pand into that realm in ways Vegan Reich would have had a harder time. Raid had a very influential aesthetic role on what would become the vegan straight edge movement. Memphis is where the hardline Survival of the Fittest gatherings were first organized, which helped hardline develop and spread around the world.

RYAN DOWNEY: At a certain point, Memphis rather improbably became a hot spot for hardline, so it was selected to be the site of the first ever hardline gathering, envisioned by its organizers as a series of workshops and discus-sions, capped off by a show.

Hardball showed up from Indiana with our long hair, worn-out shoes, out-of-style tight jeans, very-unfashionable-at-the-time ragged metal T-shirts, and Raiders hats. I was definitely conscious of some class divisions, and I felt some familiar feelings of alienation. Everybody was friendly enough to us for the most part, but we were surprised to see that the majority of the hardline people native to Memphis appeared to be well-dressed ath-letic types from well-to-do families. They got their vegan food from fancy health food stores; this was years before Whole Foods. A lot of these kids came from a suburb actually called Germantown. Sean nicknamed one of the friendlier Memphis hardline guys, "John Large House," because he lived in the biggest house most of us out-of-town people had ever stepped inside in real life. Some of the Memphis hardliners had real class rings with "hardline" written on them. I couldn't fathom affording or even wanting a class ring. Still, I was envious of the hotbed of hardline they had created down there. Hardline had supplanted their local hardcore scene.

DJ ROSE: At the first hardline fest in Memphis in 1991, I saw Raid. They were great, but most of the kids who were there were young and overly serious. I didn't find anyone that I connected with. I thought some of what they believed to be awesome, but some of it seemed like religious dogma to me.

STEVE LOVETT: At first, hardline was about veganism and radical environmentalism. Then some brought an antiabortion stance. Many others took more extreme stances, which I think became a real detriment to hardline's growth. Peoples were always trying to come up with the next extreme step, such as not eating processed flour or refined sugar.

VIQUE MARTIN: The hardcore and the straight edge scenes in the U.K., kind of like in mainland Europe, were always more politically left-wing than in the U.S. Pro-life beliefs and homophobia were completely intolerable concepts within any faction of the punk scene. So hardline was joked about and not taken seriously at all on our side of the Atlantic.

SEAN MUTTAQI: The original ethic of veganism which informed hardline's view on this subject was that life was intrinsically sacred, whether human and animal. In that regard, we always viewed having a pro-life view as being directly connected to our veganism. Other key animal rights activists like Ronnie Lee, founder of the A.L.F., Animal Liberation Front, felt the same. Likewise, we saw the connection between eugenicists and the white power system that sought to limit population growth amongst brown and black people as a way of maintaining their dominance. We also understood the complexity of the situation, and were never so naive as to not see that abortion could sometimes be the lesser of two evils in certain scenarios.

Today, as a practicing Muslim, my own personal views are largely informed by the various rulings within Islam regarding abortion. The opinions in that realm are really quite varied. In all circumstances, abortion is permitted if a woman's life is in danger. Beyond that, it is usually permitted for other reasons up until the point when the soul is viewed as having entered the fetus; in scholarly opinions, anywhere from forty days to four months. Where that line is drawn differs for each Muslim woman. From an ethics point of view, I find the topic interesting, but thoroughly I feel it's a woman's decision. I'm not a utopian. I recognize that the world involves suffering, and sometimes necessitates killing. But I think it's important to correctly label and understand our actions for what they are.

RAT STATEMENT: At the time, I was opposed to abortion. I saw it as the taking of a life. I saw it as laziness. Now that years have passed, I see a bigger picture, one of mass destruction of the human species. Now, although I see abortion as a waste of resources, I know that the earth doesn't need any more humans, so I no longer get concerned over people having abortions. I'm actually glad they do. The human species is just too destructive; this planet cannot survive our impact upon it. Our every move is destructive, even as vegans. The best thing for this planet and all life upon it is for humanity to end.

RYAN DOWNEY: Tension arose at that first hardline gathering when it became clear that there were two distinct camps. Some of us saw hardline as a serious revolutionary group, along the lines of John Africa's MOVE organization in Philadelphia; the American Indian Movement, or AIM, that championed Leonard Peltier; Earth First!; and similar activist collectives. Another camp looked at hardline like business as usual in straight edge hardcore, with an extra rule or two.

DJ ROSE: I didn't agree with all the stuff that came along with hardline. I was supportive, but they always tried to push me into the antiabortion and anti-homosexual camp. Those were issues that I felt that were bigger than me. The thing with hardline was that it had a leader, and leaders can change the rules or tweak them. Then you have to fall in line or be gone. Once Sean started adding stuff, all of a sudden there were rules on caffeine and strawberries.

RYAN DOWNEY: Looking back, Hardball shouldn't have performed at the first hardline gathering. We played with a fill-in drummer, our bassist was only half-interested in what was happening, and the crowd was mostly indifferent. We did stage our own smaller form of Vegan Reich–style protest.

We bought nonalcoholic "near beers" from the nearby grocery store and drank them in front of the venue. We wanted to elicit a reaction, and we did. I suppose the crowd saw it as further evidence of our incongruent white trash personas. To us, we were sending a message that hardline was supposed to be a true movement, a radical cause, not a social club based on our lifestyle choices. It was shortsighted and silly of us. We did it to be outcasts among the outcasts, in the same spirit as putting *Reich* next to the word *Vegan*, for militant shock value.

RICH LABBATE: The hardline thing kicked everything up a notch and it definitely had negative repercussions. Personally, I like the idea of someone blowing up a McDonald's or running a meat truck off the road. I never went and did it, but I'm not saying I wouldn't do it. The problem I had with it was the close-mindedness of it all. Rather than go and educate someone on meat eating, you beat them up?

TOBY MORSE: It's the same thing that happened in the '80s when straight rednecks that hated black people saw skinheads, and said, "Oh shit, I'm going to shave my head and wear boots and braces and be one of these guys. I can be hateful in a group!" Beating up someone just because of the color of their skin or just because they smoke a cigarette; I don't know what the difference is.

DAN O'MAHONY: I get how that kind of thing could be empowering to a disenfranchised kid in a backwater town, but bullying is bullying, so fuck 'em. Every single time I confronted some crossed-guns legend on tour, they shook my hand and said nada. I ain't that tough, either, so it was a pose.

RYAN DOWNEY: I remained active in the hardline community, going back to Memphis for the second hardline gathering in 1992. I even organized a third gathering in Indianapolis the following year. After that, I found the label too constricting for my expanding worldview. I left hardline not long after Sean Muttaqi had left it behind, mostly for the same reasons.

SEAN MUTTAQI: Vegan Reich continued on maybe a year after our final tour, which had numerous dates canceled due to phoned-in threats or complaints to the promoters and clubs. We were finding it harder and harder to get booked at hardcore or punk shows due to our notoriety. We found ourselves limited to playing skate and surf events—nonpolitical "music for music's sake"–type settings. That seemed entirely pointless in regard to what we had started the band to do. We finally made the decision to put the band identity to rest. The same lineup went on to form Captive Nation Rising, which initially was a sort of hardcore-and-reggae fusion act, but quickly left hardcore behind entirely and became a traditional reggae act with horns, keyboards, and percussion. We would open for touring Jamaican bands in Southern California.

I feel a little bittersweet about hardline's emergence as a sub-scene within straight edge. On the one hand, there's no denying that hardline really took off within straight edge. On the other hand, residing in that milieu caused hardline to be misunderstood.

STEVE LOVETT: I try to have no regrets, but there were many ugly parts to the hardline scene. Speaking as someone who helped develop it, I feel that we should have kept the radical environmental and animal rights ideas and dropped the more conservative social issues. Clearly the conservative moral outlook damaged hardline's rep in the music scene, and was unnecessarily exclusive. And though the violent, over-the-top lyrics may have attracted some people, they detracted from our more positive message. I was a kid. I saw the world as a young activist would. I learned some important life lessons through the creation and eventual rejection of hardline.

JOEY VELA: During the 1990s, I wasn't filled with so much straight edge love. Those years were filled with a lot of shady people that did a lot of shitty things in the name of being straight edge. Most, if not all of them that I am thinking about, are not straight edge anymore. I don't care if someone decides that straight edge isn't for them anymore, but I do have an issue with kids beating the shit out of someone ten on one only because they are drunk or look punk rock. It all became so stupid, and really turned me off to claiming straight edge. It became something I did not relate to anymore, and something I didn't want to be a part of.

KEVIN SECONDS: I look at straight edge, at least the more outspoken militant side of it, in the same way I look at religion. At its core, the values are decent and the intent is sincere, but we humans are terribly flawed. We are always searching for more—more love, more meaning, more acknowledgment, and more approval. And in our quest for all of those things, we do stupid shit, like imposing our will on other people until we bastardize the initial meaning and intent of what is basically a good thing.

RAT STATEMENT: We all move on over the years. Our ideas change in certain ways. I think mine have gone more extreme. People don't like having their lack of morals questioned, and will react in a confrontational manner. That's expected. I got plenty of shit about it all, but I just had to stand my ground. I still do.

SEAN MUTTAQI: My initial vision for the whole thing had been something that merged anarchism with elements of universal spiritual esotericism, incorporating things from Rastafarianism, Buddhism, Taoism, Islam, and—from others in our circle—Christianity and Judaism. Having been through earlier punk and anarchist movements that were derailed by drug and alcohol use, and being heavily immersed in martial arts, there was definitely a notion of creating an almost monastic movement, whose sole purpose was self-negation for the sake of the struggle. We wanted to create an effective revolutionary force. I don't think that was a wrong impulse at the time. Unfortunately, other streams of thought came to dominate the general culture of straight edge—namely a rigid mind-set, and a sort of general conservatism. Hardline couldn't be perceived outside of that mentality, which affected how others viewed us, and even how certain people within hardline viewed themselves. Purity ceased to be a tool for self-negation, for the sake of the greater good, and instead became a basis for self-aggrandizing, and worship of the self. I'm still torn about hardline's association with straight edge.

Raid, stage diving against cultured sadism. COURTESY OF STEVE LOVETT

The Refused. UMEÅ HARDCORE ARCHIVE, FOLKRÖRELSEARKIVET I VÄSTERBOTTEN

DESPERATE STATE: UMEÅ STRAIGHT EDGE

DENNIS LYXZÉN: When I was a young punk in the north of Sweden in 1988, a friend of mine gave me a Youth of Today record. I didn't know what straight edge was, but I liked the record a lot. They played in Sweden in 1989. My friend went to the show, but I couldn't go because my skateboard broke. I had to make the choice of either going to see Youth of Today or getting a new skateboard. My friend called me the next day and said, "Lethal Aggression were great, but Youth of Today sucked! They're straight edge!" I was like, "What's straight edge?" He explained that they didn't drink or do drugs. I read their lyrics, and they were pretty cool.

Where I grew up, if you drank and did drugs you weren't that rebellious—everybody did it. It was expected of you. So I was like, "Fuck it, I'm going to have a clear mind, I'm going to be sober, and I'm going be focused." It was much more controversial to claim to be drug-free and straight edge than it was to do drugs.

In 1989, some friends and I started the band Step Forward. We got the New York hardcore compilation *The Way It Is* and we stared at the photos on that record. There was no moving footage we could get, just photos. We tried to style Step Forward from the photos on that record. For the first show we played, we just decided we'd go crazy. We were jumping constantly for the whole set. For the last song, our guitar player smashed his guitar, and our drummer threw his cymbals stands into the fuse box so the whole place went black. That was our first show! People thought we were crazy.

JOSE SAXLUND (ABHINANDA, DESPERATE FIGHT RECORDS): I was a metalhead into Slayer, Sepultura, and Metallica, and I went to a local show in Umeå in the early '90s. Meshuggah was playing, and this band Step Forward was one of the opening acts. I was totally blown away by them and their energy. That was my way into hardcore and with that came the message.

I started to hang out with Dennis Lyxzén, who was the only straight edge dude around, and he introduced me to the music of Youth of Today and Gorilla Biscuits. Thinking back, I don't know if Step Forward was a band with all straight edge members, but I'd say Refused was definitely all straight edge.

CHRISTOFFER JONSSON (DS-13, BUSTED HEAD RECORDS): I guess the weird thing is I got into straight edge hardcore through local bands in Umeå. I discovered Suicidal Tendencies at the same time that I heard the first Refused demo tape from 1991. The straight edge scene in Umeå in the early to mid-'90s was very openly straight edge, there was no hiding it or beating around the bush. Refused was maybe the first openly straight edge band in Sweden. They wore X's on their hands. Their demo had X's all over it, as did their flyers. Dennis got the ball rolling here and then it just kept rolling.

DENNIS LYXZÉN: In our hometown, Refused were one of those bands that started the hardcore scene. We were very instrumental in making what it turned into. A lot of those people who started their own bands and became vocal in the scene and did other things; they were all there in the beginning. We kind of grew with them in a way that we didn't with the rest of the world.

JOSE SAXLUND: In the beginning, we were the few and the proud in Umeå. After a while, a few more kids came in and the scene just kept growing, the more shows we organized.

CHRISTOFFER JONSSON: Umeå didn't even have much of a punk scene before the straight edge thing got big. It wasn't like Gothenburg and Stockholm, where you had this huge scene full of leather, studs, and spiky-haired punks who wanted to get fucked up. Straight edge was the first punk that reached Umeå. All the shows were at these community youth houses; places you could go hang out after school let out. They were run by the city, and you couldn't drink or smoke on the premises. They had stages and equipment you could use. All the people there were underage, so they weren't going to see a band in a bar. That's why straight edge caught on here—you wouldn't be allowed inside if you showed up at the youth house drunk.

The other thing with Umeå is we never had violence at our shows. Everyone was super friendly to one another, and no one was harassed. We had no Nazi skinhead presence whatsoever. You felt safe, and you always had a good time. Looking back at it, you could say it was wimpy, but at least it was fun.

JOSE SAXLUND: We were highly influenced by everything we could get our hands on, since back then it wasn't that easy to get ahold of stuff, not like today. We had our pen pals to whom we sent concealed cash, so they could send us the latest New Age or Revelation seven-inch. We copied the look of every band we saw in every picture!

CHRISTOFFER JONSSON: The Umeå scene was always extremely fashion-conscious. The inner circle of the scene was Dennis and David from Refused and the people that were closest to them. The way they dressed, *everybody* dressed. It felt like it moved quickly from the classic Youth Crew look to the Victory Records look with the super-baggy-pants style. Then Jenny Piccolo from Santa Cruz and the Locust from San Diego played in Umeå in '96 or '97. That's when the scene went into full San Diego mode, with the Spock haircuts and the tight striped shirts. That happened pretty much the week after they toured.

DENNIS LYXZÉN: At first, we were the only group of hardcore kids in our town. The guys who ended up being in Abhinanda were hanging around with us. They started their band, and another band came soon after them. From 1992 to 1993 there were maybe ten kids into hardcore and half of them were straight edge; then it just exploded.

JOSE SAXLUND: Soon after Refused formed came my band Abhinanda. We were supposed to be a Hare Krishna band, even before knowing what exactly what Hare Krishna was. We just thought it was cool because Shelter wrote about it on their first record.

CHRISTOFFER JONSSON: The Umeå hardcore scene has always been influenced by American hardcore. Umeå never cared that much for the European scene. I remember liking bands like Heresy or Discharge when I was a kid, and being alone in my appreciation of them. A crucial moment for the Umeå hardcore scene was when Shelter came. Just having an American hardcore band coming to Umeå was such a huge fucking thing, especially since it was the guys from Youth of Today. They played to seven hundred people. At one point in the show, they got everyone at the show to chant "Hare

Krishna." Since the show was at the youth house, there were ten-year-old kids there chanting "Hare Krishna." I was sixteen years old, standing on the side of the stage, thinking that was the most fucked-up thing I had ever witnessed. It was totally bizarre.

DENNIS LYXZÉN: When Shelter came to Umeå in 1993, I was hanging out with Porcell, and I asked him, "When is Judge coming to Sweden?" He gave me this weird look and told me they had broken up two years ago. That was such a blow. That's how isolated we were! We had no idea what was going on in the world.

JOSE SAXLUND: After Abhinanda came Doughnuts, Shield, Purusam, and just an explosion of bands. We couldn't find a label to put out our own record, so we decided to just do it ourselves. Dennis and I started Desperate Fight Records. I don't think we had a big plan, but things kept developing. After a couple of releases we realized we had a label. By the time Abhinanda released our first album, *Senseless*, we went from being something of a joke to having a following and being able to tour Europe. That was an achievement I'm proud of. Four hardcore kids that didn't even know how to play instruments when we started moved onto recording albums and touring in just a couple of years.

CHRISTOFFER JONSSON: The peak of straight edge hardcore in Umeå was 1996, when Refused came out with their second LP, *Songs to Fan the Flames of Discontent*. That was huge. The scene got so big here in the mid-'90s that when I put on a show for Ignite from California and only three hundred kids showed up, I thought it was a bust. Every other show had at least six or seven hundred people!

JOHANNES PERSSON (REVIVE, ECLIPSE, CULT OF LUNA): The first show I ever played with my first band, Revive, we played in front of five hundred people. Straight edge was really huge at the time.

DENNIS LYXZÉN: For a lot of people, it wasn't about ideology, but more about being a part of what was going on. The shows were fun and there were a lot of cool bands coming through town then. People just wanted to be part of something that was happening, and it was quite exciting to be a part of.

JOSE SAXLUND: I'd say the straight edge scene in Umeå reached its peak between 1993 and 1997. To be honest, I think the beginning of the end was

DS-13, Punkfest, 1998, Umeå, Sweden. COURTESY OF CHRISTOFFER JONSSON

when some scenesters started to burn down trucks owned by Sweden's biggest meat producer. They started to burn down food trucks that served meat, and kept on doing more direct actions like that.

DENNIS LYXZÉN: Refused went on a European tour in the fall of 1994 with the American Hare Krishna band 108. I was dating Sara Almgren, who played in the Doughnuts at the time. I called home, and she told me, "We blew up a bunch of meat trucks last night." I was like, "Really?" It got real. The local slaughterhouse got firebombed, and mink farms got liberated.

JOHANNES PERSSON: In 1996, the straight edge scene separated, with one group getting more into the music and one group getting more into activism. In 1996, there were two hundred animal rights crimes recorded around Sweden. By this point, I had read Pete Singer's *Animal Liberation* and it really spoke to me. You have to understand how large this animal liberation movement was in Umeå. We had a high school with six hundred people. Two-thirds of the students were vegetarian, and one-third was vegan. It was huge. I started to become involved in some direct actions in the name of animal liberation. I have no regrets regarding the things I did, because I did not do stupid shit. I didn't do anything that I would consider lethal.

CHRISTOFFER JONSSON: There was a huge movement in Umeå with Animal Liberation Front activities. They freed animals in laboratories at universities and things like that. They bombed three meat delivery trucks that got burnt to a crisp.

JOHANNES PERSSON: There was a rise of militant animal rights activism when the meat trucks got burned, because it got a lot of coverage in the national media.

CHRISTOFFER JONSSON: They smashed the windows of stores selling fur and burned food trucks selling hot dogs. No one was ever caught for the stuff, because there was never any evidence.

JOHANNES PERSSON: All of a sudden, it became a race of who could be most extreme in their direct actions. There was talk of calling in a bomb threat to a circus, and putting nails through planks and laying them in the street so the trucks carrying the animals would be stopped. I spoke up and said I didn't want to partake in these activities as they could harm both innocent people and animals.

DENNIS LYXZÉN: If we came out and said, "We're very nice and peaceful, please don't eat the cows," it wouldn't have had the same impact. We forced the capitalist system to start producing meat alternatives. That definitely had a big impact. I think for some people that was a fucking big deal. In this city, there are a lot of vegetarians and vegans, but now that's not even like a huge statement.

JOHANNES PERSSON: A little while after the circus came, there was a demonstration at a laboratory where they experimented on cats. Some of the demonstrators got into the lab, and there was a commotion with fighting in there between the demonstrators and the security and the doctors. During all this, someone near me outside broke a window. The person who broke the window ran away, of course, and I was caught, prosecuted, and sentenced for the action.

After all that, I got into a verbal fight with the woman who broke the window. I had to pay for the repair, and I felt she owed me money. During the argument, I used a Swedish word that is the equivalent to "chick" in English and she went totally crazy. A few days later, there was a show in Umeå. Outside the show, people from her activist group—I would call it a cult—were giving out flyers about what happened, and how I had used the word *chick*.

DENNIS LYXZÉN: A lot of the people that did those things were crazy people, like really crazy. The actions attracted some crazy people, but in the end— you know what? We learned! We learned a lot about solidarity and equality and socialism. These were fucking great things that we could take on and move forward with in our lives.

CHRISTOFFER JONSSON: Many of those people who were die-hard vegan straight edge, and who did those actions, became drug addicts or got involved in organized crime when the animal rights trend died out.

JOHANNES PERSSON: Afterward, I went to the other side of the pendulum. I was hanging out with people who weren't straight edge anymore, and smoking pot. The only reason I was hanging out with them was because they were simply nicer people than the activists.

DENNIS LYXZÉN: At a point, it got to be very frustrating to be in Refused. We were on Victory Records from the U.S., but the Victory crowd thought we were way too political and punk. The political crowd was into stuff on

Ebullition Records, and they just lumped us in with the other tough-guy bands on Victory. We were constantly in this flux between the political hardcore scene and the tough-guy hardcore scene. Our next album, *The Shape of Punk to Come*, was sort of a reaction to that whole thing of not fitting in anywhere.

CHRISTOFFER JONSSON: As time went on, people into straight edge started getting into their late teens and early twenties and thinking to themselves, "You know, I just want to drink a beer and listen to Bruce Springsteen." When Refused put out *The Shape of Punk to Come* in 1998, no one cared about them here anymore. No one wrote about the album or anything. It did not become this huge international hit and influential record until they broke up.

DENNIS LYXZÉN: We peaked in popularity in Sweden with *Songs to Fan the Flames* in 1996. When we put out *The Shape of Punk to Come* in 1998, the hardcore kids perceived it as a very pretentious record—which was true, I guess. We could feel we weren't the band people wanted anymore; so when we broke up in '98, it was in defeat. Six months later, MTV in America started showing Refused videos, and we were like, "What the fuck?"

The rest of the world discovered us through "New Noise" and *The Shape of Punk to Come* after we had already broken up. But the people here discovered us when we were playing youth centers and selling our first demo. The thing with "the legacy" is that you can never make the choice yourself. It's pretty fucking crazy that we started out as a hardcore band, heavily into politics—we were just like anarchists roaming free—and we end up becoming a hugely successful rock band.

Desperate Fight also folded, because we weren't interested in running a record label anymore. That had an impact on our hometown, since we put on all the shows and put out all the records in Umeå. So when we lost interest, bands like DS-13 took over and did their own thing. They were much more underground and from the old-school DIY punk idea.

CHRISTOFFER JONSSON: In 1997, when we formed DS-13, the straight edge thing was all dead and gone except for us. Now there are still straight edge bands in Umeå, but it's much more divided than it was in the '90s. Now it's straight edge kids who are political, against straight edge kids who don't want politics in the music. Straight edge still exists here, but not like it did in the '90s. I have a hard time thinking something like that will ever happen again.

DENNIS LYXZÉN: We were just lucky to be a time, place, setting, and environment where we could make people happy. It also took a lot of hard work and dedication. We were very lucky, because we created something very special. What happened in the '90s was very special. We didn't think about it; we didn't know. We didn't have the experience to look at the rest of the world and think, "That's how it should be done." We just did it.

Earth Crisis crusades for the edge, 1994. DAVE MANDE

EARTH CRISIS: A FIRESTORM TO PURIFY

KARL BUECHNER: I felt that the generation of straight edge before us had taken the vehicle of straight edge and broken the windows out, run razors over the seats, and pushed it into a ravine. They wanted nothing to do with it—so it was our duty to pull it up out of there and rebuild it.

GREG BENNICK: In 1989, I was at Syracuse University. I was sitting in my dorm room. My new friend DJ Rose walked in with his friend Karl and said, "We're going to start a band, and we're going to call it Earth Crisis." Karl was being quiet and seemed sort of odd. I just said, "Cool name." We all looked at each other and they left. It was a weird *Napoleon Dynamite* kind of moment.

DJ ROSE: I moved to Syracuse right after I got out of college in the summer of '89. Karl and I used to skate; he played bass and he thought we should start a band. We met Dave Stein and Steve Reddy over in Albany, they were two very serious individuals. They were vegans, and they educated us on animal rights. That made us want to push hard in that direction. Karl got together a ragtag group of people, and I named the band Earth Crisis. We practiced two or three times.

KARL BUECHNER: Our name traces back to the Steel Pulse album of the same name. I thought that album cover artwork really encapsulated a lot of things that our band would stand against. Whether conventional or biological or nuclear, there was a lot going on in that cover.

DJ ROSE: We got a chance to play a show in Utica, New York. We played two or three songs, and then we covered SSD's "Glue." You know you're reaching your target audience if people go off for that song. That was the beginning and the end of my role as the vocalist for Earth Crisis. I wasn't really interested in being in a band. I wanted to book shows in Syracuse, and bring the bands to town that I wanted to see.

When I told Karl I didn't want to be in the band, he got super bummed. I think he holds a grudge against me to this day. I don't think he realized Earth Crisis would have died on the vine if I continued to be the singer. I don't have that anger Karl has, and I don't have the tenacity to stay on point with the message like he has. It was Karl's band and vision from the beginning. After I left, he pretty much stole the entire lineup of this Syracuse band called Framework. He became the singer and made Earth Crisis as it's known today.

GREG BENNICK: Fast-forward a few years to about 1993, and I was at a Kinko's with my friend Bill Baker. He was doing a label at the time, Incision Records, and was making plans to release a record by this band Earth Crisis. He put on the demo tape at 3 a.m. in Kinko's while we were manifesting zines at "low cost," if you know what I mean. It was a very '90s hardcore moment! I don't remember ever being that blown away by a demo. It was so heavy, the sound was so different, and the band was so intense.

I loved them so much right from the start, because I felt they were saying, "Fuck you! We do not care what you think! Our initiative is veganism and animal rights. If you stand in our way, we're going to mow you down!" Who had ever done that before? I truly believed Earth Crisis was going to be the bastion of changing the entire world over to veganism.

KARL BUECHNER: We came from listening to New York hardcore bands like Cro-Mags, Agnostic Front, and Warzone. The first Cro-Mags record, *The Age of Quarrel*, leaves you thinking, "These guys are down with Hare Krishna one hundred percent." When you listen to Agnostic Front, you think, "Wow, these guys are patriotic and believe in law and order and self-defense." Warzone is saying the world is crumbling around us, and we have to become our own tribe. We took those philosophies, approaches, and commitments, and built off them to create our own ideas about how we wanted to present our band.

LINS CUSCANI: We all dug that first Earth Crisis EP, *All Out War*. We saw it as something different, adding the values of the animal rights slant to the straight edge scene. Many straight edge kids in this country were vegetarian anyway; it was a natural progression to get into something musically and lyrically harder and also to support an ideology also so far removed from the norm. Personally, it was important to not only to be positive for myself, but to be positive to all living creatures. Earth Crisis gave everyone a different perspective on the whole straight edge thing, and made us more aware of our diets, lifestyle, and duties to other living species. This scene gained a lot of support, with a plethora of bands like Blood Green, Vengeance of Gaia, Slavearc, and Canvas becoming the focal point. A number of fanzines and record distributors sprang up also.

KARL BUECHNER: I think people were very ready for Earth Crisis and vegan straight edge. That's why so many other bands like Green Rage, Canon, or Gatekeeper came up at the same time. There were vegan straight edge bands all over the country, and then, eventually, all over different continents.

TOBY MORSE: Earth Crisis and the metal-edged, vegan straight edge really seemed to break up straight edge into different sectors.

JEFF TERRANOVA: I personally wasn't digging the '90s militant vegan straight edge because it didn't sound like hardcore to me. It was just that *jud-jud* riff over and over again. I would have been more into it if it was just actually Slayer up there. Imagine Tom Araya of Slayer singing about veganism the same way he sings about Satan?

I came into hardcore from metal. In metal, everything was fantasy. When I crossed over into hardcore, everything was based in reality and that's what appealed to me. Then hardcore turned into metal, both in its sound and the lyrical content. These bands wrote songs about blowing up mink farms and killing drug dealers. Are they really going to go out and kill drug dealers? Probably not. Where do you draw the line between reality and fantasy?

KARL BUECHNER: I am not a documentary filmmaker. I am not an author or an investigative journalist. I'm a musician into animal rights. I think the thing that makes Earth Crisis different from a lot of bands in the worlds of hardcore and metal is that the songs that we write contain some science fiction–esque speculation.

ANDREW KLINE: I'm an Earth Crisis fan. I love Earth Crisis, and I love the guys in the band. We toured with them a lot. But their take on straight edge is

From top: *Karl Buechner calls for the roundups to begin.* DAVE MANDEL; *Earth Crisis.* ADAM TANNER

much different than Strife's. We were never about separation or violence. We were always about acceptance.

LINS CUSCANI: Vegan straight edge made some of us less tolerant to others, not only from the outside but also within our own scene. It created positivity on one hand, but division on the other.

DJ ROSE: Lines got blurred. People associated Earth Crisis with the hardline straight edge thing from a couple years earlier, but Earth Crisis was vegan straight edge—not hardline. Some kids where we lived in Syracuse claimed hardline, but we were antagonistic toward them. None of them are vegetarian anymore. What a surprise! But those guys weren't down for any special cause. They were just crazy people.

GREG BENNICK: When Earth Crisis put out their second seven-inch, *Firestorm*, in 1993, *Maximum Rocknroll* and other people on the scene got upset.

KARL BUECHNER: The song "Firestorm" is about a people's uprising against the drug gangs and cartels. If you go and read books like *Seize the Time* by Bobby Seale, or *Will You Die with Me?* by Flores Alexander Forbes, or other books written by Black Panthers, "Firestorm" falls in line with what they were trying to do just to exist.

GREG BENNICK: The song had lyrics like, "Let the roundups begin." Was Earth Crisis saying they were going to round up drug dealers, block by block? You would imagine them walking down the streets in jackboots. But in no way is that what they were suggesting. To me, they were on the path of righteousness and compassion, and that appealed to me.

JASON KNOTT (CLEAR): When Earth Crisis' *Firestorm* came out, that brought me a whole new sense of pride, attitude, and purpose. That record was inspirational for us to form our band Clear in Salt Lake City, Utah.

VIQUE MARTIN: In 1993, I went to More Than Music Fest in Dayton, Ohio, with two British straight edge men, future Turbonegro singer Tony Sylvester and Strength Alone guitarist Barry Thirlway. We loved the *Firestorm* seven-inch but hated the pro-life politics of Earth Crisis. I think we went up front for the songs we liked, and then walked outside while the screaming started about politics. That kind of thing did not happen in the U.K.—it was all a bit overwhelming!

KARL BUECHNER: Someone might get freaked out over a song like "Firestorm," but one song over on the lyric sheet is a song about ghosts at Wounded Knee. On our next record, *Gomorrah's Season Ends*, there was a song about survivors after a nuclear war. Whether the subject is nuclear war or extinction, the songs still address the reality of what's going on now. We could tell the stories of the Animal Liberation Front or Earth First! or the Sea Shepherds in a more direct way, but I don't think it would capture people's imaginations. It didn't matter. People would pick one line out of a song. They didn't want to understand the words within the context of the rest of the lyrics. They wouldn't come up and talk to us at a show, or try to understand what we were trying to say.

DJ ROSE: In the beginning, it didn't matter. We were going to say what we were going to say. What's the worst that was going to happen? Someone would get punched?

STEVE REDDY: Whenever Shelter went to Syracuse to play, there was always a philosophical battle between Vedic culture and their vegan Reich-isms. There was always some big debate where it got to a point where I'd say, "Okay, who wants to get physical? Let's go!" But I knew all those guys. DJ Rose would come see Youth of Today in Albany, and I also had a good relationship with Karl. Nothing would have happened.

DJ ROSE: We loved the hardcore scene. We weren't there to threaten anyone. But even our good friends wouldn't book us in their town or play shows with us. People had this preconceived idea of Earth Crisis, that we were going to show up at a show and be mean to people and tell them they were wrong. We were all likable, normal people. All we wanted to do was present our views.

KARL BUECHNER: In the song "The Discipline," I sing, "I separate from the poison." Having said that, I never tried to separate myself from other people. When someone has a different political view or philosophy than me, that's what makes life interesting. I don't hate them. Instead of bringing people together on commonality, people wanted to demonize the opposition. To me, hardcore was always a marketplace and a community of ideas and philosophies. I always thought it was weird when someone would disagree with one or two aspects of what we were about and shut us out. You don't want to support our band because of that? You actually want to create enemies within our community?

DJ ROSE: If you don't like our views, that's fine. But don't fuck with us when we're not fucking with you. When Earth Crisis played the first More Than Music Festival in Ohio in 1993, the people booking it had this attitude that no one gave a shit about the band. They acted like they were doing Earth Crisis a favor by letting them play as maybe second or third band of a night with probably ten bands. We brought carloads of people with us from Syracuse. Before they started, I remember Rob Fish from Resurrection was trying to unplug their equipment and shit like that. Then the band started, and people went fucking ape-shit. Afterward we watched a video of the set, and we counted *four hundred* flashbulbs going off during the first song, "Firestorm." That's a lot attention for an opening band. That's when we knew people were ready.

That festival lit the fire of interest in the band. I had given an Earth Crisis demo to Tony Brummel from Victory Records, and he threw it out the car window without even listening to it. Now he wanted to put out their record.

GREG BENNICK: The only thing I can't back about Earth Crisis was their antiabortion stance. Over the years, Earth Crisis has gotten a pass on their early days with their antiabortion stance in the same way the Bad Brains get a pass for being homophobic. We're very selective in our thinking about history sometimes.

KARL BUECHNER: For most of the band, we were and still are in two hundred percent agreement that most abortions are the outright murder of a defenseless human being. Ultimately, it's no different than what happens to an animal in a slaughterhouse. Both beings are victims for either someone's convenience or profit. Obviously, these are not things that people want to hear, because they are in direct contrast to what the powers that be deluge our minds with such as, "A fetus doesn't feel pain; animals exist for us to slaughter and devour." These lies lead to death, misery, and regret.

DEMIAN JOHNSTON: In the winter of 1993, Undertow drove our van down to California, picked up Strife, and drove across the country to Syracuse to join Earth Crisis on tour. We traveled with Earth Crisis for two weeks, and we got to know them pretty well. They were nice guys. Our drummer Ryan "Murph" Murphy and I were vegan at the time, so we were stoked to hang out with those dudes. They knew where all the good vegan places were to eat. But they had that line in one of their songs that was like, "For the fetus we will attack." We were like, "What the fuck, man? That shit's fucked up!" We had a pro-life versus pro-choice argument that never ended, and we would not see their side whatsoever. I remember Daisy Rooks from *Not Even* zine and Karl had it out a few times.

ROB MORAN: If Earth Crisis got people to stop and think about what they were eating, then I was all for it. I think things always soften up with age, as they eventually did. Earth Crisis was cool what they were doing with their music and messages. I might not have agreed with a lot of it, but I still enjoyed it.

DJ ROSE: Earth Crisis and the vegan straight edge scene in Syracuse started to gain some media attention. A hardcore kid in Atlanta called Jon Rej worked at CNN. He connected us with this show *Network Earth*. From there, people invited us to spread our ideas. We did shows like MTV's *Smashed* and *48 Hours*. When I was on those shows, I always talked like I was speaking to someone's grandma or mother, because that's who watches those shows! I'm forty-six years old now, and I still get people coming up to me saying, "My mom started letting me go to hardcore shows because she saw you talking on TV."

KARL BUECHNER: When we were younger, we went to see all kinds of live music. We would go see Fishbone and the Red Hot Chili Peppers. Then we'd go see the Exploited or G.B.H., and then the next week, Agnostic Front and Breakdown. We were just into music. When it came time for us to tour, we had the same attitude. "A tour with Gwar, why not? Let's tour with Sepultura! Let's go to Europe with Warzone." We wanted to spread this message outside of our comfort zone.

TOBY MORSE: Earth Crisis still tour to this day, spreading messages of veganism and animal rights. Those guys still live like that to this day. It's fucking awesome and I love them for it.

KARL BUECHNER: We still tour because nothing has really changed! The multinational corporations have seized control of the media. They want their profit system maintained, and they want it to flow forward. That's why there's an incredible amount of resistance against things like alternative energy and veganism. That's why they use their power to portray animal rights activists or environmentalists as people with irrational or unrealistic ideas.

GREG BENNICK: I'm going to go out on a limb here and suggest Earth Crisis did more for veganism and straight edge than Youth of Today.

ANDREW KLINE: When Earth Crisis hit the scene, and people took them as this militant straight edge band, a lot of people said, "Fuck this, if this what straight edge is now. I don't want to be associated with anything like this." It pushed a lot of people away from proclaiming to be straight edge and they all went to different music scenes.

JOHN MCLOUGHLIN: When things got crazy with kids pushing straight edge and animal rights really hard, I just wasn't feeling like this was something we wanted to be a part of. I was never militant about my edge. I tried to keep our lyrics as non-preachy as possible. I'm not into cramming my beliefs down anyone's throat, nor did I want yours crammed down mine. I always welcomed new kids into the scene, so the newcomer grommets didn't bother me, but the distortion of the message did. I didn't form Wide Awake to recruit my friends into a cult or a collective or a religion. But in my mind, the movement became misguided. The message was being distorted beyond something I even recognized—and never mind identifying with it at that point.

IAN MACKAYE: When the militant thing came about, obviously these people's issues were not just about being sober. They were about power and violence and anger, and how to get that shit out of their system. There was a period of time where I thought, "If someone kills me, it's probably going to be some militant straight edge guy."

Salt Lake City's Insight standing strong at Spanky's, Riverside, CA, circa 1990. DAVID SINE

SALT LAKE CITY: IDENTITY CRISIS

REVEREND HANK PEIRCE (ROAD MANAGER FOR SLAPSHOT, UNIFORM CHOICE, C.O.C.): The whole hardline vegan thing started blowing up in Utah, and I was interviewed about straight edge by a local television station. I told them I don't think blowing things up to make your point is the best idea. But have you ever been to Utah? It's super-conservative, and super-conformist. If I lived out there I would probably go crazy and want to blow things up, too.

TROY TRUJILLO (TATTOO ARTIST): Salt Lake City has a surprisingly rich history in punk and hardcore, from the Massacre Guys and L.D.S. in the mid-1980s, to straight edge hardcore bands like Better Way and Insight that were inspired by the East Coast Youth Crew and Orange County's Insted and Uniform Choice. You might say hardcore punk was thriving in the '80s and '90s simply out of need for a counterculture to the Latter-Day Saints Church. That might be true for some, and for others it may not have been a factor. I can only speak for myself.

MARK STARR: I think straight edge was initially accepted in Salt Lake City because of the religious influence on life there. I didn't grow up religious, but I feel people outside of the punk scene could get behind kids going to hardcore shows that had straight edge bands.

TROY TRUJILLO: I remember being a little kid with an abusive alcoholic father, and knowing from a very young age that there was absolutely no way I would turn out like him. I grew up in a working-class family, half brown in a ninety percent white state. I was pissed! I was pissed at the way I was treated for having a Hispanic last name; pissed off at having friends that I could play with at school but couldn't go to their house because I wasn't a member of the church; pissed off because we were borderline poor and most of my new clothes were my older brother's hand-me-downs; and I

From top: *Clear, the band with the edge in Salt Lake City during the 1990s.* TRENT NELSON; *Insight performs at City Gardens, Trenton, NJ, August 27, 1989. Most of this day was not spent celebrating my 17th birthday, but rather trying to help Insight and Chain of Strength fasten a hitch onto their van, which had been stranded in front of my friend Jason Jammer's house for over a week. In the end, they rented a U-Haul, and continued the rest of their tour.* MIKEY GARCEAU was pissed that nobody seemed to care that I came to school with black eyes from my own father at times. Not to take anything away from my mother, who is the most loving and caring person I know. She supported us working nights. My brother and I spent a lot of time hiding in the basement pretending to be asleep, or sneaking out of our window to walk to a relative's house to escape the drunken stupor of our father.

In 1990, I was fourteen or fifteen years old, and a group of older friends I met through skateboarding told me that I was straight edge. I had no idea what that meant, but they convinced me. It was explained to me by means of a mixtape that had songs by Minor Threat, Youth of Today, 7 Seconds, and Judge, as well as a bunch of other random bands. I was enthralled by the idea of drug-free punk. Most of the friends I had were drinking alcohol and doing other drugs. Soon after, I saw one of Insight's last shows at a small club called the Speedway Cafe. It was surreal to see slam dancing, stage diving, and dog piles while people in bands were talking about living drug- and alcohol-free lifestyles.

ANDREW MOENCH: I was raised Mormon, but I wouldn't say the church had a big influence of me getting into straight edge. In the summer after eighth grade in 1993, I started skateboarding after learning how to snowboard a few years prior. One of my childhood buddies moved to a different neighborhood. He met some kids who were also into skateboarding, and they happened to be straight edge kids. That's when I was introduced to hardcore and straight edge.

In the skateboarding scene, there were the straight edge kids and the stoner kids and there was no middle ground. I saw these stoner kids, and I didn't want to be a part of that. Their whole life was getting stoned and skating. So when I met the straight edge kids who skateboarded, I was into that.

JASON KNOTT: By 1995, the first straight edge bands in Salt Lake City like Insight and Better Way weren't around any more. A whole new group of kids was just waiting for another straight edge scene to start in the city. There was a buzz and excitement. At our first show, three hundred people showed up. Then the Lazarus Project formed after us, and then you had Lifeless, who actually started a little bit before us. All of this activity gives you a good idea of the potential for a new scene starting up here.

Back in the day, bands like Insight and Better Way were at an advantage, because they played shows at clubs in the industrial area. There wasn't a whole lot of attention on them. There was no police presence, and no one really bothered them for what they were doing. As time moved on, the city grew and developed, and the industrial area wasn't abandoned any more. It was much easier for the mid-1990s scene to land on the radar of police and other people. That's when people started to pay attention. All it took was a group of five kids that all looked the same walking down the street for them to be considered a "gang."

ANDREW MOENCH: When I was fourteen, one day I was in a car with a bunch of kids going downtown and we had way too many people in the car. We got pulled over for this, and immediately the gang cops were called. Two or three squad cars came flying into the parking lot. These gang cops were taking things way too seriously, asking what kind of gang activity we were involved in that night; what our gang signs and colors were, who our gang leaders were, and all this silly stuff.

TROY TRUJILLO: As I got a little older and started going to shows regularly, I took the idea of straight edge very seriously. It was my way of dealing with my home life and a way to project a future for myself that didn't involve the substance escapisms. Many of my friends grew up in similar circumstances, so it's no surprise we all gravitated toward straight edge. Although Salt Lake City is generally pretty safe compared to a lot of other cities, most of the kids I hung out with grew up in areas that had gangs, drugs, and violence. A lot of the gangbangers I grew up with I knew from grade school. I never had a problem with any of them until my senior year in high school.

I had a large group of friends that would skateboard together. Some of us were edge and some weren't. It didn't bother us; most of us had family and friends we loved that smoked or drank, so the fact that people chose different lifestyles than our own was not a factor to us. Some of the kids we would go skateboarding with came back to school after summer vacation and were now doing more drugs and drinking more alcohol. That just didn't vibe well with us, and naturally we started splitting up into two groups. Eventually, some of these kids were offended that we were no longer skateboarding or hanging out with them. Long story short, they jumped one of our friends because they took it personally that he was straight edge.

The next day at school, there was supposed to be a one-on-one fight between an individual from each group of friends. Assuming I was not a part of the fight, I walked out normally, and I unexpectedly got jumped and hit in the head with a small pipe. All of my edge friends came running around the corner, and we got into a huge fight with these kids. The cops showed up and made a huge deal out of it. That night on the evening news, a reporter called straight edge "the fastest-growing gang in Salt Lake City."

ANDREW MOENCH: By the Salt Lake City gang police's definition, a gang was any "group of two or more individuals where one of those individuals is involved in a criminal act." That's everybody! Almost everybody hangs out with a group of people in which at least one person is going to be involved in some sort of crime according to that strict definition. Of course, the "crime" could be anything from an assault to shoplifting to speeding.

There was absolutely no basis for the police force in Salt Lake City to classify my friends and me as a gang. We didn't have any kind of organized criminal activity. There was no hierarchy, no leadership, colors, or initiation. We had no mandated rules like all these gangs that are out there. None of us wanted to be considered gang members. We saw ourselves as like-minded individuals who hung out and did stuff together, like any other group of friends. Just like there were jocks and goths, we were just a group of straight edge kids. But good luck to anybody like us trying to prove that to the Salt Lake City police or the local media.

TROY TRUJILLO: Almost immediately after that news report, we had problems with gangs who thought we were trying to impose on their arena. False stories started popping up that we were out beating people up for smoking. So people would constantly want to test us with the same nonsense: "You beat up my cousin for smoking," or "You hate me because I smoke." Regardless of how hard we tried to avoid it, we often ended up fighting.

ANDREW MOENCH: We got into fights, but there we never got into a fight that wasn't provoked. Having said that, did we overreact sometimes? Yes. Did we react too quickly? Yes. We were kids and we were dumb and the violence was sort of a rush. But we never went out to pick fights with people. Someone always instigated the fight.

DJ ROSE: We started hearing all this stuff in the media about a straight edge kid in Salt Lake City carving an X in the back of someone's head with a broken bottle at Lollapalooza. But then we heard through the grapevine that wasn't even close to what happened.

TROY TRUJILLO: Nobody carved an X in anybody's back. The guy that made that claim blew marijuana smoke in the face of somebody that was simply wearing a straight edge shirt at a show. A fight broke out, a bunch of people got kicked out, and he got hit with a chain outside. Instead of telling the truth about starting the fight, he lied and said he was attacked for smoking.

JASON KNOTT: All of this was the equivalent of getting into a fight at school and wanting someone to have your back. Kids have that sense of pride and unity and don't want to let their friends down. It was a street mentality. As a young person, I didn't want to see my friends get hurt by any means. But once the violence happened and got news attention, a side of things emerged that I never personally liked in our scene. Our shows started to become more violent, and it was starting to bum me out.

JEFF NELSON: When I see something on some dumb TV show about straight edge gangs gone crazy, I wondered how it went from being this totally positive, life-affirming thing to a gang where you're hurting anybody physically. Straight edge became a religion, and it's a very strange feeling to be one of the unwitting founders of this religion.

MARK STARR: After Insight split in 1990, I moved from Salt Lake City to Huntington Beach, California. When I came back two years later, I got threatening crank calls all the time. I moved again before any really crazy straight edge gang stuff there started blowing up. What I heard really bummed me out. I was also bummed at the news stories I saw that had Insight's name mentioned. I know Insight really wanted to bring everyone together in all scenes. We all had friends who were into all kinds of things, whether it was music, drinking, or eating meat. We really wanted to stay away from judging; though I do think when you do sing about being straight, animal rights, and being positive, of course it comes across as being judgmental.

TROY TRUJILLO: Contrary to popular belief, we weren't out looking for trouble, but we were no saints, either. Keep in mind, we grew up around gangs that would take all your stuff if you didn't stand up for yourself when confronted. In a sense, we were products of that environment. We were often

A gang of straight edge kids attack bouncers during a show at Spanky's in Salt Lake City, October 10, 1996. The ruckus was so severe that headliners Madball almost did not play. Note brass knuckles raised to strike a mighty blow. TRENT NELSON

quick to respond with violence, which we perceived as self-defense. In most cases, these confrontations asking if we were straight edge were really about power; people wanted to test us and be the ones to beat up the straight edge kids.

JASON KNOTT: There were people here who wanted to get on the map, and they didn't mind the media attention all this violence brought. Some kids in the city at the time took pride in being part of "the mean streets of Salt Lake City" and all that. Then there was national news coverage about a straight edge kid stabbing someone to death here; that ruined everything for me.

ANDREW MOENCH: On Halloween of 1998, I got out of work early. I was driving to my friend Troy's house, and I got pulled over for speeding while I had a warrant out for unpaid parking tickets. The cop gave me a speech about how it was Halloween and he had to look out for kids, so he was just going to give me a ticket and not bring me in.

Afterward, I met up with two friends, and we drove downtown in one of their cars. We were driving down State Street, the main street in downtown Salt Lake City. I saw some kids that I recognized skating, so we pulled over to hang out with them. While we were hanging out, a couple carloads of guys pulled up. Someone in one of the cars said something, and one of the skaters said something back. Apparently one of the guys in the car said something like, "Do you want to be dripping in blood?" which was some gang saying.

One of the guys got out of one of the cars and punched a kid and knocked him out cold. One of the skaters walked toward the guy, and the guy pulled out a gun. Everybody started yelling, "Gun! Gun! He's got a gun!" We all scattered.

There were a lot of younger kids hanging out there, including my friends' little brothers. I lagged behind to make sure no one got left. By the time I got back to the parking lot, the two guys I had come with were gone. Just then, one of the cars belonging to the people harassing us came flying into the parking lot, and full-on ran over a skater kid.

My mind was racing. I was looking around for a way to make sure everyone else was safe, while also figuring out how I could get away. I saw this skater kid on the sidewalk, curled up in a ball, while four guys from one of the cars were beating on him. To my left in the parking lot, I saw a pickup truck with some kids I didn't know in the back; one of them was holding a baseball bat. I ran up to them, like, "Hey! Give me that bat!" Wielding the bat, I ran toward the guys beating the kid, and they started to scatter. I picked the one closest to me and chased him across the street. While he was running, he slipped and fell down, so I beat him up with the bat. I overreacted and caused some serious damage to him. I looked around and noticed everyone clearing out. The two guys I came with were coming back, so I jumped in the car and we left.

After I left, another guy who was with the skaters stabbed the guy I had beaten with the bat. He said he just ran up and stabbed the guy while he was on the ground. Not much rhyme or reason to that, but there really wasn't much rhyme or reason to anything that night.

It turned out that the guys in those cars were all were documented gang members. Most of them were in their twenties. Earlier that night, they had been at a party starting fights, and they had left once the cops were called. The people throwing the party filed a report. I have all the documentation of this. These guys were looking for trouble, and they found it.

Someone told the media that the gang members were on their way to a church function, minding their own business, when we viciously attacked them. That story was put out by the media. I was vilified when the story got national media attention, and I had to just sit there and listen to it.

I was convicted of aggravated assault, which carries the sentence of one to fourteen years. I spent thirteen years in prison, then spent the last two years of my sentence on parole, and I've been off parole for three years. The guy who stabbed him is still in prison. The medical examiner couldn't determine which act initially killed this guy, so we were both charged with murder.

The media tried to play the event as a hate crime because the guy was Hispanic. When I went to prison, that didn't help my situation at all, because a lot of Hispanics had it out for me. The first few years in prison were rough.

JASON KNOTT: Around this time, our shows actually became less violent, because the majority of those people knew we'd stop playing if a fight broke out. We weren't a band that preached, but we would make it be known we wouldn't tolerate violence at our shows. But there was just too much inner turmoil within the scene for us or anything else to continue. The media attention just made it worse, even though all gang stuff started to fizzle out just as Clear was ending.

ANDREW MOENCH: Once the other guy and I were convicted, no one cared anymore. The media got their good story with a happy ending. By no means do I think anyone should have died that night. I will always feel awful that this guy died, and I will always live with that regret that I really didn't have to act the way I did that night.

TROY TRUJILLO: The death was a pretty well-publicized story. I was not there, but my understanding is that a lot of what we were told by the same media that sensationalized our drug-free lifestyle and exaggerated our ideology and beliefs was unsurprisingly inaccurate. Regardless of what happened that night, because it's not my story to tell, the only way that it can be directly linked to straight edge is the fact that the two people that went to prison for the crime happened to be straight edge. The fight had nothing to do with straight edge, even though straight edge was a huge part of the reporting. Again, that's no surprise given the fact that the local news outlets had been vilifying straight edge for some time by that point. Let's face it, Salt Lake City has problems, but it's actually pretty boring compared to larger cities where straight edge for the most part goes relatively unnoticed and is completely irrelevant to law enforcement and news outlets.

JASON KNOTT: It was exactly that same thing was when all people want to concentrate on regarding black metal is the one guy who burned down a church in Norway. The death had nothing to do with the ideals of straight edge or what straight edge represented. It was just violence, plain and simple.

ANDREW MOENCH: What happened that night had nothing to do with straight edge or hardcore. It seems like anytime Salt Lake straight edge gets brought up, the violence is brought up instead of the music. I don't mind talking about it. I'd rather people have the correct information about what went on. I always think about that cop who pulled me over at the beginning of that night. If only that cop had just brought me in. It would have been nice to spend just one night in jail rather than thirteen years.

Insight at City Gardens, Trenton, NJ, August 27, 1989. MIKEY GARCEAU

FRIDAY NIGHT, SEPTEMBER 7TH
FAREWELL PERFORMANCES BY

xnsIGHT

BRAINSTORM
with special guests **SEARCH**
COVER $5.00
DOORS OPEN AT 8:30

THE SPEEDWAY CAFÉ
PRESENTED BY
SALT LAKE UNDERGROUND
SLUG
PRODUCTIONS

FRIDAY JUNE 16TH

INSTED

Reason To Believe
FROM CALIFORNIA

Insight
BETTER WAY

SPEEDWAY CAFE
505 WEST 500 SOUTH • 532-5733

Anthony Pappalardo of Ten Yard Fight gets crucial air. TODD POLLOCK

YOUTH CREW REVIVAL: DO YOU REMEMBER HARDCORE?

ANDREW KLINE: All the kids who were excited about straight edge and animal rights faced a backlash from kids who wanted it to be known that they were not a part of the militant vegan thing. There were people who still wanted to be a part of straight edge, and they started bands in the style of what they considered to be classic straight edge hardcore. These kids were into straight edge and hardcore, but not into where hardcore was heading with beatdowns and breakdowns. Bands like Floorpunch came in, and a Youth Crew revival began.

CHRIS WRENN (BRIDGE NINE RECORDS): The early '90s was full of bands who promoted a straight edge lifestyle, but sounded more metal and played slower. Then the mid-'90s brought bands made up of older guys from the late '80s who wanted that more traditional sound. There were younger guys who wanted that as well. So around 1996 or 1997, a full Youth Crew revival happened.

JOHN SCHARBACH: By the late '80s, the mind-set about straight edge became codified, and something you had to live up to. In the early '90s, when those same people stopped living up to those established straight edge principles, a backlash emerged in fanzines, lyrical content, and even the visuals. Being straight edge and then "breaking edge" or stopping being straight edge became a big deal. People were extremely vocal about it. Every straight edge song from the '90s was about staying true and not falling like someone before you. The lyrical motifs turned to betrayal and selling out and turning your back on your friends. The scene really got hammered into place during this time. To this day, if you start a straight edge band, you sing about friendship, straight edge, and people betraying you or breaking the edge.

TIM MCMAHON: I think the classic, traditional straight edge sound and style started to dip around 1994 because the scene started going in so many different directions. Bands like Earth Crisis really caught on, so the metal thing took off like wildfire and the militant vegan thing also took off. Aside from that, bands were going in all sorts of different directions. Rock, emo, noisy, experimental, poppy: You name it and bands were experimenting with it. The scene pretty much became an anything goes–type deal. Shows ended up looking more like DIY flea markets, with hippies selling vegan foods and ripped-up canvas patches while handing out pamphlets addressing all kinds of political agendas. Some of it was sincere, some of it was just kids following trends.

CHRIS ZUSI: I can describe the early-to-mid-'90s hardcore scene in five words: zines with soy-based ink.

JOHN LACROIX (TEN YARD FIGHT): Nineteen ninety-five was weird. Hardcore was not popular in the actual hardcore scene. It felt very uncool to say you liked hardcore. You could say you liked an emo kind of band on Dischord Records like Hoover, but you couldn't admit you were into Youth of Today.

ANTHONY PAPPALARDO (TEN YARD FIGHT, IN MY EYES): By 1994 in Boston, you had these options: Go see New York bands like Black Train Jack and Sick of It All in a club for the "astronomical amount" of twelve dollars. You could go see a post-hardcore band in a venue where you couldn't stage dive. Or you could go to shows put on by a "collective" called the Treehouse, where the singer of Three Studies for a Crucifixion might cry if someone asked the score of the Red Sox game while he was talking about what dyes to avoid in your clothing. That last one actually happened, by the way! We weren't against the changes, but we also really liked hardcore to be interactive, not a fucking jazz concert.

JOHN LACROIX: Anthony Pappalardo, Anthony Moreschi, and I lived in an apartment together. We'd come home after a show, and be like, "That show was cool, but it was not fun!" We wanted shows where people could go off, but not in this tough-guy way that was popular at the time. So we started the band Ten Yard Fight. We didn't care if anyone liked it. If they hated it, well—then we won. We didn't know the guys who would form Floorpunch were having these same conversations in New Jersey.

Clockwise from top: *While many signed out of straight edge, Tim McMahon remained with Hands Tied.* TRACI MCMAHON; *Sweet Pete and Anthony Pappalardo of In My Eyes.* ROBBIE REDCHEEKS; *Floorpunch's Bill Hanily powers through a sea of vegan gruel to give the kids what they want.* TRACI MCMAHON

CHRIS ZUSI: By 1995, the scene was so different than it was when I first got into hardcore that it was hard to recognize. With the exception of Mouthpiece in New Jersey and then Cornerstone from Connecticut, no band was playing fast straight edge hardcore. Individuals and bands were doing all that they could to distance themselves from that late-'80s look and sound. I didn't have a problem with people doing something different. Hell, I was doing something different with Resurrection. But there was a vibe in the scene that people had grown out of the Youth Crew thing and were doing more "mature" music now. It's like they were embarrassed to admit that they liked Youth of Today. You also had people and bands that were distancing themselves from being straight edge, saying things like, "Oh, we're straight but we're not a straight edge band." That environment gave birth to our band, Floorpunch. We said that if people wanted melody, angst, cardigan sweaters, and pseudo-intellectual lyrics, then we would hit them over the head with mosh parts, varsity jackets, straight edge, and songs about being in crews.

Since the beginning hardcore has been a series of reactions. Hardcore started as a reaction to punk; Youth of Today started as a reaction to the scene going metal; tough-guy core started as a reaction to the Youth Crew; post-hardcore started as a reaction to tough-guy core; and so on. So I think Floorpunch was a natural reaction to what was going on in the scene at the time. And New Jersey has always taken a certain amount of pride in straight edge. I mean, the *edge* is fucking strong in New Jersey—so whenever straight edge falls out of fashion, someone from New Jersey is going to start a straight edge band to remind people what it's all about.

ARI KATZ: When Floorpunch started happening, I wasn't straight edge any more, and I think they all hated me; like, every single member of the band hated me! 7 Seconds' *The Crew* was one of the first records that spoke to me, because I liked their angle that, by being positive, you were almost being *extra* punk since no one would expect that from a punk. The positivity and P.M.A. in straight edge appealed to me because I was a sad kid. From there, vegetarianism came next for me, and Krishna consciousness came into the picture for some friends of mine. Through hardcore, people got turned onto a lot of things they wouldn't have discovered in the normal world, and it benefited their lives. That's what hardcore meant to me: always progressing and always moving forward. And if hardcore stops being your thing, hopefully you should feel comfortable to get out and keep moving, finding out about more music and things that keep you happy. I just always felt you should keep progressing. So that Youth Crew revival thing with Floorpunch wasn't my thing. It just seemed like stagnation.

BRETT BEACH (*HARDWARE* ZINE, IN MY BLOOD RECORDS): Bill Hanily and Marc Zeveney were doing a band called Spirit at the time and were looking to start a new band. They asked me to try out as the singer. It didn't go very well. I was friends with Chris Zusi, who was in Release and also Resurrection, who had broken up earlier that year. We all ended up at an Ignite and Mouthpiece show up in Chatham, New Jersey. I mentioned to Mark Porter that he might want to try out to be the singer for Bill and Marc's new band. Within an hour he announced he was singing for this new band. "We're gonna call it Floorpunch," he said, "because that's how we dance." And Floorpunch was born.

CHRIS ZUSI: Floorpunch formed in the early summer of 1995, and we played our first show later that summer. I was on break from Notre Dame. At some point after I got back to school in the fall, I heard about Ten Yard Fight.

ANTHONY PAPPALARDO: This is not revisionist, but I completely remember us saying we wanted Ten Yard Fight to be like the over-the-top gag band Crucial Youth, but serious. We were all straight edge, but we wanted this thing to be over the top, so that people would pay attention and, most importantly, have fun.

JOHN LACROIX: We always thought bands like Crucial Youth and Grudge were funny, but they were making fun of straight edge. We wanted to be goofy, but the message of straight edge was something not to be fucked with as far as we were concerned. We wanted to be like Slapshot, except we picked a different sport. We picked football instead of hockey. And we took it one step further and sang in sports metaphors. That was the whole concept.

ANTHONY PAPPALARDO: If we just had a jock name and played hardcore, it wouldn't have worked. We needed our singer, Anthony "Wrench" Moreschi, to wear a football jersey and eye black. We needed to start the show by having a bunch of dudes in football costumes jumping through a rally banner—which we did—and we needed football lyrics.

When our demo came out, with a straight face I told an interviewer, "Why are metaphors about nature so profound, but sports aren't? We're just talking about feelings and shit, man."

BRETT BEACH: Right about when Floorpunch was coming together, Ten Yard Fight hit the scene. We immediately formed a pretty tight bond with those guys when Floorpunch played in Boston.

JOHN LACROIX: When Ten Yard Fight started corresponding with Floorpunch, we were almost like two organized crime families coming together. They saw our demo with a picture of a fucking football guy on it, and that was that: We had to be friends. It was some of that collective consciousness–type shit.

ANTHONY PAPPALARDO: When we found out Floorpunch had a demo called *Goal Line Stand*, it was on. Lynn Roberts booked them to play Boston immediately. We played on the floor, in a church, and it was great. No stage, no problem.

CHRIS ZUSI: We played a show in Chatham, New Jersey, with Earth Crisis, and there were probably five hundred people there. It was a big show. We were one of the opening bands with only a demo out, having played only a few shows. The place exploded during our set. We figured out that, at least in the tristate area, a lot more people were *with* us than were against us. After that came Fastbreak from Connecticut and Rain on the Parade and Rancor from Pennsylvania. Around that time, Mouthpiece broke up and Hands Tied formed from the ashes.

TIM MCMAHON: On the Mouthpiece 1995 summer tour, our guitarist Matt Wieder, our roadie Ed McKirdy, and myself started having conversations about starting a new band. Matt ended up moving to Kentucky to join the band Guilt, so the concept sort of ran into a brick wall. Mouthpiece continued on throughout a good portion of 1996 as we played our last string of shows. All the while, Ed and I kept pushing to get the new band started.

Floorpunch had started in 1995. While doing Mouthpiece, I went out of my way to get them on as many shows of ours as I could. Some of Mouthpiece's greatest shows toward the end of our run were with Floorpunch. When we started Hands Tied, our hopes and intentions were to continue where Mouthpiece left off and keep playing shows with Floorpunch when possible and continuing to establish that connection, which is pretty much

The state of straight edge hardcore flyer art in the late 1990s.

what did happen. When Hands Tied finally started, we planned to be a total throwback to the bands of late-'80s straight edge hardcore. With everything going on in the scene, the flood of metallic hardcore and experimental sounds, we wanted to keep it as straightforward and traditional as possible. Our main influence was Youth of Today and we wore that on our sleeve, but not in an over-the-top, goofy sort of way.

ANTHONY PAPPALARDO: There were bands that were thinking of it as a revival one hundred percent, right down to the look, the sound, and the feel. I wasn't into that. If you start playing classical violin now, you aren't called a classical revivalist; you just play classical music. It wasn't a Civil War re-enactment to me. I cringe, because it sounds like we had meetings at some secret location, deciding who was going to wear the Side by Side shirt and where we could find vintage Jordans, in an attempt to reprogram the youth. I never felt that way. Like I said, I liked so much other shit, hardcore was just my passion, but it wasn't in a sealed capsule.

TIM MCMAHON: I never referred to it as a "Youth Crew revival." To me, the Youth Crew was Youth of Today, a few of the bands that they hung out with, and a handful of their friends. I always felt like the whole Youth Crew label was thrown around way too loosely. I don't get offended when that term is used, and I don't argue over it. I just don't really refer to it like that myself. I think fast, traditional, straight edge hardcore became popular again just due to a combination of bands coming up at the time.

BRETT BEACH: Hardcore needed some new energy and enthusiasm; it really did. People were going through the motions. Once I heard the first couple of Floorpunch songs, I knew it was going to work. People started gravitating to the band. I'm telling you, I knew it was going to work. I said, We've got to do this right, play some shows and get a demo out. Then we'll do a seven-inch. I'll put it out. We'll do everything the way bands used to do it—ourselves. We'll show people we can get this done without a label like Victory or Revelation, just making grassroots hardcore. It had to be done. I spelled it right out in an ad we made for the first Floorpunch seven-inch, which read: "Do You Remember Hardcore?!"

VIQUE MARTIN: In 1992 I started doing a zine called *Simba*, and exchanging letters and zines with straight edge girls in the U.S. I became part of a crew known as "Chicks Up Front Posse." I spent a lot of time on the East Coast between 1993 and 1997. We went to a lot of shows, and we were always up front. Two of us were still up front at the Revelation Records 25th anniversary shows in 2012, both in California and New York! We showed the boys that we weren't going to stand at the back holding coats. We weren't going to allow the rules of being up front to be dictated to us. They spouted all that bullshit of, "If you don't like the pit, then get out." We countered with, "It's not *your* fucking pit. You don't get to make the rules. We aren't fucking going *anywhere*." And there were a lot of us. We had a lot of boys in our gang, too, who thought we had the right to stand wherever the fuck we wanted. So yeah, I think we changed things back then. We did zines, we put on shows, and we made our presence known. w

TIM MCMAHON: Bands came up playing that style, new kids came into the scene and picked up on it, and older kids that loved that style in the past now had something to get excited about again. I guess there was also a bit of a backlash against all the metal that had been considered hardcore for the few years prior. Granted, kids still loved the metal stuff, but I think some kids appreciated an alternative.

JOHN LACROIX: Ten Yard Fight had a falling-out with Anthony Pappalardo, which was actually the best thing that could have happened, because he started In My Eyes, with "Sweet" Pete Maher singing.

ANTHONY PAPPALARDO: I was living with John LaCroix and the singer for Ten Yard Fight, Wrench, at the time and didn't really get along with them. We disagreed over dirty dishes, someone hogging the landline, or inviting over crust punks that smelled and left the couch reeking of that vinegary "Food Not Bombs" stench. I was the obvious outcast, which really came to light after we signed with Equal Vision. Steve Reddy proposed that he make Ten Yard Fight basketball jerseys. He lived near the Champion outlet, and they had a nice mark up. But why would a football band make basketball jerseys? This was a big fucking deal to me, because what else is a big deal when you're nineteen and in a band? Also, I hated basketball jerseys, and embroidered band beanies, and any other shit that wasn't a T-shirt or a hoodie.

I don't know if anyone really even cared, but me rallying against that so hard made it really obvious that people were super sick of me and how headstrong I was about random shit like how a song started, what color shirts we should make, and how a seven-inch should be designed. Things got worse as we started writing songs for our first LP. I heard the guys playing some songs I didn't recognize. I was like, "What's up with that? It sounds like Strife." They told me it was for some other thing. Then they got mad serious, told me I was an asshole, and kicked me out with a very detailed telling of everything wrong with me.

I moved down the street to 103 Calumet, where Sweet Pete and two skater friends from college were living. We basically just shoved Baked Lays into our mouths and played Madden football. We started In My Eyes based on hanging out together with no stress. Pete was really instrumental in saying that we were going to be a straight edge band that didn't have songs about straight edge and didn't put X's all over everything. By 1997 the tipping point had been reached and everyone was doing that again, so we went the other way.

Within two months we recorded our demo. Craig Mack booked us at the New Milford Teen Center on March 7, 1997, as "this new band that Sweet Pete sings for." Right before we went on, I regrettably suggested the name In My Eyes. The rationale was that we'd pick the most straight edge song as our name, since we weren't going to write straight edge songs. That's how we ended up with that name. When you'd tell it to norms, they'd always ask, "Like the Peter Gabriel song?"

TIM MCMAHON: Hands Tied released a seven-inch on Equal Vision and eventually went on a tour of Europe in 1998. I remember coming back from that tour and being on such a high. Everything in Europe had gone perfectly. The shows were great and we had such a good time; then we got home and everything fell apart.

We had come back to play a big show in Philadelphia with Burn, and we ended up being the opener. Ninety-five percent of the crowd was still outside, waiting in line to get inside, when we hit the stage. If I had to guess, there were probably thirty people in the venue when we played. I think we still gave it our all, but there's no question that it was demoralizing. Our guitarist Dan Hornecker looked over at me when the set was over and said, "I'm done."

CHRIS ZUSI: After the *Fast Times at the Jersey Shore* LP came out in 1998, we did a summer tour of the U.S. Then in the winter of 1999 we toured Europe. I know this is going to be a shocker, but after being in a van together for months at a time we needed a break from each other. Six weeks apart turned into six months, and so on. We never officially decided to break up, but during that time Mike Kingshott and Marc Zev stopped being straight edge, so there wasn't really a reason to keep the band going. Then in 2000 we got asked to play a show at CBGB with Breakdown and the Cro-Mags. We decided that we wanted to play our final show as a band at home rather than in Europe. Playing CB's with our two favorite bands that May seemed like a fitting time for the "final mosh" and the end of Floorpunch

Everyone's experience in hardcore and straight edge is relative. For me, I missed out on Minor Threat, SSD, and the A7 in New York. Instead, Youth of Today, Judge, CB's and Revelation Records were the epicenter for my experience. Even though I was *playing* in bands during the 1987-through-1990 era, that wasn't really my scene. I did my best to participate, but I was a spectator. By the time Floorpunch came along, it felt like our scene was happening. All of our friends were doing the bands, organizing the shows, and putting out the records. I'm sure there were kids in the scene when Floorpunch was active that connected to straight edge, and felt like I did eight years earlier. Five years later, *those* kids started taking control of the scene.

Clockwise from top: *Hoods up while Stop and Think plays, thank you.* BOB SHEDD; *Have Heart's Pat Flynn shows what counts.* ADAM TANNER; *American Nightmare's Wes Eisold logically shows his Spock hairdo to an adoring crowd.* ADAM TANNER

EAST COAST 2000: THE UNBREAKABLE

JOHN SCHARBACH: The 1990s left a huge impression on people's ideas of straight edge and what straight edge meant. An element of shame or guilt crept into the culture that hasn't completely left. I think the 2000s came to terms with all of this through bands that tried to inject their own type of personality into straight edge.

TIM MCMAHON: Among the few straight edge bands that carried the torch into the 2000s, one that always struck a chord with me was the First Step, from North Carolina. Their traditional straight edge hardcore sound attracted me. They knew their history, and they were very well-rounded musicians that had clearly done their homework. They were also very sincere and dedicated kids that not only talked the talk but walked the walk. I tried to hang out with them and go on the road with them whenever I could. I really respected how they continued to be a great representation of straight edge from all angles.

AARON CHRIETZBERG (THE FIRST STEP): The First Step started around 2001. The newer bands weren't really going for a classical straight edge hardcore sound, but were suddenly going for a bit more of a thrash style, or kind of trying for more of a New York hardcore street style. We were very into Youth of Today, DYS, A.F., Cro-Mags, SSD, the Faith, Minor Threat, Bold, and Chain of Strength. We liked that those bands had really clear lyrical content and were just hard-hitting in sound, lyrics, and style. Some of those newer bands like Tear It Up and Shark Attack were really cool and interesting to me, but they just didn't hit home with me personally.

JOHN SCHARBACH: The First Step was extremely important to me in the sense that they were the first band I really traveled with. They introduced me to a lot of people. I always felt like I was in the band, even though I couldn't play an instrument. I was left with just tagging along, selling the merch and carrying gear. In my opinion, they were the premier straight edge band of the time.

PAT FLYNN: The Boston bands like Right Brigade, Ten Yard Fight, In My Eyes, Fastbreak, and Follow Through were more or less over by 2000. That was a huge bum-out to me. I had just really discovered the New York Youth Crew era when I was fifteen. I saw the late-'90s Youth Crew revival as my chance to experience something close to the romanticized shows at the Anthrax in 1988 that I read about in *Schism* fanzine.

CHRIS WRENN: In 1999, Ten Yard Fight broke up, and In My Eyes and Floor-punch broke up soon after. That was the time for the next shift. Tim Cossar from Ten Yard Fight was my roommate, and when that band was breaking up, he started putting together American Nightmare. American Nightmare wasn't really a crazy departure from Ten Yard Fight, but it was definitely darker. All of a sudden, all of the bands that had red T-shirts or royal-blue T-shirts only sold black T-shirts.

GREG W: In Boston, Ten Yard Fight and In My Eyes had been the bands that were setting the tone for kids my age. Then American Nightmare got really big in Boston. I think that was a reaction to Ten Yard Fight and In My Eyes going on for so long. Kids didn't want to be the clean-cut straight edge; they wanted something darker. Bands like Hope Conspiracy and Converge were more metal. Trust me, we were into American Nightmare, but it reached a point where every band was an American Nightmare junior. I was just so sick of seeing T-shirts with scratchy fonts and all that.

CHRIS CORRY (STOP AND THINK, STEP FORWARD, NO TOLERANCE): From 1999 to 2003 a lot of people in straight edge seemed to be almost ashamed to have anything to do with hardcore. So they would do these bands that sort of sounded like a hardcore band but had very personal emo lyrics, and lots of Ian Curtis from Joy Division and Morrissey references. They wore expensive clothes from London and Paris. It was just so self-serious and such a drag. At the time I thought some of it was okay, but, man—in retrospect, it was awful.

PAT FLYNN: When the whole dyed-black-hair Noel Gallagher Britpop mod-core scene appeared, straight edge seemed like a dorky little-kid pastime. Meanwhile, this overtly bastardized coagulated hardline metalcore scene was trying to bring back the glory of mid-'90s idiotic straight edge–based violence. I saw the emergence of these two scenes—tough-guy militant straight edge and Britpop-core—as almost entirely worthless. Neither had anything to do with a real sense of individuality or community and honest creativity.

The decline of the Youth Crew revival was also a bummer to fifteen-year-old me because the more artsy-fartsy Boston college screamo sound and mod aesthetic was beginning to emerge as the only way to look in the hardcore scene. Suddenly, if your shirt wasn't black with Morrissey on it and was not a size small and your hair was not dyed black and combed forward, then you were a weirdo. At least in Massachusetts, I started to feel like the weirdo. More and more, the fashion-obsessed mentalities that I saw in the screamo scene became the norm of the hardcore scene, along with high praise for bands like American Nightmare. Straight edge didn't seem to be really of much importance by 2001.

GREG W: When we formed the band Mental, it was a reaction to bands in our area like American Nightmare and Panic. We wanted to do something that was different to what was going on at the time. Luckily, the older people who got me into hardcore as a kid put me onto classic New York hardcore. I could never connect to any of that baggy-pants Victory Records stuff too much. The guys in Mental and I were *so* into old New York and D.C. hardcore. We worshipped it, and we wanted to bring that style of music back.

PAT FLYNN: Mental brought a version of straight edge that was not so dominated by asshole tough-guy bullshit. They came out as a straight edge band that didn't want anything to do with stuff like Throwdown or Embrace Today.

AARON CHRIETZBERG: We often played with bands that were different than us. Sometimes a few friends might be like, "Why are you playing with American Nightmare?" But we'd remind them American Nightmare were really kind to us as hardcore kids. They were awesome live, and they often hooked us up—they were a really cool band. Because we were so into the whole straight edge thing and style, people thought we just didn't like anything else. They wanted to relate to us that way, as some sort of oppositional band, but that wasn't the case.

CHRIS CORRY: Mental really got going in 2002, and I thought they were great. They brought youthful enthusiasm and fun back, but never became too jokey with it. There was still sincerity there, and they weren't afraid to be a hardcore band. After a couple years of hardcore bands where the members obviously were more interested in Britpop and electronic dance music, it was really heartening to hear a band that loved Underdog and Straight Ahead playing one-minute hardcore songs that were really simple and good. It wouldn't have worked if they didn't have good songs and a charismatic singer, but they had those things. They were so cool, looking back on it all.

GREG W: Mental just played a shitload of shows and practiced a lot. We did everything real grassroots. I feel a lot of the bigger bands at the time consisted of ex-members of the last band that was big on the scene. That was the tradition for a while. Mental didn't have any of that. We had a circle of friends who came to our first shows. As we kept up, eventually we met people and built up a following. That straight edge crowd was a natural fit for us. I was definitely X'd up, and I put that out there as my image for sure.

CHRIS CORRY: Most straight edge bands at the time were doing a very bland Boy Scout routine, playing a very defanged version of the '80s Youth Crew bands. Mental just disregarded any of that. Their songs were simple and catchy, and it felt like they were having fun with the crowd when they played. They had a reverence for old New York hardcore, but they had their own voice and visual aesthetic. They were polarizing, too—some people really hated them.

GREG W: Mental wanted to do a record. Some labels were interested, but nothing we were super excited about working with. We wanted to be on a label where we were associated with the bands, but we didn't have any options we liked. We did have two thousand dollars in the band account, so we decided to do it ourselves. At that time, I was selling bootleg "Yankees Suck" shirts outside of Fenway Park, where the Red Sox play, so I had cash coming in pretty easily. I just started pressing records. Dan Ducas, who played guitar, was interning at Bridge Nine Records, doing mail order and crap, so Chris Wrenn, the head of that label, helped me connect the dots to start my label, Lockin' Out Records. The label was heavily inspired by Revelation and Schism, two labels that put out records for their friends. I'm really into hip-hop, so Roc-A-Fella Records was another inspiration.

I just thought it was cool to have a label where the bands were playing shows together, influencing one other, and sharing members.

NED RUSSIN (TITLE FIGHT, DISENGAGE): When I was coming of age in hardcore, I was most attracted to the Lockin' Out scene. Mental, Righteous Jams, Dump Truck, Jaguarz, Crunch Time, and Justice all had this undeniable energy. My favorite was Mental. All those bands were writing interesting music; they were putting a lot of effort into every aspect from lyrics to aesthetics; and they were all generally having fun. I think I was so in awe of those bands because they were so okay with presenting themselves in a way that seemed totally atypical of what I was used to. Reading *Trumbull* fanzine and listening to the Mental set live on WERS made me realize those guys were really carving out their own paths, combining all of their interests in one place in a way that never existed. Mental toured a lot, and inspired bands and scenes across the country. They created a whole imposter scene in their wake, almost like Youth of Today in 1987.

JUSTIN DETORE (MENTAL, BOSTON STRANGLER, MIND ERASER, NO TOLERANCE): You could still find pockets of straight edge hardcore in the suburbs, too, with bands like Think I Care and XFilesX.

CHRIS CORRY: Think I Care was probably my favorite band that identified as straight edge. They were like splitting the difference between Infest and SSD, which I really liked a lot. They didn't sound polished or safe, and they really seemed content to do their own thing for a while.

PAT FLYNN: I looked up to the older fellas in the New Bedford, Massachusetts, hardcore scene, like Brendan Radigan, Craig Arms, Chris Brown, and Trevor Vaughan. They were pretty resistant to the outgrowth of a pretty fashion-obsessed social club that overtook the more popular hardcore scenes of Massachusetts. Their bands, XFilesX and Say Goodbye, wrote songs with lyrics that were pretty explicitly opposed to this phenomenon of fashionable hardcore that appeared to have very little to with straight edge and old '80s hardcore.

JUSTIN DETORE: In my opinion, the straight edge scene in Boston didn't get a jump start until Stop and Think formed.

PAT FLYNN: I was excited for Stop and Think's demo in 2002. They were perceived as the new band that would carry the torch of straight edge in a way that wasn't so apishly in your face.

CHRIS CORRY: The guys in Stop and Think wanted to have hard riffs without that tough-guy element. They wanted to be like Straight Ahead or Youth of Today but maybe with a little Breakdown or Outburst flavor, which was not really a common thing at the time. People liked those bands, but no one was really trying to start that kind of band.

GREG W: There was a point where Stop and Think was the only Boston straight edge band, but they weren't on that level of a Ten Yard Fight or In My Eyes, where they were a big draw. They are good example of a band that was bigger after their time. They probably only played half a dozen shows in Boston. Of course, they were awesome shows, because everyone went off for them. The energy was through the roof, due to the personalities involved. Then Joey Contrada went on to be in Righteous Jams and the vocalist A. J. McGuire was our manager and roadie.

NED RUSSIN: I would say that Mental was the most important straight edge band of the early part of the first decade of the 2000s, and Have Heart the most important of the later part. They are polar opposites, but they both gained popularity because they were honest in their approach.

GREG W: Have Heart came in toward the end of Mental's life cycle, and they were the next wave for straight edge in Boston. When Mental started, we were all straight edge, so we just ended up being a straight edge band by default. But our lyrics didn't go in that direction. I think Have Heart was the big straight edge hardcore band in Boston after In My Eyes because they really laid it out in their lyrics.

CHRIS WRENN: I saw Have Heart picking up the straight edge torch after Mental. Bands like American Nightmare and No Warning only had black T-shirts. When Bridge Nine Records started working with Have Heart, Pat's only concern was that we didn't make black T-shirts for the band, and I don't think we ever did; red and royal blue definitely, but not black.

PAT FLYNN: I read an interview with Sweet Pete from In My Eyes where he said something along the lines of, "I don't care if you are straight edge or not, or if there are five or five hundred kids at our shows. I'm most happy when there is a genuine sense of connection amongst diverse people trying to create a positive scene." That struck a chord. Hearing that from a well-respected member of the Massachusetts hardcore scene relieved me, a fifteen-year-old kid, from any pressure to fit into some stupid mold of the perceived hardcore scene.

I needed that greater sense of confidence to start the band that became Have Heart, and to try and spread this idea of honest individuality within a creative community. By the time Have Heart started playing shows in 2003, the sentiment of Sweet Pete's quote was more or less nonexistent in the Massachusetts scene. Bane shows were a place to just be who you were, but even then there was a vibe or either dumb-ass collective violence or fashion-based snobbery.

I don't know if Have Heart were picking up where the late-'90s bands left off, but, at least for me, I wanted to inject my state's hardcore scene with a greater sense of nonviolence and inclusion. Being straight edge was either perceived as a tough-guy joke or a lame path from the '90s designed for prepubescent hardcore kids. With Have Heart, I hoped that maybe being straight edge could be perceived as more of a personal thing that did not add or detract from one's sense of community.

NED RUSSIN: Have Heart crossed a lot of boundaries and really connected with people for that. The last Have Heart show was the craziest show I've ever been to, something like three thousand people in one room losing it for a current band.

AARON CHRIETZBERG: We first started hanging out with John Scharbach when he was super young. He had this crazy bleached long hair and was always wearing the Revelation reissued T-shirts at the time. We went to the Posi Numbers Fest in Pennsylvania. John was super stoked on the band Right Brigade. We were younger kids from the middle of nowhere. John had Air Jordan 1's on and his hood up. His style was the most forward of our crew. At that fest, people definitely looked at us like we weren't cool. But John went off for Right Brigade. A few months later, we were talking with Jesse Standhard from Right Brigade and he asked about John. He was like, "Who is that guy? He's like the most crucial human ever!" He was definitely psyched on how uncommon John's style was; that's how he got the name "Crucial John." A few years later, John and I were talking at another Posi Numbers Fest. He was like, "Dude, remember a few years ago everyone was wearing black? We were like one of a the few kids wearing cargo shorts and old sneakers—now every kid has them on!" So we were definitely out of sync with what went on in the scene when we started. We were just like, "Fuck it—people already don't get us, so we'll just take it even further!"

GREG W: I still do Lockin' Out, but I have a job and a kid now. I break even, and it's a stupid business to be in if you even care about that sort of thing. But it's just a hobby. I have days when I wake up and I don't want to do it, because hardcore is one of the hundred things that are important to me, compared to when I was twenty and it was one of the three things that mattered. But then some band will come along that I like a lot, and I get that feeling like I need to put their record out. So I e-mail them, and they get excited to do a record, and I'm like, "Fuck, I guess I'm doing this still!"

HOSTED BY DJ 12XU

RECORD RELEASE PARTY

JULY 1ST 2005

STOP AND THINK * INVASION

MARK PORTERS FLOORPUNCH

COLD WORLD * JUSTICE * IRON AGE

ALT+ & DFYA
Present

KUALA LUMPUR
EDGE DAY
sober living for the revolution

2014
Featuring

SXC SECOND COMBAT   **KOTM** KIDS ON THE MOVE

THY REGIMENT   **SHARON STONED**   Massacre by Fall

HOMERUN   **TOUCHDOWN**   **HEART ATTACK**

KIDS SPIRIT   **UNFOLD**   **CARBON 14**

STUBBORN   **ONYOURSIDE**   **SKATANIX**

RM25 SUN 19OCT14 3PM@ALT HQ, FAHRENHEIT88 B.BINTANG

FREE CD FOR THE 1ST 20 TICKET

NO DRUGS X NO ALCOHOL X SMOKE ELSEWHERE...

UNITED X FRONT PROUDLY PRESENT

YOUTH OF TODAY
LIVE IN MALAYSIA

SUPPORTING BANDS
STAID
PHILIPINES
STRAIGHT ANSWER
INDONESIA
KIDS ON THE MOVE · THY REGIMENT
NAKED WEAPON · BREAKIN' CHAINS
SECOND COMBAT

DOORS	PRESALE	VENUE	DATE / TIME
RM 60	RM 50	MCPA HALL (UPPER LEVEL)	15/10/11 1 PM UNTIL END

SUPPORTING LABEL

To get presale tickets kindly contact below details.   012 674 5451 / 017 402 1449

Backlab Proudly Present
XEDGEDAYX 2016
BREAK FREE ★ NO SURRENDER ★ NOSTALGIA
HOMERUN ★ PATRIOTS ★ THY REGIMENT
NEVER REGRET ★ KIDS SPIRIT
HACKTICK! ★ BENZOATE

29th OCTOBER 2016
MAKESPACE QUILL CITY MALL
3:00PM RM15

Forum: Perbezaan HC/Punk dulu & sekarang
Ein/Fizi/Azam/Hutch

Supported by

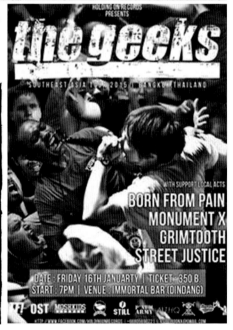

HOLDING ON RECORDS
PRESENTS

the geeks
SOUTHEAST ASIA TOUR 2015 / BANGKOK THAILAND

WITH SUPPORT LOCAL ACTS
BORN FROM PAIN
MONUMENT X
GRIMTOOTH
STREET JUSTICE

DATE : FRIDAY 16TH JANUARY | TICKET : 350 B.
START : 7PM | VENUE : IMMORTAL BAR (DINDANG)

OST   MOSSKIDS   STILL   ARMY   ALT HQ

THE VALUE'S HERE: ASIA & THE WORLD'S EDGE

JOHN PORCELLY: Gorilla Biscuits and Judge played in South America in 2014. The show was huge and I saw *X*'s on so many hands. When we realized that all the members of Project X were there, we said, "What the hell?" and we played a Project X set. When we played "Straight Edge Revenge," I could see the looks on these kids' faces. I could see all the shit they were taking at school from people thinking they were weird for not drinking. Thirty years later, it's still the same old song. I could see that frustration and anguish. They weren't just singing along—it was like primal scream therapy.

KI SEOK SEO (THE GEEKS): When I was in junior school, Korea was still a pretty poor country, so two students had to share one table. My tablemate was trading American punk rock tapes with other classmates and I was very curious about it, so he let me borrow Nirvana's *Nevermind*. That was my way into a whole new world. Through them, I got into the neo-punk movement of Green Day and the bands on Epitaph Records. Our information was pretty limited. But when Korea was opened to the global market, all these import CDs came into our country. I found Youth of Today's *Break Down the Walls* CD, and the cover was so striking and the music's positive message blew me away.

Break Down the Walls inspired my friends and me to start writing our own songs in 1997. We couldn't form a band, because that would have been impossible in Korean high school. You had to be at your desk by 6:30 a.m., and you studied until midnight. So we didn't have the time, and we didn't have the courage. When we enrolled in university, we got more freedom. We were good students who liked to study, but we loved hardcore punk. So we called our band the Geeks, because that was a reflection of how people viewed us at the time. We formed in 1999.

KAWAMURA TAKASHI (INSIDE): In 2000, I was fourteen years old. I got into hardcore punk and went to the local record store every weekend. I found an Earth Crisis CD, and that's how I found out about straight edge. I thought their version of straight edge was too radical, and didn't fit me at that time.

When I was twenty, I was a university student, and everyone around me drank alcohol and behaved sloppily. I really hated that. It looked dirty and so many people missed class because of it. At that time, I joined the band Umbrage. The singer was straight edge, and I thought I should try to do it because I wanted to change myself.

KI SEOK SEO: Thirty or forty years ago, Korea was one of the poorest countries in the world. My father and my grandfather worked to build the economy here, and the only thing that was a relief and kept people together and alive was drinking. Drinking together was the only way people came together and socialized. Reportedly, Koreans drink three times more than Russians on a daily basis. There's a strong feeling that you need to conform and comply with this ritual. So when I started to claim I didn't want to smoke or drink, people became really upset. For example, during my mandatory two years of military service, one of my superiors offered me a drink. When I declined him very politely, he got really upset and he almost punched me. But I did not give up. I persuaded everyone that it was my life and my choice. Somehow I survived.

KAWAMURA TAKASHI: In old Japanese society, there was a custom that people were forced to drink alcohol at their business parties. So it can be a little bit difficult for adult people to be straight edge. The average daily life in Tokyo is very different from straight edge life. Many people get drunk every day after work, and smoke inside buildings like music venues. I think it's the worst!

KI SEOK SEO: The Geeks' very first show was in a small basement, and people didn't get it. Most of the people into punk in Korea didn't even know what straight edge was at that time. We were trying to start our own scene, so we began educating the punks on straight edge. Slowly we had unity.

KAWAMURA TAKASHI: There is no straight edge scene in Tokyo. The first straight edge band in Tokyo was Till I Die in the late 1990s. As recently as 2017, there was only Inside, Stand United, and One Word.

KI SEOK SEO: We are the first Korean hardcore band to play Hong Kong, Malaysia, and Thailand. Southeast Asia is more accepting of straight edge, as it's a more liberal region than Korea. There a lot of straight edge people in Malaysia, as well as bands like Second Combat and Kids on the Move and then there is the Edge Fest.

I've been straight edge for twenty years, and the Geeks will be celebrating our eighteen-year anniversary soon. Straight edge is one of the best decisions I made in my life. The reason I still live it is to show that it's real. I can go out and be a party animal, but I don't have a sip of alcohol. I'm living by example, and I think it's making a dent in our society. I'm proud of that.

KAWAMURA TAKASHI: People are so weak and so many yield to temptation and ruin their lives. That is the same in the hardcore punk scene. Some people use drugs, some people drink or smoke. I don't care about what other people do, but we've got the straight edge, so we don't make mistakes like that. That's the difference, and that difference is very important to us.

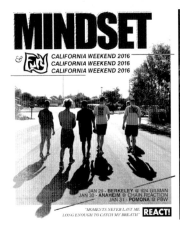

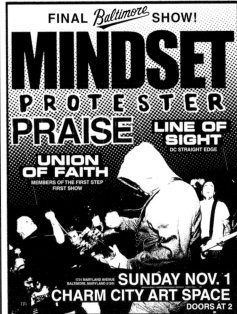

From top: *Maryland's Mindset leaving no doubt that the edge is alive and well.* MICHAEL ANDRADE; *Praise's Andy Norton walks to the edge.* ANNE SPINA; *Mindset completely blowing apart a confined space.* ANGELA OWENS

BACK TO D.C.: BUILDING TOMORROW

PAT FLYNN: I think straight edge is in a good place today. When the majority of people laugh at "Kill Your Local Drug Dealer" T-shirts and would rather be caught dead than wearing straight edge clothing line T-shirts, I think that's a good thing. Less capitalizing on the concept of straight edge is a good thing in my book.

ANDY NORTON (DESPERATE MEASURES, PRAISE): Straight edge is still a part of hardcore today, but I think the way people view it is different. It seems like a much more personal thing, not talked about much unless it's an outwardly straight edge band. If people break edge, it's not this huge deal like it was ten or so years ago.

PAT FLYNN: To be straight edge in 2016 is no real giant proclamation that must be heard by everyone in the room. I don't see the exclusionary and violent stance in straight edge right now that I saw when I was going to shows in the early 2000s. I think people have grown up and seen the reality of how people will change. It's unlikely that every fifteen-year-old that says they will be straight edge for the rest of their lives will actually go on and follow through with that. Perhaps the whole pride aspect of straight edge has died down. I think that's a good thing, especially since "straight edge pride" was marked by violence and mob behavior in the '90s and early 2000s.

MICHAEL CLARKE (MINDSET): I personally think straight edge and hardcore are as great as they've ever been. I do think there's been a bit of a dark age for straight edge since maybe the early 2000s. That's not to say there haven't been bands, but there hasn't been a strong straight edge scene, and it certainly hasn't been the cool thing. As a matter of fact, it seems like the cool thing in hardcore for the last ten years has been trying to act like a criminal, and trying super hard to be edgy. But the straight edge bands worth hearing fight their way into the general hardcore scene and gain fans because they're great bands—not because straight edge is the "it" thing at the moment.

PAT FLYNN: Since they started around 2008, Mindset from Baltimore carried the straight edge torch in what I believe was a positive, healthy manner for young people to see.

MICHAEL CLARKE: I think our primary goals when forming Mindset were promoting empowerment, unity, straight edge, vegetarianism, and DIY ethics. I do think we accomplished all of those things to some degree. I was always very proud of the mixed crowds at our shows, seeing girls stage diving, trans people, punks, skins, straight edge, longhairs, and whatever. That may be what I'm most proud of in regard to Mindset, that our crowds were diverse and there has never been a fight at a Mindset show. We were always vocal about straight edge and vegetarianism, hopefully in a way that was more like, "Here's an alternative option."

PAT FLYNN: But Mindset called it quits in 2016. I hope there will be another band that does the same thing they did.

MICHAEL CLARKE: There's value in things that are finite, and we wanted to close the book on Mindset and be at the top of our game, with no regrets. Bands keep reuniting and fucking up their original project. Hardcore is so contextual to me. When you see a fifty-year-old dude singing about things he wrote when he was eighteen, and then you read interviews where he says, "Straight edge and hardcore don't mean anything to me anymore," that doesn't make any sense to me, and that compromises the integrity of the original. If you make something cool, leave it the fuck alone. So we closed our book. We're definitely all moving on to new projects, and we're still as enthusiastic about straight edge and hardcore as ever.

ANDY NORTON: Mindset encompassed everything I love in a straight edge band. They had something to say, and they articulated it well. They had a great aesthetic that was executed perfectly on every platform including records, shirts, and getting the most live and wild a band can get. They operated on their own terms. They never did a package tour or had a booking agent, and they essentially put out their own records. I think that they were the straight edge band that was needed for this time period and it's sad to see them go. Doing a straight edge band that takes influence from the late '80s is very hard to do tastefully. It often comes off cliché and corny. Mindset wasn't either of those things.

CHRIS BRATTON: I will deeply miss Mindset, who I loved watching demolish the stage every night when Chain of Strength toured with them. Seeing singer Ev Wivell get big parts of his face smashed open bloody and a big chunk of his head gashed open right there onstage and then just shake it off and keep right on singing hard was sick as fuck. That defined what it meant to be hardcore. Ev had to go directly to the emergency room after he finished one set to get multiple stitches to his face. He got his head metal-stapled shut, then went ahead and played his set the following night like nothing had happened.

MICHAEL CLARKE: I've found that most of the straight edge bands out there today are the real deal, because they're not trend-driven. There may be fewer of us, but we have a much more favorable lifer-to-poser ratio. My favorites right now are Praise, Violent Reaction, No Tolerance, Protester, and Line of Sight.

Praise is our generation's 7 Seconds—that is to say, they are a melodic, exposed, vulnerable band, cutting right through the tough-guy vibe. Their songs are incredibly well-written; the lyrics are chilling and touching. They really saved melodic-style hardcore from whatever horrible direction it was heading in.

ANDY NORTON: Praise is a straight edge band. When Praise started, I wanted everyone to be on the same page and share similar ideas. On top of that, most of the people I wanted to play music with were straight edge. I don't think it's the focus of the band or part of our aesthetic, but we are definitely a straight edge band. On the other hand, I don't think it's something I need to write about or a flag that we need to fly.

MICHAEL CLARKE: Violent Reaction are U.K. boys, and I love their blend of U.K. '82 and Oi! meets Youth of Today. I came up in the punk scene, so seeing dudes in boots playing straight edge songs that sound like Last Rights is a perfect combo.

TOM PIMLOTT (VIOLENT REACTION): The intent behind Violent Reaction was to just to do an all-out straight edge band with a slightly different sound to the Youth of Today and Earth Crisis clones. We started by doing a U.K. '82 or Oi!-type thing, mixed with Poison Idea and Out Cold. The latter part of the equation faded out after the demo and first seven-inch, partially due to my inability to write songs outside of the Ramones box. Now we lean more on the simpler, hard-and-fast style of Negative Approach, S.O.A., and Agnostic Front. I guess you could say we don't really sound like what most people think of when you talk about straight edge hardcore. For some over here in Liverpool, we don't dress punk enough, so we are macho right-wing jocks to the punks, but we are too punk and elitist for the mosh kids. That laughable stuff aside, straight edge in the U.K. is pretty strong at the moment. Most of the U.K. hardcore bands doing cool stuff these days are represented by at least one U.K. edge alumni. I'd say we are as accepted as we need to be!

MICHAEL CLARKE: No Tolerance is a classic-style hardcore band, but very aggressive. Corniness or a lack of attitude will turn me off on a straight edge band right away. Sometimes you hear a straight edge band and you can tell they've never heard Negative Approach. No Tolerance is the antithesis of that.

JUSTIN DETORE: No Tolerance wasn't started to preach a particular message. Don't get me wrong, the lyrics are from the heart, but it's all been said before more eloquently than Chris Corry or myself could put it. The band exists to show that it's still possible to do a good straight edge hardcore band that pays tribute to a sound and aesthetic of a particular era but isn't soft.

MICHAEL CLARKE: Protester is high on my list because they rip, they're young, and they're from D.C. They play a very classic style, not as some sort of weird fetishism, but more of an extension of a great idea. Line of Sight is a very new band, also from D.C. We were lucky enough to play a few shows with them before Mindset broke up. Austin Stemper is a great front man who perfectly balances the line between aggression and thoughtfulness. Everyone in the band is a great musician, so hearing those songs live and watching them play was energizing. There are a lot of great straight edge bands coming out of D.C. at the moment.

NED RUSSIN: I think Washington, D.C., in particular right now has a really interesting scene, with a single group of people doing an obscene number of bands. I think they are influenced by Youth of Today and the like, but the bands are also doing a lot of different things influenced by a lot of different bands. D.C. is doing something interesting right now without limiting itself.

JOHN SCHARBACH: It's nice that someone is noticing what's happening in a scene I feel heavily involved in. At this point, there is a lot of mixing sonically and visually, and it's producing various results. D.C. just seems to have a heavy influx of excited kids lately, and the scene is growing. I can't tell if people move here and feel the pressure of getting involved, or if they want to be involved so bad that they move here.

MICHAEL CLARKE: Straight edge takes some of the most fundamentally accepted, time-honored, championed traditions in our society, and goes directly against them. Most young kids come into the punk and hardcore scene as insecure, angry, confused outsiders in some way or another. So to me, it's important for Mindset and other straight edge bands to present the alternate option, that it's okay to reject something, even if you're the only one. Even when other people look at you like you're nuts, you do what's right for you, and do it with confidence. Most of the time, people will come around to respecting you for it. For the ones that don't, you don't give a fuck about them anyway, because you're good with your choices.

From top: *Ray Cappo senses crucial times with the reunited Youth of Today, This Is Hardcore Festival, Philadelphia, August 4, 2016; Mike Ferraro wonders "where it all went."* PHOTOS BY ANNE SPINA

EXPLANATION FOR ACTION

JEFF NELSON: Within only thirty-five years, straight edge has led to so many inaccuracies and legends. I have read that *I* invented straight edge, because I was laying out some graphics and it occurred to me that a "straight edge" was a ruler. But I wasn't the guy in Minor Threat who wrote that song! Seeing the nonsense and the scrutiny and the importance to the origins is no different than the importance placed on the early beginnings of religion. It's both weird and amazing. Straight edge became a religion, and it's a very strange feeling to be one of the unwitting founders of this religion. And I say this as a devout atheist: Architecture and music are the only good things religion has brought.

DAVE SMALLEY: Straight edge by itself is nothing. It's what you do with it that matters. Let's use Ernest Hemingway as an example. He was notorious for being a big drinker and womanizer, but he wrote some of the most beautiful things in the English language. He did something with his life that was irrespective of drinking or not drinking. But if someone was straight edge and was just a nasty person and hurt people and never achieved anything with their life, is that person better than Hemingway? Of course not.

JON ROA: I never thought being straight edge was an end to itself. People can say, "I'm straight edge." So what? What have you done? What have you accomplished besides not drinking? Greg Ginn from Black Flag and SST Records smokes lots of pot, but he gets a lot more done than any kid who went to an Inside Out show

DAVE SMALLEY: The whole term came from the idea that it gave you an edge in order to achieve something. Straight edge is not the goal. Straight edge is a tool for some people to get to a goal. It's to use that sharpness from not being dulled to achieve something great.

JON ROA: I remember when I met Tim Yohannan, the late editor of *Maximum Rocknroll*. He drank and smoked, and I thought, "This guy's getting a lot done." That made me think. Then I'd hear about these straight edge kids who would come over to the *Maximum Rocknroll* house and steal his records. That's when I started to contemplate, "Well, who's the better person here?"

KENT MCCLARD: To me, straight edge is a political thing as much as it is a social thing. Look at a band like M.D.C. They weren't promoting straight edge, but they were very close to it in a way. They were promoting this act of consumer rebellion and fighting corporations. To me, it was all connected. All these hardcore bands were showing that what you do has an impact.

GREG BENNICK: I learned so much from straight edge, questioning right and wrong and questioning myself and my potential impact on people. I've been doing motivational speaking for a few years, and I have been the keynote speaker at many large events. When I go out to speak, I'm not writing down every bit of a speech before I get onstage. In fact, it's the opposite; that comes from walking out with just a microphone in my hand to an unpredictable and intense audience.

I founded an organization called One Hundred for Haiti. I put in a lot of time fundraising for the group. We have initiatives about clean water and against sexual assault. I go to Haiti on a regular basis to help people there transform their own communities, rather than me being the great hope from America who swoops in and saves the day. Straight edge led me creatively to where I am now.

TOBY MORSE: I have founded a nonprofit organization called One Life, One Chance. I go into schools and talk about the choice of a drug-free lifestyle. When I first go in front of a class, the first thing I ask is, "What's the first thing you think about when you see me? Raise your hand if you think I party." Every kid raises his hand. I tell them I never tried anything, and they don't believe me. They all think I've gone to rehab and cheated on my wife, because that's what you're supposed to do if you're a tatted-up musician.

I show a PowerPoint presentation that includes the definition of straight edge and a picture of Minor Threat. I talk about the Bad Brains and P.M.A. I show pictures of friends of mine who passed away because of drugs. Then I show people who are straight edge who are super successful, like my friend C. J. Wilson, who was a pitcher for the Los Angeles Angels. I try to show people who are straight edge that kids can relate to in the real world. But my main thing is breaking the stereotypes of heavily tattooed punk rock musicians being partiers.

After I spoke at a school in Massachusetts, I was on the cover of the newspaper with a picture of Minor Threat behind me. My friend sent it to Ian MacKaye. He thought it was awesome. I think he's stoked that somebody took something he created and presented it in a positive way to kids in schools.

The message of straight edge is so important that I want to share it. I've spoken in thirty-six schools so far. I look at my presentation as the opposite of "scared straight." I don't come out there and say I was a junkie who lost my house and my wife. I show them my life. I show them they don't have to take the normal path to have a great life. I show them people who have done drugs and not made it. I show them people who were straight edge and made it. It's super real and raw. And with that I try to inspire one or two kids.

PAT FLYNN: Had I not discovered Youth of Today when I was fifteen, there's a good chance I would have gotten wrapped up in a lot of the same toxic, damaging shit as many of my friends and family members. I'm grateful for that. From being exposed to thought-provoking minds like Ray Cappo, Kevin Seconds, or Sweet Pete, I also learned how to be myself. Straight edge isn't only about how drinking and doing drugs may complicate your life. In my understanding, straight edge goes far beyond the basic commonly thought-of ideals and extends more toward just being a kind, honest, self-reflecting individual, and a contributing member of a community. That's a lot more than "Don't smoke, don't drink, don't fuck."

REVEREND HANK PEIRCE: I failed out of college and ended up roadying for bands like Slapshot, C.O.C., and Uniform Choice. I used to do weekend tours with Gang Green, and they had this attitude of, "You're straight edge, you can take care of everything while we act like idiots." They didn't realize that babysitting was not in my job description.

I remember C.O.C. touring with Metallica, and seeing one of the Metallica roadies sulking around wearing his satin tour jacket. I thought, "I don't want to be one of those guys, man." I wanted to have an impact on the world. So I went back to finish college. I studied religion at UMass Boston, and from there I entered the seminary.

I'm a Unitarian Universalist minister. We are the most liberal of liberal religions. You don't have to believe in God. We have no creed. We want people to find the best pathway to enlightenment. We have people influenced by Buddhism and Christianity. It's a church full of heretics, basically.

JON ROA: "Straight Edge" was a great song that turned into a way to get things done without being inhibited by outside forces. If you can get it done by other means, I'm not going to judge you. Somewhere down the line, straight edge became something where you judge someone else for drinking a beer. If someone wants to smoke a joint but not eat at McDonald's or buy Nikes, and still rejects notions of self-destruction, then I don't see anything wrong with that. To me, it's more important to see people being nice to each other.

GREG BENNICK: The definition of straight edge has no more significance than what we want to apply to it. The question is whether we know ourselves based on those definitions. It's very easy to say you're straight edge and have no sense of self and be like everyone else. It's what we know of ourselves within those definitions that make us who we are and creates the psychology behind straight edge.

ARTHUR SMILIOS: I know that a guitar isn't going to change the world, but what comes out of it can inspire the real movers and shakers. I have met a few incredible activists who have made a difference, and I was told that some of the music I helped make served as the impetus for their actions. We may be clowns, pounding stages, but we can serve a purpose.

Insted still making the difference at their reunion at CBGBs, New York City, 2004. PHOTO COURTESY OF RICH LABATTE; *Civ from Gorilla Biscuits lends the reunited Judge his vocal authority.* ANNE SPINA

LIFE AFTER STRAIGHT EDGE

ARI KATZ: When I was done being straight edge, I knew I was done. I didn't call it bullshit or anything. I just felt I didn't need it anymore, and it was time to go onto something else. I think you hit a certain age and hopefully don't feel the need to identify yourself with a phrase or a look.

JOEY VELA: I'm still straight edge in technical terms. I don't drink, smoke, or do drugs. But I don't relate to straight edge at all. It doesn't mean the same thing to me that hardcore does.

JOE SNOW: Straight edge was a great tool of my youth, but it does not translate well to my adult life. That said, I am as straight edge as I was back then, but I would never dream of calling myself "straight edge" ever again.

JONATHAN ANASTAS: I ended up breaking edge to fit in when I got into advertising. I did the same thing I did back in high school. I took two sips of a drink and poured out the rest in a plant somewhere. I was insecure when I was just starting at the company. I thought that if I announced I didn't drink, people would assume I had some past issues with alcohol and they wouldn't want to do business with me.

JEFF NELSON: One thing I find appalling is this notion that you are straight edge for life, or not at all. This idea that once you are straight edge you can never leave straight edge and come back—to me that seems to be utter bullshit. It's ridiculous and ludicrous, and as dumb than any of the dumbest religions in the world.

DEMIAN JOHNSTON: When I find out about guys in their forties who are still calling people who drop straight edge sellouts, I'm like, "Seriously?" I'm happy they're still pissed off and everything, but could they at least be pissed about their mortgages or something relevant to adult life?

TIM MCMAHON: I felt betrayed. I took it all so seriously. When I saw people that just moved on to what looked to be the next trend, I felt like they disrespected something that I felt was important and vital in creating who I was. To me, straight edge was a progression in life—learning lessons, applying them, and continuing to move forward. When people got out of straight edge, I felt like they were taking steps backward and regressing— taking lessons learned and knowing what's right and wrong, and turning back around; giving up and hopping back in line with the rest of the world that couldn't see the light.

BRIAN BAKER: I spent about twenty-five years of life completely fucked up on drugs and alcohol. Trust me, the irony is not lost on me. Having spent my life on both sides of that coin, I can tell you right now there's not a down-side to being sober.

TOBY MORSE: Some people fuck up most of their life and become straight edge when they're forty. Some people fall off straight edge at thirty and come back later. And there are kids who pushed straight edge hard and then got into serious hard drugs and didn't come back.

ANTHONY PAPPALARDO: After a while, you see your non–straight edge friends living normal, productive lives, not lying in a corner with a needles stick-ing out of their arms, begging for change. Nope, they get shit done; they travel, they open businesses, they do things.

ANDY STRACHAN: I wish I had the commitment to stay straight edge like the other Boston guys Jaime and Al from SSD, and Choke. I was a bike mes-senger in Boston and got caught up in partying more and more.

JEFF NELSON: It should be a personal decision if you're not going to drink or smoke or do anything else you consider distracting from the best-lived life. You should do it because you want to do it, not because someone told you to do it or it's the cool thing to do at the moment. We're all humans and have moments of weakness. Why should someone be penalized for changing their mind or even changing their mind back and deciding they're better off not drinking? Why on earth would you hold that against them? That rigidity is repellent to me.

ARI KATZ: When I was twenty-two, I started smoking pot and drinking. I just knew I was done with it. It's not like I called straight edge bullshit or any-thing, but I lost all my fucking friends because of it. A really good friend of mine threw me into a garbage can when he heard about it! When you decide to lose your edge, you lose all your friends. I think it might be easier to leave a Hasidic family than it is to leave straight edge.

JOE NELSON: I broke my edge at Kevin from Insted's wedding as a joke. I drank six beers in twenty minutes. I never drank before in my life, so I was fucked up. I tried to dunk a basketball in this hoop in the backyard and ended up splitting my head open and passing out in the bushes. Brad X from Doggy Style and Gwen Stefani took care of me. I remember Gwen being like, "Did you drink, Joe?" I was like, "Yeah, Gwen! I had six beers in twenty minutes, okay? I broke my edge for Kevin's wedding!" But I never looked back; it was a new direction!

DAMIAN ABRAHAM (FUCKED UP): I was diagnosed as having generalized anxiety and having some bipolar issues, so I went on antianxiety pills, and I've been on them throughout the course of the band. I decided to stop taking my antianxiety pills—which is not advised for anyone. In a moment of weakness in Denmark, I had to go to a mental hospital, and it was a big ordeal. So out of desperation, soon I was like, "Yo, let me hit that joint." You could almost hear the needle screeching off the record. The rest of my band looked at me like, "What?" So I smoked pot that night, and it really worked at curing my anxiety. I'm not saying it's going to work for everyone, but I guess I have no regrets.

ANTHONY PAPPALARDO: I am not really sure there was any epiphany for me or key moment where I wanted to stop being straight edge, but at one point I just started thinking, "I've spent my life not walking under ladders, not even out of superstition, because that's the rule. Fuck the rules, who cares, it's a fucking ladder." I went to visit my sister in London while she was doing a semester there and ended up in a Britpop club, about five years too late, dancing to whatever and doing shots with some girl whose name I couldn't understand because her accent was so thick. Then some random bros from Reykjavík wanted to smoke up in their minimalist flat after hanging out at some pub allegedly owned by Jarvis Cocker, during a snowstorm, while listening to psych -rock LPs. It was fun. Some college girl from a "ladies drink free" night calls me up to take drugs on a random Tuesday? Sure. Why not?

PAT DUBAR: I'm half Native American, part Celtic, and part Viking. I come from all these warrior societies, which makes sense, looking at the way I acted when I was younger. There was a lineage of pain with my relatives due to growing up in the South and being Indian. I felt that pain myself, and in my late twenties it led me to a medicine man. I told him I was at a point in my life where I didn't want to live anymore. He told me I had to come with him to a ceremony and get healed. I said, "Fuck it! What are we doing?" He told me we were going to the Amazon.

I signed a waiver of death and we flew into Iquitos, Peru. We went on a fucking boat up the Amazon for four hours, and then we hiked for another three hours. We finally got there and did ayahuasca—the most potent hallucinogenic in the world. The natives of the Amazon call it death training, because it makes your physical body feel like it's dying. When the drug starts to kick in, the reptilian part of your brain where fear, hunger, and anger exist start to fight against each other. But you can connect to your subconscious mind, so even though you feel like you're on another planet, you're steering the ship. You have to make this split-second decision whether to tell yourself, "I'm not going to die. I'm going to get through this and be a warrior." Or you just say, "I'm going to die!" and you flip out. There were people in the temple all around me screaming bloody murder, thinking they were dying.

I went into my subconscious and communicated and relived experiences in my life that were traumatic as a kid. You can review your life back to the earliest moments of childhood and figure out what led you to where you are. You go through everything and recognize what made you what you are, and what led you there. After all that, you realize all you have to do is set the bags down and walk away, you know?

I had anger issues and I was violent. I thought violence was the first answer to a problem. After that, I learned to respond instead of react, and I haven't lifted my hand to someone in seventeen years. I don't want to hurt anyone ever again. So I've been to the top of the mountain and back down. That experience in the Amazon changed my life as much as straight edge, because it redefined things for me. I was in the jungle for three weeks with giant snakes and jaguars and no electricity. My life has come full circle. I've had all these experiences. I still don't ever drink.

ANDY STRACHAN: Some friends and I became Sikhs through practicing yoga. I currently live in Española, New Mexico, where there is a large yoga community. There is no meat, no alcohol, and no smoking. I started that about fifteen years ago. That got me back to the tenets of straight edge, and I was like, "Thank God!" So I guess I'm straight edge again. It's a much more preferable and easy way of life compared to others.

BRIAN BAKER: The main thing about being sober is there is one less thing in the way of figuring out what all this is all about. I think that's the original intent of straight edge. You don't want to put blocks in your way. You don't want to slow yourself down with stupid shit. It's incredibly valid and I'm very proud of being a part of something that was so beneficial to people.

ANTHONY PAPPALARDO: I used to like pro wrestling with Dr. Strange and the fucking Road Warriors. I had a Lizzy Borden cassette. I loved all that shit, but I could not care less about it now as a grown man—it has no feeling to me. I still think a Uniform Choice T-Shirt is as cool as is their music. I still think Minor Threat is one of the greatest bands, not just punk bands, of all time. If I see someone wearing an X-Rated Swatch watch, I still get the same little flicker of excitement that I did as a kid. Occasionally I'll find some Youth of Today video on YouTube that I've never seen, and I'm mesmerized. I'm not a part of it anymore, but it's a part of me. If I found a copy of the Straight Ahead twelve-inch in some bin at a random store in upstate New York this weekend, I would be texting or posting it to Instagram immediately and losing my mind. That feeling doesn't leave me.

JOHN PORCELLY: I used to get pissed off about people doing the whole "true till college" thing and ditching straight edge. I was a straight edge lifer and it really bummed me out that people would turn their back. But I meet a lot of people who say Youth of Today had a huge impact on them. They tell me how they went to college and started drinking, but how they got married, had kids, and came back full circle to the ideals. All the things instilled in them are still there. They're teaching their kids to keep a positive mental attitude. So now I realize the value of the ideals, rather than the rules. The ideals are the most important thing. Whether they went off for a few years and drank or did drugs doesn't matter. In the end, straight edge is still a success.

DAVE SMALLEY: I wouldn't be who I am at this very minute without straight edge. It was not a temporary thing for me. If that's what it was for some kids, that's fine, too. If it helped them to not do things when they were highly susceptible to falling into some bad things, that's great. People change and grow.

TIM MCMAHON: As I grew older, I started looking at people on an individual basis, taking from them what they truly were as people. That comes with maturity and experience. I'm still just as serious about straight edge as I was, but what other people do doesn't affect me anymore. I've seen so many people come and go, nothing surprises me and nothing really fazes me.

DAMIAN ABRAHAM: I like to think that I probably could still be straight edge if I wasn't in Fucked Up, but marijuana has really helped me deal with the anxiety of touring. It's not to say that straight edge wasn't awesome. I have no regrets about being straight edge for sixteen years, like, none at all.

RYAN DOWNEY: I tried alcohol once since the age of fifteen, when I was twenty. I had a Guinness with another ex-hardline straight edger, and then a wine cooler about two weeks later. Both experiences reinforced what I had already figured out at age fifteen. Drinking isn't for me. I've been straight edge again ever since, for well over twenty years. Believe it or not, there are still people on occasion who will say I can't claim straight edge, thanks to these two drinks twenty years ago. I've got two middle fingers for these people.

Clockwise from top left: *The reunited Judge won't let you get in their way.* ANNE SPINA; *H₂0's Toby Morse does it right.* DAN RAWE; *John Porcell brings it down in 2016.* ANNE SPINA; *Mouthpiece in the new millenium.* KEN SALERNO

WHAT REMAINS: KEEPING THE EDGE

IAN MACKAYE: Occasionally, I'll hear an interview with somebody who is not a music person at all, and they'll say, "I'm straight edge!" I love it. About ten years ago, "straight edge" entered the dictionary. I said to my dad, "I made it into the goddamned dictionary!" It's not that I'm thinking about it, like, "Finally, my philosophy has taken hold!" What I'm fascinated by is how this idea made its way into the culture.

AL BARILE: I'm probably the most proud over the years of how straight edge has continued spreading. I read stories about C. M. Punk, the pro wrestler, and C. J. Wilson, a pitcher for the Los Angeles Angels, talking about straight edge. If that type of demographic has been penetrated, that means, strangely enough, that probably everyone in the world knows what straight edge is. That's unbelievable, because you have to understand that this thing started with maybe two or three people in D.C. and two or three people in Boston.

C. J. WILSON (TEXAS RANGERS, LOS ANGELES ANGELS): Being edge is something that people will always associate with me for the rest of my career. It's in my Twitter name, on my glove, and always in my biographical info. I think it's awesome when people come up to me and say, "I didn't even know what straight edge was until you, and it inspired me."

KARL BUECHNER: Straight edge being in professional wrestling through the WWE's Straight Edge Society, and being mentioned on sitcoms and shows like *The Sopranos* is great. Here's why: I think many people don't even know there's another way to live, since the media has everyone under a giant cloud. Every comedy movie coming out is about some fun-loving potheads who have a journey of mayhem. It's presented in this very deceptive way. None of those movies ever end with the character in court because he ran over a five-year-old girl when he was drunk or high. It's all fun and games. There are no repercussions and no long-term effects. No one becomes an alcoholic. No one becomes a drug addict. The fact that straight edge is out there in the mainstream—even if it is just a buzzword—means it can still end up being someone's point of origin. If TV gets some kid to ask, "What is straight edge?" then that's great.

AL BARILE: When I was growing up, I don't think that choice existed, and I don't think it was a fair fight. I do feel from what I hear now—generations after me—that the effect that I was looking for took hold exactly the way I wanted. I think there are multiple choices now. When I grew up, there really weren't. There was only one choice. I hope I'm getting that across. I believe in creating choices, not eliminating choices.

TOM PIMLOTT: Straight edge is punk as fuck, and just as valid now as it was in 1981. Everyone drinks and gets fucked up, at least in the U.K. To me straight edge is the most obvious way to separate yourself from normal society. Secondly—and I'm stealing this theory from a non–straight edge friend that wrote this in her zine while drunk years ago—hardcore needs straight edge. Straight edge is a phenomenon that came out of hardcore and hardcore alone. If straight edge is allowed to die out, or stops being present in the music, then, in a way, hardcore will have let itself down and will lose a bit of legitimacy as a bona fide subculture.

DEMIAN JOHNSTON: The important thing is that straight edge was subversive. I was doing something that cops and jocks hated and didn't understand. I loved that, because my attitude toward cops and jocks was, "Fuck those people." Once I got past that anger, I looked outward to more real issues. Straight edge came from nothing, and accomplished some pretty good stuff.

VIQUE MARTIN: From straight edge, I learned that it's okay to go against the entire culture that you are from, and say no and declare that something isn't for you. Britain has a huge pub culture and it's very unusual for someone to abstain from drinking. There's a lot of peer pressure to conform. And I think not conforming to anything is great practice for being able to stick to what you believe in; for forging your own path and deciding what works for you.

NED RUSSIN: Straight edge is important because it is a very simple and easy approach to live your life in a positive way—yet somehow it manages to offend and confuse people. I'm not saying it's important simply because it offends people, but when you look at what people care about and why, you realize that there are plenty of other options available outside of what's considered normal. That's not a bad thing. When I started to realize that *normal* isn't synonymous with *good*, I started to question everything in my life. This realization has allowed me to live a life and do things I wanted to do, regardless of cultural approval.

GREG BENNICK: To this day, people always ask why I have to label myself straight edge as a grown man. For me, it's really empowering and lets me have a sense of self-identity. We are creatures who strive for meaning in the midst of an abstract existence. You and I could be sitting here talking on the phone about a concept like straight edge, and then one of us could hang up the phone and suddenly die. I'm not meaning to sound morose, but that's just the reality. We are all trying to define things as we go along, just so we can keep our heads level and not go insane. So to identify my-self as straight edge and to identify myself as vegan—these are the ways in which I maintain a psychological balance in an unsure world.

KENT MCCLARD: I don't think people understand what a poisonous idea straight edge is to the mainstream. If you're serious about it, you're going to walk a path that makes life hard. There are not a lot of people in our society that are cool with someone not drinking. It's something everyone does. Unless you're a part of a recovery or religious community, this is what people do. If you don't do those things, you're considered a freak. I've been straight edge thirty years, but I don't consider it my identity.

TOBY MORSE: I'll be straight edge until the day I die, I know that. But I don't wake up every morning screaming, "I'm straight edge!" I just know I don't drink and I don't smoke and there's a name for it. I'm not going to drink a beer in the same way I'm never going to shoot a gun. These are just things I'm not interested in doing.

KARL BUECHNER: The wide array of people who chose to be involved in straight edge always fascinates me. They could be bipolar or suffer from the emotional scars of abuse. They could have listened to Satanic black metal or become Nazi skinheads or gangster kids that robbed people and sold crack. Of all the things they could have done, they got into animal rights or environmentalism or straight edge. How awesome is that? Now that we're adults and look back on all this stuff, we can see none of these guys were trying to cause trouble or trying to add more chaos. These people were trying to find solutions.

PAT DUBAR: All those bands that had something smart to say about me or Uniform Choice, it doesn't matter. We have giant sacks full of mail written to us by kids who quit drinking because of our record. Even if we look back on it all today and think straight edge is silly, the bottom line is, it helped someone somewhere at some point. Outside of all that bullshit we put up with from other people, that music had a positive effect on someone, and that's that.

RON BAIRD: I went through my whole life thinking, "I wish I could have lived in a time where I could have made a change," and, "I wish I lived through the civil rights movement." The funny thing is, I look back now as a fifty-year-old man and say to myself, "Dude! You were a part of history!" When I was a fifteen-year-old kid preaching straight edge and having full cans of beer thrown at my face, I never thought in my wildest imagination that would be the case.

CHRIS ZUSI: At the end of the day, I think the straight edge message continues to endure because it connects with people through the music. There is a power in the message delivered via hardcore music. Even in this day and age where every youth subculture has been commercialized and co-opted, being straight edge still sets you apart from most people. That will always appeal to kids.

TOM PIMLOTT: A lot of kids today are just like me when I was a teenager: avoiding drinking and drugs as much as possible while trying not to attract ridicule from their peers. These are the types finding punk and hardcore and keeping straight edge going. I was lucky enough to discover Minor Threat before anyone could convince me to behave otherwise. I realized that there were other people like me, and we had a name to call ourselves. You can't underestimate the importance of being able to identify with something when you're a teenager. Discovering this really vivid world behind the name was an amazing feeling. "Straight edge" is a visually strong phrase, and with the bold lettering, X'd fists, high-tops, sing-along lyrics, and stage dives. It's no wonder straight edge hooked me in and captivates kids generation after generation.

JOHN PORCELLY: We were out to create a revolution. Seriously. We loved the power and energy of hardcore, but we really, really weren't into the whole self-destructive punk ethos. We were into being healthy and in shape and living clean, mean, and smart. We honestly thought vegetarianism was important and revolutionary and part of a whole new way of living. When I was in high school, everyone was into junk food, shitty meaningless music, burgers, and keg parties. That was youth culture at the time, and Youth of Today was a stance against it. To this day, I stand against all that media-fed crap. I exercise, do yoga every day, meditate, read, and try my best to live an uplifted life. Seriously, I hope to Krishna that a new, empowered Youth of Today–type band comes along one of these days to get this new generation of kids off their mind-numbing video games and out of their sedentary, shitty, social media–driven lives. Seriously, we need a whole new revolution. New edge kids—*get on it*.

Connecticut's Wide Awake and pals stroll through Manhattan's Lower East Side in 1988 after recording their self-titled seven-inch at Don Fury Studios. Left to right: *Burn vocalist Chaka Malik;* Smorgasbord *editor Chris Daily; the late Doug Byrnes, original vocalist for Connecticut's Pressure Release; Gorilla Biscuits drummer Luke Abbey; Wide Awake EP cover artist Ted Nelson; Pressure Release and Burn bassist Alex Napeck; Wide Awake roadie Craig Coloruso; Youth Crew all-star Dylan Schreifels; Pressure Release guitarist Tom Kuntz; Wide Awake guitarist John McLoughlin; Wide Awake drummer Scott Frosh; scenester Jay "Turbo" Weller; Wide Awake vocalist Tom Kennedy;* Boiling Point *editor Tom Rockafeller; and later Pressure Release vocalist Ben Smith.* JOHN PORCELLY

CAST OF CHARACTERS

DAMIAN ABRAHAM: vocalist, Criminally Insane, Fucked Up

JONATHAN ANASTAS: bassist, DYS, Slapshot

GREG ANDERSON: vocalist, False Liberty; guitarist, Brotherhood

RON BAIRD: vocalist, Stalag 13

BRIAN BAKER: guitarist, Minor Threat, Government Issue, Dag Nasty, the 400, the Meatmen, Junkyard, Bad Religion

AL BARILE: guitarist, SS Decontrol; owner, X-Claim! Records

BRETT BEECH: coeditor, *Hardware* zine; owner, In My Blood Records

GREG BENNICK: vocalist, Trial

RICHIE BIRKENHEAD: vocalist, the Numskulls, Underdog, Into Another; guitarist, Youth of Today

CHRIS BRATTON: drummer, Justice League, Chain of Strength

ALEX BROWN: guitarist, Side by Side, Project X, Gorilla Biscuits; coeditor, *Schism* zine

KARL BUECHNER: vocalist, Earth Crisis, Freya, Path of Resistance

CURTIS CANALES: vocalist, Chain of Strength

TOM CAPONE: guitarist, Beyond, Bold, Quicksand

RAY CAPPO: vocalist, Youth of Today, Shelter, Better Than a Thousand

AARON CHRIETZBERG: guitarist, the First Step

MICHAEL CLARKE: guitarist, Mindset

JORDAN COOPER: owner, Revelation Records

CHRIS CORRY: guitarist, Stop and Think, No Tolerance

JOHN COYLE: vocalist, Back to Back, Outspoken

LINS CUSCANI: vocalist, Break It Up, Thirty Seconds Until Armageddon, Vengeance of Gaia

CHRIS DAILY: editor, *Smorgasbord* zine; owner, Smorgasbord Records

JUSTIN DETORE: vocalist, No Tolerance

RYAN J. DOWNEY: vocalist, Hardball, Burn it Down; journalist

PAT DUBAR: vocalist, Uniform Choice, Unity

TONY ERBA: vocalist, Face Value, Gordon Solie Motherfuckers, Cheap Tragedies, Fuck You Pay Me; bassist, H-100s

MIKE FERRARO: drummer, Death Before Dishonor, Youth of Today; vocalist, Judge

ROB FISH: vocalist, Release, Resurrection, 108, the Judas Factor

PAT FLYNN: vocalist, Have Heart, Clear, Free, Sweet Jesus

MIKE GITTER: editor, *xXx* zine; A&R, Atlantic Records, Roadrunner Records, Razor & Tie, Century Media

CATHERINE GOLDMAN, AKA KATIE THE CLEANING LADY: coeditor, *Forced Exposure* zine; co–radio show host, *Faster Than Anyone Else*

ISAAC GOLUB: vocalist, A Chorus of Disapproval

SAB GREY: vocalist, Iron Cross

RON GUARDIPEE: vocalist, Brotherhood, Resolution

STEVE HANSGEN: bassist, Minor Threat; guitarist, Second Wind

ROB HAWORTH: guitarist, No for an Answer, Hard Stance, Inside Out, Farside, State of the Nation

PETER HOEREN: owner, Crucial Response Records

RYAN HOFFMAN: guitarist, Justice League, Chain of Strength

DEMIAN JOHNSTON: bassist, Undertow

CHRISTOFFER JONSSON: bassist, DS-13; owner, Busted Head Records

ARI KATZ: drummer, Enuf, Up Front; vocalist, Lifetime

JACK "CHOKE" KELLY: vocalist, Negative FX, Last Rights, Slapshot, Stars and Stripes

SIMON KELLY: editor, *Punch in the Face* zine

ANDREW KLINE: guitarist, Strife

PETE KOLLER: guitarist, Sick of It All

RICH LABBATE: bassist, Insted

JOHN LACROIX: guitarist, Ten Yard Fight

DAVE LARSON: editor, *Excursion* zine; owner, Excursion Records

STEVE LARSON: drummer, Insted

IAN LECK: vocalist, Steadfast, Voorhees

PAT LONGRIE: drummer, Unity, Uniform Choice

STEVE LOVETT: vocalist, Raid

TOM LYLE: guitarist, Government Issue

DENNIS LYXZÉN: vocalist, Step Forward, Refused, International Noise Conspiracy

IAN MACKAYE: vocalist, Teen Idles, Minor Threat, Embrace; guitarist/vocalist, Fugazi; co-owner, Dischord Records

SEAN MARCUS: vocalist, Aware

VIQUE MARTIN: editor, *Simba* zine; distribution manager, Revelation Records

KENT MCCLARD: editor, *No Answers* zine; owner, Ebullition Records

MARK MCKAY: drummer, Terminally Ill, Slapshot, Stars and Stripes

JOHN MCLOUGHLIN: guitarist, Wide Awake

TIM MCMAHON: vocalist, Mouthpiece, Hands Tied, Face the Enemy, Triple Threat, Search

TIM MONROE: guitarist, Unit Pride

ROB MORAN: bassist, Unbroken

TOBY MORSE: vocalist, H_2O, Hazen Street

SEAN MUTTAQI: vocalist/guitarist, Vegan Reich; owner, Hardline Records, Uprising Records

ADAM NATHANSON: guitarist, Life's Blood, Born Against

JEFF NELSON: drummer, Teen Idles, Minor Threat; co-owner, Dischord Records

JOE NELSON: vocalist, Triggerman, the Killing Flame, Ignite

ANDY NORTON: vocalist, Praise

GENTLEMAN JIM NORTON: bassist, Crucial Youth

DAN O'MAHONY: vocalist, Carry Nation, No for an Answer, 411, God Forgot, Speak 714, Done Dying

GAVIN OGLESBY: guitarist, No for an Answer, the Killing Flame, Triggerman, Blood Days

ANTHONY PAPPALARDO: guitarist, Ten Yard Fight, In My Eyes

REVEREND HANK PEIRCE: road manager, Corrosion of Conformity, Slapshot, Uniform Choice

JASON PETERSON: guitarist, Youth Under Control, Wind of Change

TOM PIMLOTT: vocalist, Violent Reaction

JOHN PORCELLY: guitarist, Youth of Today, Judge; vocalist, Project X

STEVE REDDY: vocalist, Wolfpack; owner, Equal Vision Records

JON ROA: vocalist, Justice League, End to End, Eyelid

CAINE ROSE: vocalist, Touchdown

DJ ROSE: vocalist, Path of Resistance

BILLY RUBIN: editor, *Think* zine; vocalist, Half Off, Haywire

NED RUSSIN: vocalist/bassist, Title Fight; vocalist, Disengage

JOHN SCHARBACH: vocalist, Breakthrough, Give

WALTER SCHREIFELS: bassist, Youth of Today, Project X; guitarist, Gorilla Biscuits; vocalist/guitarist, Quicksand

JAIME SCIARAPPA: bassist, SS Decontrol, Slapshot

KEVIN SECONDS: vocalist, 7 Seconds

SAMMY SIEGLER: drummer, Side by Side, Youth of Today, Judge, Project X, Gorilla Biscuits, CIV

DANNY SLAM: vocalist, America's Hardcore

DAVE SMALLEY: vocalist, DYS, Dag Nasty, All, Down by Law

ARTHUR SMILIOS: bassist, Gorilla Biscuits

JOE SNOW: photographer

JOHN STABB: vocalist, Government Issue

MARK STARR: vocalist, Insight

RAT STATEMENT: whole band!, Statement

ANDY STRACHAN: guitarist, DYS

NATHAN STREJCEK: vocalist, Teen Idles, Youth Brigade

JEFF TERRANOVA: bassist, Up Front

DREW THOMAS: drummer, Youth of Today, Crippled Youth, Bold

OLAV VAN DEN BERG: drummer, Lärm, Man Lifting Banner, Seein' Red, Colt Turkey, Profound

PAUL VAN DEN BERG: guitarist, Lärm, Man Lifting Banner, Seein' Red, Colt Turkey, Profound

JOEY VELA: vocalist, Breakaway, Second Coming

GREG W: vocalist, Mental; owner, Lockin' Out Records

MATT WARNKE: vocalist, Crippled Youth, Bold

CHRIS WRENN: owner, Bridge Nine Records

DAVE ZUKAUSKAS: editor, *Run It!* zine

CHRIS ZUSI: guitarist, Release, Resurrection, Floorpunch

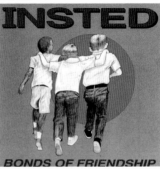

STRAIGHT EDGE ESSENTIALS

ESSENTIAL FULL-LENGTH RECORDS

SS DECONTROL *The Kids Will Have Their Say* (1982)

SS DECONTROL *Get it Away* (1983)

MINOR THREAT *Out of Step* (1983)

DYS *Brotherhood* (1983)

STALAG 13 *In Control* (1984)

ILL REPUTE *What Happens Next?* (1984)

7 SECONDS *The Crew* (1984)

UNIFORM CHOICE *Screaming for Change* (1986)

DOGGY STYLE *Side by Side* (1985)

JUSTICE LEAGUE *Shattered Dreams* (1986)

LÄRM *Straight on View* (1986)

SLAPSHOT *Back on the Map* (1986)

YOUTH OF TODAY *Break Down the Walls* (1986)

YOUTH OF TODAY *We're Not in This Alone* (1988)

BOLD *Speak Out* (1988)

INSTED *Bonds of Friendship* (1988)

SLAPSHOT *Step on It* (1988)

UP FRONT *Spirit* (1988)

NO FOR AN ANSWER *A Thought Crusade* (1989)

GORILLA BISCUITS *Start Today* (1989)

JUDGE *Bringin' it Down* (1989)

UNITY *Blood Days* (1989)

TURNING POINT *It's Always Darkest... Before the Dawn* (1990)

DIE HARD *Looking out for #1* (1990)

INSTED *What We Believe* (1990)

FOUR WALLS FALLING *Culture Shock* (1991)

A CHORUS OF DISAPPROVAL *Truth Gives Wings to Strength* (1991)

MAN LIFTING BANNER *Ten Inches That Shook the World* (1992)

OUTSPOKEN *A Light in the Darkness* (1992)

RAID *Above the Law* (1992)

CORNERSTONE *Beating the Masses* (1995)

MOUTHPIECE *What Was Said* (1994)

RESURRECTION *I Refuse* (1994)

UNBROKEN *Life.Love.Regret* (1994)

STRIFE *One Truth* (1994

UNDERTOW *At Both Ends* (1994)

EARTH CRISIS *Destroy the Machines* (1995)

THE PATH OF RESISTANCE *Who Dares Wins* (1996)

TEN YARD FIGHT *Back on Track* (1997)

FLOORPUNCH *Fast Times at the Jersey Shore* (1998)

IN MY EYES *The Difference Between* (1998)

BATTERY *Whatever it Takes* (1998)

FOLLOW THROUGH *Taking it Back* (1997)

TRIAL *Are These Our Lives?* (1999)

CARRY ON *A Life Less Plagued* (2001)

SPORTSWEAR *Building, Dwelling, Thinking* (1999)

MAINSTRIKE *No Passing Phase* (1999)

COUNT ME OUT *110* (2000)

RIGHTEOUS JAMS *Rage of Discipline* (2004)

HAVE HEART *The Things We Carry* (2006)

THE FIRST STEP *What We Know* (2006)

DAMAGE CONTROL *What It Takes* (2003)

JUSTICE *Escapades* (2007)

BOSTON STRANGLER *Primitive* (2012)

COKE BUST *Confined* (2013)

MIND-SET *Leave No Doubt* (2012)

PRAISE *Lights Went Out* (2014)

NO TOLERANCE *You Walk Alone* (2015)

VIOLENT REACTION *Marching On* (2015)

HOUNDS OF HATE *s/t* (2013)

PROTESTER *Hide From Reality* (2017)

ESSENTIAL SEVEN-INCH EP'S

TEEN IDLES *Minor Disturbance* (1980)

MINOR THREAT *Filler* (1981)

MINOR THREAT *In My Eyes* (1981)

7 SECONDS *Skins, Brains & Guts* (1982)

7 SECONDS *Committed for Life* (1983)

ILL REPUTE *Oxnard Land of No Toilets* (1983)

MINOR THREAT *Salad Days* (1985)

LAST RIGHTS *Chunks* (1984)

JUSTICE LEAGUE *Think or Sink* (1985)

UNITY *You Are One* (1985)

DOGGY STYLE *Work as One* (1985)

YOUTH OF TODAY *Can't Close My Eyes* (1985)

CRIPPLED YOUTH *Join the Fight* (1986

LÄRM *No One Can Be That Dumb* (1986)

SIDE BY SIDE *You're Only Young Once* (1988)

NO FOR AN ANSWER *You Laugh* (1988)

PROJECT X *s/t* (1988)

JUDGE *New York Crew* (1988)

GORILLA BISCUITS *s/t* (1988)

VARIOUS *X Marks the Spot* (1988)

WIDE AWAKE *s/t* (1988)

CHAIN OF STRENGTH *True Till Death* (1988

UNIT PRIDE *s/t* (1988)

BREAKAWAY *s/t* (1988)

TURNING POINT *s/t* (1989)

HARD STANCE *Face Reality* (1989)

INSTED *We'll Make the Difference* (1989)

RELEASE *The Pain Inside* (1989)

FOUR WALLS FALLING *s/t* (1989)

INSIGHT *Standing Strong* (1989)

BROTHERHOOD *No Tolerance for Ignorance* (1989)

BOLD *s/t* (1989)

YOUTH OF TODAY *Disengage* (1990)

CHAIN OF STRENGTH *What Holds Us Apart* (1990)

PRESSURE RELEASE *Prison of My Own* (1990)

AMENITY *This Is Our Struggle* (1990)

AGAINST THE WALL *Identify Me* (1990)

POWERHOUSE *s/t* (1990)

COLT TURKEY *Christmas Sucks!* (1990)

OUTSPOKEN *Survival* (1990)

INTEGRITY *In Contrast of Sin* (1990)

CONFRONT *Payday* (1991)

VARIOUS *Words to Live by Words to Die For* (1991)

MAN LIFTING BANNER *Myth of Freedom* (1991)

CONVICTION *A Question of Commitment* (1991)

BATTERY *s/t* (1991)

MOUTHPIECE *s/t* (1991)

RESURRECTION *s/t* (1991)

UNBROKEN *You Won't Be Back* (1992)

UNDERTOW *Stalemate* (1993)

EARTH CRISIS *Firestorm* (1993)

STRIFE *My Fire Burns On* (1992)

HARD STANCE *s/t* (1993)

MAINSTRIKE *Times Still Here* (1995)

FLOORPUNCH *Division One Champs* (1996)

TEN YARD FIGHT *Hardcore Pride* (1996)

HANDS TIED *s/t* (1996)

RANCOR *Flip the Switch* (1997)

SPORTSWEAR *Keep it Together* (1997)

FASTBREAK *Don't Stop Trying* (1996)

FOLLOW THROUGH *Not This Time* (1996)

TRIAL *Foundation* (1997)

COUNT ME OUT *What We Built* (1998)

CARRY ON *Roll With the Punches* (2000)

THE FIRST STEP *Open Hearts and Clear Minds* (2002)

FAR FROM BREAKING *The Identity* (2003)

DAMAGE CONTROL *Can't Keep Us Down* (2002)

MENTAL *Get an Oxygen Tank!* (2003)

HAVE HEART *What Counts* (2004)

JUSTICE *Look Alive* (2004)

STEP FORWARD *10 Song EP* (2006)

NOOSE *The War of All Against All* (2012)

NO TOLERANCE *No Remorse, No Tolerance* (2011)

HOUNDS OF HATE *No Redemption* (2011)

COKE BUST *Degradation* (2010)

VIOLENT REACTION *Dead End* (2014)

MINDSET *Nothing Less* (2016)

PROTESTER *No Identity* (2015)

DRUG CONTROL *s/t* (2015)

SEARCH *Between the Lines* (2017)

'80S EAST COAST DEMO TAPES

GORILLA BISCUITS *s/t* (1987)

SIDE BY SIDE *s/t* (1987)

WIDE AWAKE *Hold True* (1987)

PRESSURE RELEASE *s/t* (1987)

UP FRONT *s/t* (1987)

TOUCHDOWN *Reach for the Top* (1988)

TURNING POINT *s/t* (1988)

RELEASE *s/t* (1988)

ENUF *s/t* (1988)

SECOND THOUGHT *s/t* (1988)

FED UP! *Courage to Change* (1988)

ON EDGE *By Your Side* (1987)

'80S WEST COAST DEMO TAPES

UNIFORM CHOICE *s/t* (1984)

AGAINST THE WALL *Where the Strength Lies* (1988)

PUSHED ASIDE *s/t* (1989)

OUTSPOKEN *Look Beyond* (1990)

INSTED *Be Someone* (1986)

HARD STANCE *End the Hate* (1988)

FREE WILL *s/t* (1988)

IMPLEMENT *s/t* (1989)

UNIT PRIDE *Holding Strong* (1987)

BREAKAWAY *s/t* (1988)

YOUTH UNDER CONTROL *Live and Learn* (1987)

BROTHERHOOD *Brotherhood of Friends* (1989)

LATE-'90S REVIVAL DEMO TAPES

FLOORPUNCH *Goal Line Stand* (1996)

CORNERSTONE *The Truth Hurts* (1994)

IN MY EYES *s/t* (1997)

TEN YARD FIGHT *s/t* (1995)

RIGHT BRIGADE (1998)

FASTBREAK *Youth Pride* (1994)

HANDS TIED *s/t* (1996)

RANCOR *I Won't Take Part* (1994)

EARLY 2000S DEMO TAPES

STOP AND THINK (2001)

THE FIRST STEP (2001)

MENTAL (2001)

DUMP TRUCK *Feelin' Good* (2003)

RIGHTEOUS JAMS *Righteous Jams in 2003* (2003)

INVASION *Face up to It* (2001)

COKE BUST (2006)

NWOSEHC (THE NEW WAVE OF STRAIGHT EDGE HARDCORE) DEMO TAPES

PROTESTER *s/t* (2014)

NO TOLERANCE *Boston Straight Edge* (2009)

CORRECTIVE MEASURE *s/t* (2015)

CLEAR *s/t* (2012)

DISENGAGE *s/t* (2009)

LINE OF SIGHT *s/t* (2015)

FREE *s/t* (2015)

THE REAL COST *s/t* (2016)

TAKE CONTROL *s/t* (2014)

STEP FOR CHANGE *s/t* (2016)

DRUG CONTROL *s/t* (2014)

SOURCE INDEX

V. 7SECONDS: COMMITTED FOR LIFE

Tony Kinman quote: "People should realize that a drug dealer is no cooler..." from an interview conducted by Ken Lester for Public Enemy issue number 7, 1979.

VIII. UNIFORM CHOICE: SCREAMING FOR CHANGE

Gavin Oglesby quotes, "I first became aware of Uniform Choice..." and "It's unfortunate they were...," from an interview conducted by Brian Jordan and Tim McMahon for the Double Cross website.

Joe Nelson quote, "There's actually a great video of Pat's brother Courtney...," from an interview conducted by Brian Jordan and Tim McMahon for the Double Cross website.

IX. YOUTH OF TODAY: TAKE A STAND!

Ray Cappo quotes, "It was February 1985...," "The other guys in my band Violent Children...," "My whole dream in a hardcore band was to preach straight edge...," "We were really bold and we'd challenge the crowd...," from an interview conducted by Ron Guardipee that appeared in *Bringin' It Back* issue #2.

John Porcelly quote, "We were straight, loud, proud and outspoken...," appeared in the book *All Ages: Reflections on Straight Edge*.

John Porcelly quote, "In the beginning, the Youth Crew was Youth of Today and our small circle of friends," from the article "John Porcelly and the Origins of Youth Crew," written by Anthony Pappalardo and published by Green Room Radio.

X. SLAPSHOT: BACK ON THE MAP

Ray Cappo quote, "We invited Slapshot to play a show at CBGB...," from an interview conducted by Ron Guardipee that appeared in *Bringin' It Back* issue #2.

Curtis Canelles quote, "We played in Boston with Youth of Today and Slapshot...," from an interview conducted by Brian Jordan and Tim McMahon for the Double Cross website.

XI. BOLD: JOIN THE FIGHT

Ray Cappo quotes, "With Violent Children, we always wanted a brother band...," "Finally, Crippled Youth played at the Anthrax...," "They lived right near Porcell and we became friends with them...," from an interview conducted by Ron Guardipee that appeared in *Bringin' It Back* issue #2.

XII. YOUTH CREW ACROSS AMERICA

John Porcelly quotes, "I booked our first tour myself..." and "By the time we came back...," from the article *John Porcelly and the Origins of Youth Crew* written by Anthony Pappalardo and published at Green Room Radio.

Jason Patterson quotes, "We met Ray and Porcell..." and "Youth Under Control played with Youth of Today...," from an interview conducted by Brian Jordan and Tim McMahon for the Double Cross website.

XIV. YOUTH CREW STYLE: MORE THAN FASHION

Chris Bratton quotes, "What would later crystallize the Youth Crew look..." and "Interestingly, in an old RUN DMC interview...," from the article *The First Chain of Strength Interview in Twenty Years Is Mostly About Clothes* by Anthony Pappalardo.

Mike Ferraro quote, "When I was a freshman in high school...," from an interview conducted by Brian Jordan and Tim McMahon for the Double Cross website.

John Porcelly quotes, "We figured it was more authentic...," "I always half joke about...," and "Something was happening in the scene...," from the article *John Porcelly and the Origins of Youth Crew* written by Anthony Pappalardo and published at Green Room Radio.

XVI. HALF OFF & THE SLOTH CREW

Ray Cappo quote, "Billy Rubin from Half Off…," from an interview conducted by Ron Guardipee that appeared in *Bringin' It Back* issue #2.

Drew Thomas quote, "We had a lot of fun out in Southern California…," from an interview conducted by Brian Jordan and Tim McMahon for the Double Cross website.

John Porcelly quote, "At the last Project X practice…," from a Project X interview conducted by Chris Daily that appeared in *Smorgasbord* issue #2.

XVII. THE ANTHRAX: HOLD TRUE

John Porcelly quotes, "The thing about The Anthrax when it started was there was pretty much no straight edge scene…" and "Next to CBGB, as far as being a landmark place and a place to change the face of Punk or hardcore…," from an interview conducted by Brian Jordan in *Impact* issue #2.

XIX. JUDGE: FED UP!

Mike Ferraro quotes, "*Maximum Rocknroll* had made Youth of Today…," "I was pissed off at the people coming down on Youth of Today…," "I wanted to say to *Maximum Rocknroll*…," "Calling the band Judge was about the band being an authority figure…," and "People took quickly to the message of Judge…," from an interview conducted by Brian Jordan and Tim McMahon for the Double Cross website.

XXII. NO ONE CAN BE THAT DUMB: THE U.K. & EUROPE

Peter Strandell of Svart Parad quotes courtesy of Daniel Ekeroth, from interviews for his book *Swedish Hardcore*.

XXIII. THE NEW BREED

Isaac Golub quote, "At the time Chorus of Disapproval got going…," from an interview conducted by Brian Jordan and Tim McMahon for the Double Cross website.

XXV. DESPERATE STATE: UMEÅ STRAIGHT EDGE CITY

Dennis Lyxzén quotes, "Where I grew up…," "The rest of the world…," and "We were just lucky…," from an interview published on the Dying Scene website, February 2011.

Dennis Lyxzén quotes, "In our hometown...," "If we came out and said...," and "A lot of people...," from an interview published on Aux, April 2013.

XXVI: EARTH CRISIS: A FIRESTORM TO PURIFY

Karl Buechner quote, "For most of the band...," from the book *Burning Fight: The '90s Hardcore Revolution in Ethics, Politics, Spirit and Sound.*

XXXIII. LIFE AFTER STRAIGHT EDGE

Damian Abraham quotes from an interview conducted by Steven Hyden for the Onion AV Club, June 2011.

XXXIV. WHAT REMAINS: KEEPING THE EDGE

John Porcelly quote, "We were out to create a revolution...," from the article *John Porcelly and The Origins of Youth Crew* written by Anthony Pappalardo and published at Green Room Radio.

C. J. Wilson quote, "Being edge is something that people will always associate with me...," from an interview conducted by Julian PMAKid, August 2011.

Sammy Siegler of Youth of Today contemplates the edge between songs at the Anthrax. BOILING POINT ZINE

AUTHOR ACKNOWLEDGMENTS

THANXX TO THESE YOUTH CREW ALL-STARS

Jordan Cooper, Drew Stone, Chris Wrenn, Chris Minicucci, Casey Jones, Pat Dubar, Mike Gitter, Nancy and Al Barile, Jeff Nelson, Joe Nelson, Jon Roa, Mike Ferraro, John Porcelly, DJ Rose, Ron Baird, Joe Snow, Billy Rubin, Steve Larson, Kevin Hernandez, Chris Zusi, Andrew Kline, Sean Muttaqi, Ari Katz, John Scharbach, Michael Clarke, Aaron Jinpa, Jack "Choke" Kelly, Gail Rush, Bridget Collins, Alison "Mouse" Braun, Mikey Garceau, Toby Morse, Ian McFarland, Vique Martin, Ian MacKaye, Sammy Siegler, Chris Bratton, Chris Daily, Joe Snow, Brett Beach, John LaCroix, Anthony Pappalardo, and Adam Lentz.

EXTRA SPECIAL THANKXXX

Tim McMahon for the access to the Double Cross Archives and Anthony Civorelli for the intro.

GREATEST THANKS OF ALL

Danielle Jelley-Rettman, The Rettman family, The Jelley family, Carlin, Sandy, Mish, Cole and Belle.

TONY RETTMAN ONLINE

Instagram: @straightedgebook
Facebook: @sXebook
web: www.straightedgebook.com

THE TIME IS NOW: FURTHER READING FROM BAZILLION POINTS

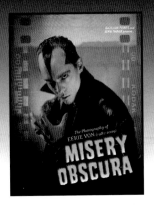

MISERY OBSCURA
The Photography of Eerie Von, (1981–2009), by Eerie Von
Hardcover, 160 pages

Essential Misfits/Samhain photos
"Mesmerizing"—Kirk Hammett
"Some of the most awesomely, brutally theatrical moments in punk rock history"—Pitchfork

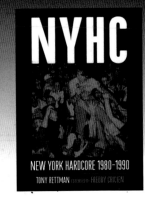

NYHC *New York Hardcore 1980–1990*, Tony Rettman
Softcover, 384 pages

"I'm floored! An amazing read."
—Roger Miret, Agnostic Front

"A great oral-history book."
—New York Times

CITY BABY *Surviving in Leather, Bristle Studs, Punk Rock, and G.B.H*
Ross Lomas with Steve Pottinger
Softcover, 304 pages

"Always doing what they felt like and having laugh…absolutely captivating."—Vive le Roc

"The full, warts and all story, a gripping read Full of crazy punk rock antics"—Sidewalk

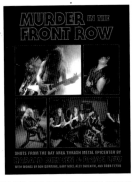

MURDER IN THE FRONT ROW
Shots From the Bay Area Thrash Metal Epicenter
Harald Oimoen and Brian Lew
Hardcover, 272 pages

"The definitive story of the scene"
—Kirk Hammett, Metallica

"The true essence of thrash metal"
—Dave Lombardo, Slayer

EXPERIENCING NIRVANA
Grunge in Europe, 1989
Bruce Pavitt
Hardcover, 208 pages

An early microhistory and photojournal

"The book is amazing, so perfectly representative of the time"—Dave Grohl

WE GOT POWER!
Hardcore Punk Scenes From 1980s Southern California
Dave Markey & Jordan Schwartz
Hardcover, 304 pages

w/essays by Henry Rollins, Keith Morris, Pat Fear, Mike Watt, more.

"Vital to understanding the birth of American punk rock" —L. A. Times

Points

D.I.Y. DELIVERANCE AT BAZILLIONPOINTS.COM

CHOOSING DEATH
The Improbable History of Death Metal & Grindcore
Albert Mudrian; forewords
by DJ John Peel & Scott Carlson
Softcover, 400 pages

Best Books of the Year, *Kerrang!*
"So damn honest and real"
—Tomas Lindberg, At the Gates

SUB POP U.S.A.
The Subterraneanan Pop Music Anthology, by Bruce Pavitt
Deluxe softcover, 400 pages

The complete *Subterranean Pop* fanzines and Seattle Rocket columns

"Awesome."—*Entertainment Weekly*
"Wonderful"—*Classic Rock*

SWEDISH DEATH METAL
by Daniel Ekeroth
Softcover, 450 pages

The ultimate blow-by-blow account of Sweden's legendary death metal underground.

Book of the Year, *Decibel*
Starred review, *Publishers Weekly*

TOUCH AND GO: *The Complete Hardcore Punk Zine '79–'83*
Tesco Vee and Dave Stimson
Deluxe softcover, 576 pages

"As a hardcore punk primer you couldn't do better."—*Time Out Chicago*

WHAT ARE YOU DOING HERE? *A Black Woman's Life and Liberation in Heavy Metal*
Laina Dawes
Softcover, 208 pages

"Essential reading..."—PopMatters

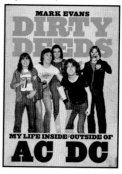

DIRTY DEEDS: *My Life Inside/ Outside of AC/DC*
Mark Evans
Softcover, 288 pages

The first insider account of the classic Bon Scott years of AC/DC.

Unity, breaking down the walls of hate, apathy, sexism, negativity, abuse, racism, ignorance, and fascism.

Clockwise from top left: *Ian MacKaye circa 1983; Minor Threat, the Cathay de Grande, Hollywood, circa 1983.* PHOTOS BY PAT LONGRIE; *Minor Threat rocks out under the Nevada dusk sky while Kevin Seconds shows he's happy and proud.* CARI MARVELLI

Clockwise from top: *Kevin Seconds skanks it up to Reno, NV's, legendary Bix Bigler Band while they perform their classic song, "There's a Scientific Name for Your Dick.";* Backyard sing-along with an early three-piece line up of 7 Seconds; Kevin Seconds and Bessie Oakley say "Fuck Your America" in the most direct way possible. PHOTOS BY CARI MARVELLI

Springa "looking like David Lee Roth" at SSD's final L.A. show, the Olympic Auditorium, March 30, 1985. CASEY JONES

Clockwise from top left: "Lil Bill" Tuck of Pillsbury Hardcore. CASEY JONES; *Wishingwell Records ad.* COURTESY OF FRED HAMMER; *Who wears short shorts? Jon Roa of Justice League.* CASEY JONES; D.C. worship in the O.C. with a classic D.C. flyer by Tomas Squip revised for a local outing; Pat Dubar of Uniform Choice recites the poem from Screaming for Change. CASEY JONES

From top: *Pat Dubar warns, "You better listen!"; Uniform Choice moves the youth of Orange County to declare, en masse, "No Thanks." Note bald-headed Billy Rubin (Half Off, Haywire) in the mix, as well as an out-of-place teen in a Corona beer shirt.*

PHOTOS BY CASEY JONES

BILLY RUBIN

Facing page, clockwise from top: *Youth of Today performs outdoors in Southern California.* COURTESY OF CHRIS DAILY; *The exterior of the Anthrax's first location, prior to becoming the hub of East Coast straight edge.* CHRIS SCHNEIDER; *Ray Cappo of Youth of Today, Gilman Street Project, Berkeley, CA, 1987.* TRENT NELSON; *Billy Rubin of Half Off dresses the part of a straight edge kid while asking, "Who Writes Your Rules?"* COURTESY OF CHRIS DAILY; *Matt Warnke of Bold.* CHRIS DAILY. This page, clockwise from top: *Kevin Hernandez of Insted, the Country Club, Reseda, CA, 1989.* MIKEY GARCEAU; *By the 1990s, Insted were the lone straight edge holdover from the '80s. Their final U.S. tour in 1991 brought them to City Gardens in Trenton, NJ. Note your author in backwards red baseball cap, gleefully yelling along.* LENNY ZIMKUS; *Insted hits the road in the fall of 1988.* COURTESY OF RICH LABBATE; *Against the Wall's Randy Johnson, Spanky's Cafe, Riverside, CA, 1990.* MIKEY GARCEAU

John Porcelly and Ray Cappo of Youth of Today. TRENT NELSON

YOUTH OF TODAY
NEW YORK HARDCORE

MILANO
SABATO
11
MARZO

FROM NEW JERSEY
LETHAL AGGRESSION

OSSABUCHE PROD.

CENTRO SOCIALE LEONCAVALLO
VIA LEØNCAWALLØ 22

HARDCORE ◆ MUSIK FÜR DIE NEUNZIGER

YOUTH OF TODAY
NEW YORK CITY STRAIGHT EDGE HARDCORE

LETHAL AGGRESSION
NEW JERSEY WASTELAND HARDCORE

ON TOUR !

TEL 0511
INFO 703942

SPV

Facing page photos, clockwise from top left: *Holland's Lärm.* PETER HOEREN; *Ray Cappo tells the kids of Italy they're not in this alone.* FREDDY TWICE; *Cappo makes a point, Chatham Oaks Hall, January 2, 1987.* CHRIS DAILY; This page, clockwise from top left: *Wally Schreifels and Tom Capone of New York City's Quicksand.* LENNY ZIMKUS; *Pushed Aside and Against the Wall's Randy Johnson doing some early photo bombing as Judge plays, Gilman Street Project, Berkeley, Summer 1989.* MIKEY GARCEAU; *Mike Judge, Unisound, Reading, PA, 1990.* JAMIE DAVIS; *Uniform Choice on their "Where Are the Bald Guys" tour in 1987.* COURTESY OF PAT LONGRIE; *New Jersey's Turning Point and Hi-Impact Records CEO Darren Walters in front of CBGB, June 1989.* COURTESY OF DARREN WALTERS

Clockwise from top: *Tim McMahon of Mouthpiece at the band's final show, Princeton Arts Council, August 17, 1996.* JOE WHISKEYMAN; *Floorpunch's Mark Porter clears the path for the Youth Crew revival in 1996.* ROBBY REDCHEEKS; *Refused takes fashion tips from San Diego's Jenny Piccolo.* VIQUE MARTIN; *Turning Point gets a prime parking spot in front of a show.* COURTESY OF DARREN WALTERS; *Chicks Up Front Posse shows straight edge is not just boys' fun.* COURTESY OF VIQUE MARTIN

Clockwise from top left: *Umeå's DS-13 are hardcore, and you're not.* COURTESY OF CHRISTOFFER JONSSON; *Earth Crisis's Karl Buechner ready for all-out war at the More Than Music Fest, Dayton, OH, Spring 1993.* VIQUE MARTIN; *Raid wants your hands off the animals, please.* COURTESY OF STEVE LOVETT; *Strife knows there is one truth.* DAVE MANDEL

Clockwise from top left: *Tim McMahon of Hands Tied keeps the edge alive.* TRACI MCMAHON; *Have Heart.* ADAM TANNER; *Mindset's Evan Wivell "being the spark."* ANNE SPINA; *Ray Cappo's yoga mastery, Youth of Today reunion, This Is Hardcore Fest, Philadelphia, 2016.* ANNE SPINA; *Protester doesn't hide from reality.* ANNE SPINA; *Mike Judge, still fed up in 2016.* ANNE SPINA

Clockwise from top: *Toby Morse of H₂0 won't forget his roots.* DAN RAWE; *Strife's Rick Rodney stands as one.* ADAM TANNER; *Walter Schreifels and Tom Capone move into the 1990s with their post-hardcore band, Quicksand.* LENNY ZIMKUS; *Mouthpiece, Revelation Records 25th Anniversary show, New York, 2012.* ADAM TANNER

From top: *Seattle's Trial, still for the kids, the Metro, Chicago, Spring 2008.* MATT MILLER; *Youth of Today and youths of today.* ANNE SPIN